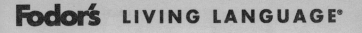

Fodor's LIVING LANGUAGE®

D0373219

French
for
Travelers

Fodor's Travel Publications   New York, Toronto, London, Sydney, Auckland

ENGLAND

Boulogne

La Manche
(English Channel)

Cherbourg

Dieppe

Amien

Le Havre

Rouen

Seine

Caen

Brest

St. Malo

NORMANDY

BRITTANY

Mont St-Michel

Chartres

Rennes

Le Mans

Orlé

Angers

Blois

Nantes

Loire

Tours

VAL DE LOIRE

ATLANTIC OCEAN

Poitiers

La Rochelle

Cognac

Limoges

Bay of Biscay

Bordeaux

Garonne

Dordogne

Bayonne

Biarritz

Pau

Toulouse

LANGU

MIDI-PYRÉNÉES

Lourdes

Carcassonne

S P A I N

ANDORRA

Calais

BELGIUM

Lille

miens

CHAMPAGNE

LUXEMBOURG

Corsica — Bastia

Ajaccio

Reims

Verdun

ILE-DE-
FRANCE

Metz

Paris

LORRAINE

Nancy

Fontainebleau

Strasbourg

ALSACE

GERMANY

Orléans

Colmar

Mulhouse

BURGUNDY

Vézelay

Dijon

SWITZERLAND

Cluny

Saône

Vichy

Clermont-
Ferrand

Lyon Rhône

Rhône

ALPES

ITALY

Grenoble

GUEDOC

Nîmes

Avignon PROVENCE

Montpellier

Arles

Aix-en-Provence

Nice — MONACO

CÔTE D'AZUR

Cannes

Marseille

Toulon

St. Tropez

Perpignan

0   50 mi

0   75 km

Mediterranean Sea

Corsica

iii

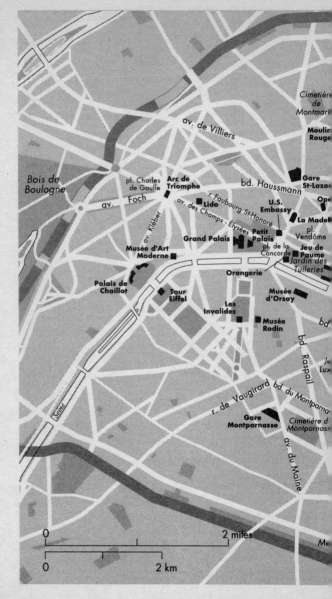

Cimetière de Montmartre

Moulin Rouge

av. de Villiers

bd. Haussmann

Gare St-Lazare

Bois de Boulogne

pl. Charles de Gaulle

Arc de Triomphe

av. Foch

r. Faubourg St-Honoré

Lido

av. des Champs - Élysées

av. Kléber

U.S. Embassy

Opéra

La Madeleine

pl. Vendôme

Grand Palais

Petit Palais

Musée d'Art Moderne

pl. de la Concorde

Jeu de Paume

Jardin des Tuileries

Palais de Chaillot

Orangerie

Tour Eiffel

Les Invalides

Musée d'Orsay

Musée Rodin

bd. Raspail

Seine

r. de Vaugirard

bd. du Montparnasse

Jardin du Luxembourg

Gare Montparnasse

Cimetière de Montparnasse

av. du Maine

Métro

0   2 miles

0   2 km

Parc de la Villette

Cimetière de Montmartre

Sacré Coeur

Moulin Rouge

pl. Pigalle

bd. de la Chapelle

Gare du Nord

Canal St-Martin Bassin de la Villette

Parc de Buttes-Chaumont

Gare St-Lazare

r. La Fayette

Gare de l'Est

Opéra

Folies Bergère

La Madeleine

pl. Vendôme

■ **Bourse**

Jeu de Paume
Jardin des Tuileries

Palais Royal

bd. de Sébastopol

pl. de la République

av. de la République

Musée Picasso

r. de Rivoli

Centre Pompidou

Louvre

bd. Voltaire

Cimetière du Père Lachaise

Palais de Justice

Hôtel de Ville

pl. des Vosges

bd. St-Germain

Ile de la Cité

Notre Dame

pl. de la Bastille

Ile St-Louis

r. du Faubourg St-Antoine

Sorbonne

Jardin du Luxembourg

bd. Raspail

pl. de la Nation

bd. St-Michel

Panthéon

Montparnasse

matière du ntparnasse

Gare d'Austerlitz

Seine

Gare de Lyon

pl. d'Italie

Parc Montsouris

FODOR'S FRENCH FOR TRAVELERS

EDITORS: Emmanuelle Morgen, Christopher Warnasch

Contributors: Christine Boucher, Rosa Jackson

Editorial Production: Marina Padakis

Maps: David Lindroth, *cartographer;* Rebecca Baer and Robert P. Blake, *map editors*

Design: Guido Caroti, *cover and interior designer;* Jolie Novak, Melanie Marin, *photo editors;* Kayley LeFaiver, *graphics*

Cover Photo: Daniel Thierry/DIAF

Production/Manufacturing: Pat Ehresmann

COPYRIGHT

SPECIAL SALES

Fodor's Travel Publications are available at special discounts for bulk purchases for sales promotions or premiums. Special editions, including personalized covers, excerpts of existing guides, and corporate imprints, can be created in large quantities for special needs. For more information, contact your local bookseller or write to Special Markets, Fodor's Travel Publications, 280 Park Avenue, New York, NY 10017. Inquiries from Canada should be directed to your local Canadian bookseller or sent to Random House of Canada, Ltd., Marketing Department, 2775 Matheson Boulevard East, Mississauga, Ontario L4W 4P7. Inquiries from the United Kingdom should be sent to Fodor's Travel Publications, 20 Vauxhall Bridge Road, London SW1V 2SA, England.

PRINTED IN THE UNITED STATES OF AMERICA

10 9 8 7 6 5 4 3 2 1

CONTENTS

15 ACTIVITIES AND ENTERTAINMENT   176

16 GRAMMAR IN BRIEF   189

PREFACE

You don't need to know French to get along in the French-speaking world. The hundreds of French phrases in this guide will see you through almost every situation you encounter as a tourist, from asking for directions at the start of your trip to conversing in a bar at the end. To make yourself understood, all you have to do is read the phonetics that appear after each expression just as you would any English sentence. You'll come closer to approximating French sounds if you study the pronunciation guide at the beginning of the book, and you can really polish your speech with *Fodor's French for Travelers* cassette or CD, on which native speakers pronounce the guide's key French dialogues. The words and phrases that are boldfaced in this book are recorded on the cassette and CD supplement.

If you want to understand the structure of the language and begin to learn it on your own, check out the grammar chapter, Chapter 16. Additionally, a two-way 1,600-word dictionary at the end references all the key words in the book.

To get the most out of your trip, read the travel tips and cultural information about Canada, Belgium, and France interspersed throughout the chapters. You'll find, among other things, traditional French menu items, bank and store hours, metric conversion tables, and federal holidays, all gathered by Fodor's expert resident-writers.

Before you start chatting away, be sure to familiarize yourself with the table of contents on the previous pages, so that you know where to quickly find phrases and information when you need them.

Bon Voyage—Enjoy your trip!

THE BEST OF ALL POSSIBLE WORLDS

France is neither too hot nor too cold, neither too wet nor too dry, neither too flat nor crammed with inconvenient mountains. At any rate, that is what the French say. They think that countries should be hexagonal in shape and about 600 miles across. Spain is too square, Norway is frayed at the edges, the United Kingdom and Ireland are awkwardly surrounded by cold water, Switzerland is landlocked and too small, and the United States is too large (you cross three time zones and then get the same depressing dinner). After God created France, He belatedly realized that He had gone too far: It was too near perfection. "How can I restore the balance?" He asked Himself. Then He saw what to do—He created the French. That is a French story. The French enjoy grumbling about themselves or, rather, about other French people, but in the same breath they admit that there is only one civilized way for people to live, and that is the French way, *la civilisation française*.

There is something to be said for this view. In many parts of France people are kind, patient, and friendly, behaving with natural dignity and good manners (except Parisians in the rush hour). Visitors to France, particularly Anglo-Saxon visitors, will have a better time whether they stay a week or a year if they "go native" as far as they find it practicable—and when and where they don't, they should be philosophically aware of the drawbacks of trying to behave as in dear old Birmingham, Alabama or Birmingham, England. (The term "Anglo-Saxon" is used as the French use it. To them, Louis Armstrong, Robert Burns, James Joyce, and Frank Sinatra are representative Anglo-Saxons; Beowulf and King Alfred have nothing to do with it.)

Let's look at the French timetable. Most of the French are up early, gulping a café au lait and getting to work by 9. By 10, Parisian executives are fuming because their London contacts haven't yet answered the phone (it's now 9 in England). There is no coffee break.

At noon, they are hungry. Work stops for an hour, sometimes two. *Le déjeuner* (called *le dîner* in the country) is a sacred rite. Fast-food outlets have multiplied, but the norm is a proper meal, taking at least an hour; a surprising number manage to get home for it. However, six lunches out of ten are eaten at restaurants using *tickets restaurants* [tee-KEH reh-stoh-RAH(N)] (company-subsidized meal coupons), or at staff cafeterias, where nearly everyone opts for a substantial hot meal.

After lunch it's back to work for another four-hour stretch. No tea or coffee break. Are the French mighty toilers? Yes and no. They work very hard, but on the other hand, wage earners and schoolchildren have many leisure days. The average industrial worker puts in 1,872 hours of work in the United States, 1,750 in Great Britain, but only 1,650 in France. Only since January 2002, have companies with more than 20 employees been required to respect a 35-hour work week. Five weeks' paid vacation is the official minimum, there are many public holidays. One family in ten has a second house in the country, where they go on weekends and vacations, causing astounding traffic jams as they flee the cities.

If the average French working person finishes the day's work at 6 or 6:30, will he or she call in a favorite café for a chat and an aperitif on the way home? Probably not, nowadays. In the past, the café was used as a sort of extra living room for meeting friends or making professional contacts, or even for writing novels if you were Jean-Paul Sartre or Simone de Beauvoir. But today an average of two hours and fifty minutes is spent watching television at home, which reduces the time available for social life.

The number of cafés has diminished. Fortunately, there are still a lot left, and how convenient they are for the visitor! On the terrace of a French café, you can bask in the sun or enjoy the shade of a parasol, sipping a cool beer or glass of wine and keeping an eye on life's passing show. A small black coffee entitles you to spend an hour or two—no hurry.

Some people—notably Americans—complain that the French are inhospitable and standoffish. The fact is that they are great respecters of privacy. If the Englishman's home is his castle, the Frenchman's apartment or house is his lair. People simply do not pop into one another's lairs, drinking casual cups of coffee and borrowing half a pound of sugar. They need a neutral place, such as a café, in which to socialize.

When talking with the French, there are conventions that should be observed if you don't want to be thought a barbarian by people who are unaware of Anglo-Saxon attitudes. You must say

"*Bonjour*" preferably followed by *Monsieur, Madame, Mademoiselle, Messieurs, Mesdames,* or *Messieurs Dames* much more often than you would think necessary (on entering a small shop, for instance) and "*Au revoir, Monsieur, Madame,*" etc.). Hands are shaken frequently (by colleagues at work, morning and evening, and by the most casual acquaintances). Friends and even colleagues make a ritual of *la bise* (lah beez), two, three, or four kisses, depending on where you are in France. Men generally shake hands. On going through a door, a certain amount of *après-vous*-ing is normal, with *pardon* if you go through first, turning your back. Men are still chivalrous, and women are not expected to take offense. Getting on first-name terms is a sign of much greater intimacy than in England or the United States. Rush-hour Parisian life is more brutal, of course, and, as elsewhere in the world, the driving seat of a car exerts a malign influence.

Back home from the café, *le dîner* (still called *le souper* in the country) is served around 8. It's a lighter meal than at midday, with soup replacing hors d'oeuvres in the country. The movies, after a sharp fall as television established itself in every home, remain popular. Except in Paris and a few other big cities, where they can be seen in *v.o.* (*version originale*), films are dubbed into French, a practice deplored by intellectuals.

Almost all employed people now have a two-day weekend, usually Saturday and Sunday, but Sunday and Monday for many shop workers. Sunday is a day for enjoying oneself and for the great Sunday ritual of going to church. Though 85 percent of the population declare themselves Catholics, only 15 percent of those go to church every week. Four out of ten will visit friends or relations. Sixty percent of families do more cooking on Sundays than on other days. This is also a big day for restaurants that feature a special Sunday menu. Half the French end their Sunday lunch with a fresh fruit tart or some sort of gâteau, which is why the pastry shops are open in the morning and why you see Frenchmen carefully carrying flat cardboard boxes. If invited to dine in a French home, it's polite to offer a bouquet of flowers rather than a bottle of wine that might clash with the meal.

An essay such as this has to contain rash generalizations. Is there an average French person? Obviously not. There are the rich and the poor, for example. The poor, in France, like champagne, oysters, and foie gras, but they get them less often than do the rich.

3

The same is true of other aspects of life. The gulf between one class and another is not one of tastes and aspirations; rich and poor are in broad agreement on what constitutes a pleasant life. The poor are simply farther away from it than are the rich. Both look down on conspicuous displays of wealth.

What do they think of us? Corresponding to the Anglo-Saxon stereotype that depicts the French all wearing berets and carrying baguettes or walking poodles, the French picture Americans as rich, generous, overweight, and likely in world politics or personal relationships to behave like well-meaning bulls in china shops and the English either as tall, silent, inhibited, masochistic, and scrupulously honest or as drunken, sadistic, soccer-watching vandals. Of course most people know better, but if you are going to attach a national label to yourself, you might as well be aware of the cliché lurking at the back of the mind.

"Happy as God in France" say the Germans, exaggerating a bit. Anglo-Saxons come in two sorts: those who love France and those who don't. It's a matter of taste and character. The former find it easy to slip into the French way of life for a week or a month or permanently. The latter are better off spending a short time in Paris or on the Riviera. But really, the French are canny operators when it comes to enjoying *la douceur de vivre,* the sweetness of life. If you follow their example while in France, you can't go far wrong. (One way to go wrong would be to quote almost any paragraph from this essay to them; at any rate, it will start a vigorously French argument.)

PRONUNCIATION GUIDE

Every French word or phrase in this book is presented along with its English equivalent and an easy-to-follow transcription (sound key) that provides the correct pronunciation. Simply read the transcription as you would read regular English and you will be speaking comprehensible French. Of course, there are differences between many English and French sounds. You can learn to imitate French pronunciations more accurately by using the *Fodor's French for Travelers* CD or cassette and by listening to the French speakers around you in your travels.

PRONUNCIATION CHART

The pronunciation chart presented below is your guide to the transcriptions used in the book. You will find it useful to spend some time learning what sounds are represented by the various French spellings. Then you will be able to follow the transcriptions without having to consult the chart. Pay special attention to the vowels; they determine the overall sound of the word and are crucial to comprehension.

Consonants

French Spelling	Approximate Sound	Symbol	Example
b, d, k, l, m, n, p, s, t, v, z	same as in English (see Note)		
c (before e, i, y)	s	[s]	cinéma seenaymah
c (before a, o, u)	k	[k]	cave kahv
ç (appears only before a, o, u)	s	[s]	français frah(n)seh (see Note)
ch	sh	[sh]	chaud shoh
g (before e, i, y)	s (as in measure)	[zh]	âge ahzh
g (before a, o, u)	g in game	[g]	gâteau gahtoh
gn	ny in onion	[ny]	agneau ahnyoh
h	always silent		homme ohm

French Spelling	Approximate Sound	Symbol	Example
j	s in measure	[zh]	Jacques zhahk
qu, final q	k	[k]	qui kee
r	pronounced in back of mouth, rolled like light gargling sound	[r]	Paris pahree
ss	s	[s]	tasse tahs
s (beginning of word or before consonant)	s	[s]	salle sahl disque deesk
s (between vowels)	z in Zelda	[z]	maison mayzoh(n)
th	t	[t]	thé tay
x	x in exact	[gz]	exact ehgzahkt
x	x in excellent	[ks]	excellent ehksehlah(n)
ll	y in yes	[y]	volaille vohlahy
ll	as in ill	[l]	elle ehl

Note: Final consonants are most often silent in French, e.g., *Paris* [pahree]. There are four letters, however, that are usually pronounced when final. These are *c, r, f,* and *l*. Please be *careful* about this rule!

Vowels

French Spelling	Approximate Sound	Symbol	Example
a, à, â	a in father	[ah]	la lah
é, er, ez (end of word)	ay in lay	[ay]	thé tay parler pahrlay allez ahlay
e plus final pronounced consonant	e in met	[eh]	belle behl (l is the final pronounced consonant)
è, ai, aî	e in met	[eh]	père pehr chaîne shehn
e, eu	u in put	[uh]	le luh
i	ee in beet	[ee]	ici eesee

i plus vowel	y in yesterday	[y]	lion lyoh(n)
o, au, eau, ô	o in both	[oh]	mot moh chaud shoh beau boh hôte oht
ou	oo in toot	[oo]	vous voo
oi, oy	wa in watt	[wah]	moi mwah
u	no equivalent in English—say ee, then round your lips	[ew] or [oo]	tu tew fumeurs fewmuhr
u plus i	wee as in week	[wee]	lui lwee
euille	no equivalent in English—say uh and follow it with y	[uhy]	feuille fuhy
eille	ay as in hay	[ehy]	merveilleux mehrvehyuh

Nasal Vowels

Nasal vowels are sounds produced when air is expelled from both the mouth and the nose. In French, a consonant that follows a nasal vowel is not fully pronounced. For example, the French word *on*: We pronounce the nasal vowel *o* through the mouth and nose, but we do not sound the following consonant *n*. That is, we do not touch the roof of our mouth with the tip of the tongue. In our transcription of French nasal vowels, we will therefore include an (n) or (m) in parentheses.

French Spelling	Approximate Sound	Symbol	Example
an, en	vowel in balm	[ah(n)]	France frah(n)s
em	vowel in balm	[ah(m)]	emmener ah(m)uhnay
in, ain, ein	vowel in man	[a(n)]	fin fa(n)
im, aim	vowel in man	[a(m)]	faim fa(m)
ien	y + vowel in men	[yeh(n)]	bien byeh(n)
ion	y + vowel in song	[yoh(n)]	station stahsyohn(n)

oin	w + vowel in man [wa(n)]	loin *lwa(n)*
on	vowel in song [oh(n)]	bon *boh(n)*
om	vowel in song [oh(m)]	tomber *toh(m)bay*
un	vowel in lung [uh(n)]	un *uh(n)*

STRESS

English, we stress certain syllables in a word (ri*dic*ulous) and certain words in a sentence (I *want* to go *home*). Stressed syllables are pronounced with greater force and loudness and are made longer than other syllables. In French, all syllables in a word and words in a sentence receive equal stress. Your French will be more comprehensible if you give every syllable a full, clear pronunciation.

LIAISON

Liaison means linking. French speakers pronounce *some* final consonants when the next word begins with a vowel. In this way, the two words are linked and the result is a more flowing, harmonious sound. For example:

> *Nous parlons français.* [Noo *pahrloh(n) frah(n)seh*.]

Here the *s* in *nous* is not pronounced since the next word begins with a consonant. There is no liaison.

> *Nous allons chez Philippe.* [Noo *zahloh(n) shay Feeleep.*]

Here the *s* in *nous* is pronounced since the next word begins with a vowel. This is a case of liaison. Note that *s* in liaison is pronounced *z*. In this volume, liaison consonants will be shown as the first sound in the second word.

ELISION

Another way that French preserves the ear-pleasing alternation of vowels and consonants is to drop the vowel in certain words when the next sound is a vowel. The most important of such elisions is with the definite articles *le* and *la* (masculine and feminine equivalents for *the* in English).

masculine singular	le film	*luh feelm*
but	l'ami	*lahmee*
feminine singular	la dame	*lah dahm*
but	l'orange	*lohrah(n)zh*

APPROACHING PEOPLE

COURTESY

Please.	S'il vous plaît.	Seel voo pleh.
Thank you.	Merci.	Mehrsee.
You're welcome.	De rien.	Duh ryeh(n).
Excuse me.	Pardon.	Pahrdoh(n).
It doesn't matter.	Ça ne fait rien.	Sah nuh fay ryeh(n).

GREETINGS

Good morning.	Bonjour.	Boh(n)zhoor.
Good afternoon.		
Hello. (formal)*		
Good evening.	Bonsoir.	Boh(n)swahr.
Good night. (bedtime)	Bonne nuit.	Bohn nwee.
Hello. (telephone)	Allô.	Ahloh.
Good-bye.	Au revoir.	Oh rvwahr.
See you soon.	À bientôt.	Ah byeh(n)toh.
See you later.	À tout à l'heure.	Ah toot ah luhr.
	À la prochaine.	Ah lah proh-shehn
See you tomorrow.	À demain.	Ah duhma(n).
Let's go!	Allons-y!	Ahloh(n)-zee!

QUESTION WORDS

Who?	Qui?	Kee?
What?	Quoi?	Kwah?
Why?	Pourquoi?	Poorkwah?
When?	Quand?	Kah(n)?

*You may hear people greeting each other with *Salut* [sahlew]. This is a very informal slang expression used among friends. Until you get to know someone very well, it's best to stick to the more formal *bonjour* [boh(n)zhoor].

Where?	Où?	Oo?
Where from?	D'où?	Doo?
Where are you going?	Où allez-vous?	Oo ahlay voo?
How?	Comment?	Kohmah(n)?
How much is it?	C'est combien?	Seh koh(m)byeh(n)?

ASKING FOR HELP

Excuse me,	Pardon,	Pahrdoh(n),
_Sir.	_Monsieur.	_Muhsyuh.
_Ma'am/Mrs./Ms.	_Madame.	_Mahdahm.
_Miss.	_Mademoiselle.	_Mahdmwahzehl.
Do you speak English?	Parlez-vous anglais?	Pahr-lay voo ah(n)gleh?
Do you understand English?	Comprenez-vous l'anglais?	Koh(m)prehnay-voo lah(n)gleh?
Yes./No.	Oui./Non.	Wee. Noh(n).
I'm sorry.	Je suis désolé(e).*	Zhuh swee dayzohlay.
I don't speak French.	Je ne parle pas français.	Zhuh nuh pahrl pah frah(n)seh.
I don't understand.	Je ne comprends pas.	Zhuh nuh koh(m)prah(n) pah.
I understand a little.	Je comprends un peu.	Zhuh koh(m)prah(n) uh(n) puh.
I'm a tourist.	Je suis un(e) touriste.†	Zhuh swee zuh(n) [zewn] tooreest.

*In French, adjectives agree in number and gender with the nouns they modify. *Désolé* is the masculine form and *désolée* is the feminine. Herein, the feminine endings will appear in parentheses. See also Chapter 16, Grammar in Brief (page 193), regarding the gender of adjectives.

†Note: In French, you generally add *e* to masculine nouns and adjectives to make them feminine, unless they already end in *e* (*touriste*, for example). To make masculine and feminine nouns and adjectives plural, just add *s*. So, if you're an American man, you'd say, "Je suis américai*n*." If you're an American woman, you'd say, "Je suis américai*ne*." A group of American women would say, "Nous sommes américai*nes*," while a mixed group of men and women would use the plural form, "Nous sommes américai*ns*."

I speak very little French.	Je parle un petit peu français.	Zhuh pahrl uh(n) ptee puh frah(n)seh.
Please speak more slowly.	**Parlez plus lentement, s'il vous plaît.**	**Pahrlay plew lah(n)-tmah(n), seel voo pleh.**
Please repeat.	Répétez, s'il vous plaît.	Raypaytay, seel voo pleh.
Could you please help me?	Pourriez-vous m'aider, s'il vous plaît?	Pooray-voo mehday, seel voo pleh?
Okay.	D'accord.	Dahkohr.
Of course.	Bien sûr.	Byeh(n) sewr.
Where is . . . ?	Où est . . . ?	Oo eh . . . ?
Thank you very much.	Merci beaucoup.	Mehrsee bohkoo.

EMERGENCIES

Fire!	**Au feu!**	**Oh fuh!**
Hurry!	**Vite!**	**Veet!**
Help!	**Au secours!**	**Oh skoor!**
Call the police!	**Appelez la police!**	**Ahplay lah pohlees!**
Call the fire department!	**Appelez les pompiers!**	**Ahplay lay poh(m)-pyay!**
I'm sick.	Je suis malade.	Zhuh swee mahlahd.
Call a doctor.	Appelez un médecin.	Ahplay uh(n) maydsa(n).
I'm lost.	Je suis perdu(e).	Zhuh swee pehrdew.
Can you help me, please?	**Pourriez-vous m'aider, s'il vous plaît?**	**Pooray-voo mehday, seel voo pleh?**
Stop, thief!	**Au voleur!**	**Oh vohluhr!**
Someone/they stole . . .	**On a volé . . .**	**Oh(n) ah vohlay . . .**
_my camera!	_mon appareil-photo!	_moh(n) nahpahrehy-fohtoh!
_my car!	_ma voiture!	_mah vwahtewr!
_my handbag!	_mon sac à main!	_moh(n) sahk ah ma(n)!

11

_my money!	_mon argent!	_moh(n) nahrzhah(n)!
_my passport!	_mon passeport!	_moh(n) pahspohr!
_my suitcase!	_ma valise!	_mah vahleez!
_my wallet!	_mon porte-feuille!	_moh(n) pohrtuhfuhy!
_my watch!	**_ma montre!**	**mah moh(n)tr!**
He's the thief.	C'est lui, le voleur.	Seh lwee, luh vohluhr.
Stop him/her!	**Arrêtez-le/la!**	**Ahrehtay-luh/-lah!**
Leave me alone!	Laissez-moi tranquille!	Lehsay-mwah troh(n)keel!
I'm going to call the police.	Je vais appeler la police.	Zhuh vay zahplay lah pohlees.
Where's the police station?	**Où est le poste de police?**	**Oo eh luh pohst duh pohlees?**
I want a lawyer.	**Je veux un avocat.**	**Zhuh vuh zuh(n) nahvohkah.**
I want an interpreter.	Je veux un interprète.	Zhuh vuh zuh(n) na(n)tehrpreht.
Is there someone here who speaks English?	Y a-t-il quelqu'un ici qui parle anglais?	Yahteel kehlkuh(n) nee see kee pahrl ah(n)glay?
I want to go to the American consulate.	Je veux aller au consulat américain.	Zhuh vuh zahlay oh koh(n)sewlah ahmay reeka(n).

COLORS

red	rouge	roozh
yellow	jaune	zhohn
green	vert	vehr
blue	bleu	bluh
white	blanc	blah(n)
brown	brun/marron	bruh(n)/mahroh(n)
orange	orange	ohrah(n)zh
purple	violet	vyohleh
black	noir	nwahr
gold	or/d'or	ohr / dohr
silver	en argent/ argenté	ah(n) nahr zhah(n) / ahr-zhah(n)-tay

NUMBERS AND QUANTITIES

Take the time to learn how to count in French. You'll find that knowing the numbers will make everything easier during your trip.

Cardinal Numbers

0	zéro	zayroh
1	un	uh(n)
2	deux	duh
3	trois	trwah
4	quatre	kahtr
5	cinq	sa(n)k*
6	six	sees*

*Note: The final consonants are not pronounced when the next word begins with a consonant. For example, *huit fois* (wee fwah) vs. *huit ans* (weet ah[n]).

7	sept	seht
8	huit	weet*
9	neuf	nuhf
10	dix	dees*
11	onze	oh(n)z
12	douze	dooz
13	treize	trehz
14	quatorze	kahtohrz
15	quinze	ka(n)z
16	seize	sehz
17	dix-sept	dee-seht
18	dix-huit	dee-zweet
19	dix-neuf	deez-nuhf
20	vingt	va(n)
21	vingt et un	va(n) tay uh(n)
22	vingt-deux	va(n)-duh
23	vingt-trois	va(n)-trwah
24	vingt-quatre	va(n)-kahtr
25	vingt-cinq	va(n)-sa(n)k
26	vingt-six	va(n)-sees
27	vingt-sept	va(n)-seht
28	vingt-huit	va(n)-tweet
29	vingt-neuf	va(n)-nuhf
30	trente	trah(n)t
31	trente et un	trah(n)t ay uh(n)
32	trente-deux	trah(n)t-duh
40	quarante	kahrah(n)t
50	cinquante	sa(n)kah(n)t
60	soixante	swahsah(n)t
61	soixante et un	swahsah(n)t ay uh(n)
62	soixante-deux	swahsah(n)t-duh

70*	soixante-dix	swahsah(n)t-dees
71	soixante et onze	swahsah(n)t ay oh(n)z
72	soixante-douze	swahsah(n)t-dooz
73	soixante-treize	swahsah(n)t-trehz
74	soixante-quatorze	swahsah(n)t-kahtohrz
75	soixante-quinze	swahsah(n)t-ka(n)z
76	soixante-seize	swahsah(n)t-sehz
77	soixante-dix-sept	swahsah(n)t-dee-seht
78	soixante-dix-huit	swahsah(n)t-dee-zweet
79	soixante-dix-neuf	swahsah(n)t-deez-nuhf
80*	quatre-vingts	kahtruh-va(n)
81	quatre-vingt-un	kahtruh-va(n)-uh(n)
82	quatre-vingt-deux	kahtruh-va(n)-duh
83	quatre-vingt-trois	kahtruh-va(n)-trwah
90*	quatre-vingt-dix	kahtruh-va(n)-dees
91	quatre-vingt-onze	kahtruh-va(n)-oh(n)z
92	quatre-vingt-douze	kahtruh-va(n)-dooz
100	cent	sah(n)
101	cent un	sah(n) uh(n)
102	cent deux	sah(n) duh
110	cent dix	sah(n) dees
120	cent vingt	sah(n) va(n)
200	deux cents	duh sah(n)
210	deux cent dix	duh sah(n) dees
300	trois cents	trwah sah(n)

*Note: In French, the number 70 (*soixante-dix*) is literally translated as "60-10." You must add *onze* (11) through *dix-neuf* (19) to *soixante* (60) to get the numbers 71 through 79. The number 80 (*quatre-vingts*) is literally translated as four twenties. The numbers 90 through 99 are formed the same way as the 70s, by adding the numbers *onze* (11) through *dix-neuf* (19) to the number *quatre-vingts* (80).

Practice counting aloud from 60 to 100 so you become comfortable with these numbers.

400	quatre cents	kahtruh sah(n)
500	cinq cents	sa(n) sah(n)
600	six cents	see sah(n)
700	sept cents	seht sah(n)
800	huit cents	wee sah(n)
900	**neuf cents**	**nuhf sah(n)**
1,000	**mille**	**meel**
1,100	mille cent	meel sah(n)
1,200	mille deux cents	meel duh sah(n)
2,000	deux mille	duh meel
10,000	dix mille	dee meel
50,000	cinquante mille	sa(n)kah(n)t meel
100,000	cent mille	sah(n) meel
1,000,000	un million	uh(n) meelyoh(n)
1,000,000,000	un milliard	uh(n) meelyahr

Ordinal Numbers

first (*m*)	**premier** (1er)	**pruhmyay**
first (*f*)	**première** (1ère)	**pruhmyehr**
second	**deuxième** (2e)	**duhzyehm**
third	**troisième** (3e)	**trwahzyehm**
fourth	**quatrième**	**kahtreeyehm**
fifth	cinquième	sa(n)kyehm
sixth	sixième	seezyehm
seventh	septième	sehtyehm
eighth	huitième	weetyehm
ninth	neuvième	nuhvyehm
tenth	dixième	deezyehm
twentieth	vingtième	va(n)tyehm
hundredth	centième	sah(n)tyehm

Note: In French, decimal points are indicated by commas. For example, 6.5 would be written 6,5 (*six virgule cinq*) and pronounced *sees veergewl sa(n)k*.

Quantities

a half	une moitié	ewn mwahtyay
half of	un demi de	uh(n) duhmee duh
a half hour	une demie heure	ewn duhmee uhr
a third	un tiers	uh(n) tyehr
a quarter	un quart	uh(n) kahr
two-thirds	deux tiers	duh tyehr
3 percent	trois pour cent	trwah poor sah(n)
a lot of, many	beaucoup de	bohkoo duh
a little of	un peu de	uh(n) puh duh
a dozen (of)	une douzaine de	ewn doozehn duh
a few	quelques	kehlkuh
enough	assez de	ahsay duh
too little	trop peu de	troh puh duh
too much	trop de	troh duh
a kilo of	un kilo de	uh(n) keeloh duh
a glass of	un verre de	uh(n) vehr duh
a cup of	une tasse de	ewn tahs duh
once	une fois	ewn fwah
twice	deux fois	duh fwah
last	dernier (dernière)	dehrnyehr

DAYS, MONTHS, AND SEASONS

Days of the Week

Monday	lundi	luh(n)dee
Tuesday	mardi	mahrdee
Wednesday	mercredi	mehrkruhdee
Thursday	jeudi	zhuhdee
Friday	vendredi	vah(n)druhdee
Saturday	samedi	sahmdee
Sunday	dimanche	deemah(n)sh

Months

January	janvier	zhah(n)vyay
February	février	fayvryay
March	mars	mahrs
April	avril	ahvreel
May	mai	meh
June	juin	zhwa(n)
July	juillet	zhweeyay
August	août	oot
September	septembre	sehptah(m)br
October	octobre	ohktohbr
November	novembre	nohvah(m)br
December	décembre	daysah(m)br

Seasons

winter	l'hiver	leevehr
spring	le printemps	luh pra(n)tah(m)
summer	l'été	laytay
fall	l'automne	lohtohn
in winter	en hiver	ah(n) neevehr
in spring	au printemps	oh pra(n)tah(m)
in summer	en été	ah(n) naytay
in fall	en automne	ah(n) nohtohn

THE DATE

What is today's date?	Quelle est la date d'aujourd'hui?	Kehl eh lah daht dohzhoordwee?
What day is it today?	Quel jour sommes-nous aujourd'hui?	Kehl zhoor sohm-noo ohzhoordwee?
Today is Friday, April 1.	Aujourd'hui nous sommes le vendredi, premier* avril.	Ohzhoordwee noo sohm luh vah(n)druhdee, pruhmyehr ahvreel.

*Note: *Le premier* (the first) is used for the first day of each month. Otherwise, regular cardinal numbers are used for dates.

| Today is May 18, 2003. | Aujourd'hui nous sommes le dix-huit mai, deux mille trois. | Ohzhoordwee noo sohm luh deezwee may, duh meel trwah. |

HOLIDAYS

The following are public holidays in France. When a holiday falls on a Thursday or a Tuesday, many businesses close for a four-day weekend.

January 1	Le jour de l'an	New Year's Day
March–April	Pâques	Easter
March–April	Lundi de Pâques	Easter Monday
May 1	La Fête du Travail	May Day (Labor Day)
May 8	L'armistice de 1945	Armistice Day (1945)
May–June	L'Ascension	Ascension Thursday
May–June	Lundi de la Pentecôte	Whitmonday
July 14	La Fête Nationale	Bastille Day
August 15	L'Assomption	Assumption Day
November 1	La Toussaint	All Saints' Day
November 11	L'Armistice	Armistice Day
December 25	Noël	Christmas Day
December 26	Saint-Etienne	Saint Stephen's Day
Merry Christmas!	Joyeux Noël!	Zhwahyuh noh-ehl!
Happy New Year!	Bonne Année!	Bohn ahnay!
Happy Easter!	Joyeuses Pâques!	Zhwahyuhz pahk!
Happy holidays!	Passez de bonnes fêtes!	Pahsay duh bohn feht!
Happy Patron Saint Day!	Bonne fête!	Bohn feht!

AGE

How old are you?	Quel âge avez-vous?	Kehl ahzh ahvay-voo?
I'm 36.	J'ai trente-six ans.	Zheh trah(n)t-see zah(n).
How old is he/she?	Quel âge a-t-il/a-t-elle?	Kehl ahzh ahteel/ ahtehl?

19

He's (she's) 20.	Il a (elle a) vingt ans.	Eel ah (ehl ah) va(n) tah(n).
I'm younger than he is.	Je suis plus jeune que lui.	Zhuh swee plew zhuhn kuh lwee.
I was born in 1970.	Je suis né(e) en mille neuf cent soixante-dix.	Zhuh swee nay ah(n) meel nuhf sah(n) swahsah(n)t-dees.
His birthday is December 2.	**Son anniversaire est le deux décembre.**	**Soh(n) nahneevehrsayr ay luh duh daysah(m)bruh.**

TELLING TIME AND EXPRESSIONS OF TIME

What time is it?	Quelle heure est-il?	Kehl uhr ehteel?
It's . . .	Il est . . .	Eel eh . . .
_three o'clock	_trois heures	_trwah zuhr
_three-fifteen	_trois heures et quart	_trwah zuhr ay kahr
_three-thirty	_trois heures et demie	_trwah zuhr ay duh-mee
_two forty-five	_trois heures moins le quart	_trwah zuhr mwah(n) luh kahr*
_three-ten	_trois heures dix	_trwah zuhr dees
_two-fifty	_trois heures moins dix	_trwah zuhr mwah(n) dees
It's . . .	Il est . . .	Eel eh . . .
_midnight	_minuit	_meenwee
_noon	_midi	_meedee
_three AM	_trois heures du matin	_trwah zuhr dew mahta(n)
_three PM	_trois heures de l'après-midi	_trwah zuhr duh lahpreh meedee
_six PM	_six heures du soir	_see zuhr dew swahr

*Note: After the half hour on the clock, minutes are subtracted from the next hour. The literal translation of the French for 2:45 is "it's three minus a quarter (of an hour)."

five minutes ago	il y a cinq minutes	eel yah sa(...
in a half hour	dans une demi-heure	dah(n) zewn... uhr
since seven PM	depuis sept heures du soir	duhpwee seht ... swahr
after eight PM	après huit heures du soir	ahpreh weet uhr ... swahr
before nine AM	avant neuf heures du matin	ahvah(n) nuh vuhr dew mahta(n)
When does it begin?	A quelle heure est-ce que ça commence?	Ah kehl uhr ehskuh sah kohmah(n)s?
He came . . .	Il est arrivé . . .	Eel ay tahreevay
_on time	_à l'heure	_ah luhr
_early	_tôt	_toh
_late	_en retard	_ah(n) ruhtahr

The 24-Hour Clock

In European countries, after 12 PM (noon) time is often stated as 13 hours, 14 hours, etc., similar to military time in the United States. This system—from 1 hour (1 AM) to 24 hours (12 AM midnight)—is generally used for transportation schedules and theater times. Simply add 12 to all times beyond 12 PM (noon), hence 3 PM is 3 plus 12, or 15 hours. The following chart will help you for quick reference.

Official Time Chart

1 AM	1h00	Une heure	Ewn uhr
2 AM	2h00	Deux heures	Duh zuhr
3 AM	3h00	Trois heures	Trwah zuhr
4 AM	4h00	Quatre heures	Kahtr uhr
5 AM	5h00	Cinq heures	Sah(n)k uhr
6 AM	6h00	Six heures	See zuhr
7 AM	7h00	Sept heures	Seht uhr
8 AM	8h00	Huit heures	Weet uhr
9 AM	9h00	Neuf heures	Nuh vuhr
10 AM	10h00	Dix heures	Dee zuhr
11 AM	11h00	Onze heures	Oh(n)z uhr
12 PM	12h00	Midi	meedee
1 PM	13h00	Treize heures	Trehz uhr

PM	14h00	Quatorze heures	Kahtohrz uhr
3 PM	15h00	Quinze heures	Ka(n)z uhr
4 PM	16h00	Seize heures	Sehz uhr
5 PM	17h00	Dix-sept heures	Dees-seht uhr
6 PM	18h00	Dix-huit heures	Deez-weet uhr
7 PM	19h00	Dix-neuf heures	Deez-nuh vuhr
8 PM	20h00	Vingt heures	Vah(n) tuhr
9 PM	21h00	Vingt-et-une heures	Vah(n) tay ewn uhr
10 PM	22h00	Vingt-deux heures	Vah(n)-duh zuhr
11 PM	23h00	Vingt-trois heures	Vah(n)-trwah zuhr
12 AM	0h00	zéro heure	zayroh uhr

The show you're planning to see might start at 7:30 PM or 19h30 (*dix-neuf heures trente*).

Expressions of Time

now	**maintenant**	ma(n)tuhnah(n)
earlier	**plus tôt**	plew toh
later	**plus tard**	plew tahr
before	**avant**	ahvah(n)
after/afterward	**après**	ahpreh
soon	**bientôt**	byeh(n)toh
once	**une fois**	ewn fwah
in the morning	le matin	luh mata(n)
at noon	à midi	ah meedee
in the afternoon	l'après-midi	lahpreh-mee-dee
in the evening	le soir	luh swahr
at night	la nuit	lah nwee
at midnight	à minuit	ah meenwee
tomorrow	demain	duhma(n)
yesterday	hier	eeyehr
the day after tomorrow	après-demain	ahpreh-duhma(n)
the day before yesterday	avant-hier	ahvah(n)-tyehr
this week	cette semaine	seht suhmehn
next week	la semaine prochaine	lah suhmehn proh-shehn

last week	la semaine dernière	lah suhmehn dehrnyehr
every day	tous les jours	too lay zhoor
in 3 days	dans trois jours	dah(n) trwah zhoor
2 days ago	il y a deux jours	eelyah duh zhoor
on Saturdays	**le samedi**	**luh suhmdee**
on weekends	le weekend	luh weekehnd
on weekdays (during the week)	pendant la semaine	pah(n)dah(n) lah suhmehn
a working day	un jour ouvrable	uh(n) zhoor oovrahbl
a day off	un jour de congé	uh(n) zhoor duh koh(n)zhay
in January	en janvier	ah(n) zhah(n)vyay
last January	en janvier dernier	ah(n) zhah(n)vyay dehrnyay
next January	en janvier prochain	ah(n) zhah(n)vyay proh-sha(n)
each month	**chaque mois**	**shahk mwah**
every month	tous les mois	too lay mwah
since August	**depuis août**	**duhpwee oot**
this month	ce mois-ci	suh mwah-see
next month	le mois prochain	luh mwah prohsha(n)
last month	le mois dernier	luh mwah dehrnyay
this year	cette année	seht ahnay
next year	**l'année prochaine**	**lahnay prohshehn**
last year	l'année dernière	lahnay dehrnyehr
every year	chaque année	shahk ahnay
In what year . . .	En quelle année . . .	Ah(n) kehl ahnay . . .
In 1980 . . .	En mil neuf cent quatre-vingts . . .	Ah(n) meel nuhf sah(n) kahtruh-va(n) . . .
In the nineteenth century . . .	Au dix-neuvième siècle . . .	Oh deeznuhvyehm syehkl . . .
In the forties . . .	Dans les années quarante . . .	Dah(n) lay zahnay kahrah(n)t . . .

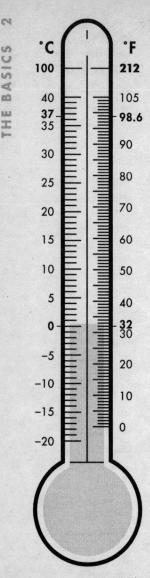

TEMPERATURE CONVERSIONS

In both France and Canada, temperature is measured in degrees Celsius, or centigrade. To convert degrees Celsius into degrees Fahrenheit, use this formula:

To convert centigrade to Fahrenheit

$$\left(\frac{9}{5}\right)C° + 32 = F°$$

1. Divide by 5
2. Multiply by 9
3. Add 32

To convert Fahrenheit to centigrade

$$(F° - 32)\frac{5}{9} = C°$$

1. Subtract 32
2. Divide by 9
3. Multiply by 5

WEATHER

What's the weather today?	Quel temps fait-il aujourd'hui?	Kehl tah(m) fayteel ohzhoordwee?
It's raining/ snowing.	Il pleut/neige.	Eeh pluh/nehzh.
It's sunny.	Il ya du soleil.	Eelyah dew sohlehy.
It's foggy.	Il ya du brouillard.	Eelyah dew brooyahr.
It's . . .	Il fait . . .	Eel feh . . .
_cold.	_froid.	_frwah.
_cool.	_frais.	_freh.
_cloudy.	_un temps couvert.	_uh(n) tah(m) koovehr.
_foggy.	_du brouillard.	_dew brooyahr.
_warm.	**_chaud.**	**_shoh.**
_hot.	_très chaud.	_tray shoh.
_nice.	**_beau.**	**_boh.**
_sunny.	_du soleil.	_dew sohlehy.
_windy.	_du vent.	_dew vah(n).
What's the forecast for tomorrow?	Quelle est la météo pour demain?	Kehl eh lah maytayoh poor duhma(n)?
It's going to rain.	Il va pleuvoir.	Eel vah pluhvwahr.
What is the average temperature at this time of year?	Quelle est la température moyenne en cette saison?	Kehl eh lah tah(m)payrahtewr mwahyehn ah(n) seht sayzoh(n)?

ABBREVIATIONS

A.C.F.	Automobile Club de France	Automobile Club of France
apr. J.-C.	après Jésus-Christ	A.D.
av. J.-C.	avant Jésus-Christ	B.C.
arr.	arrondissement	district (in Paris)
bd./boul.	boulevard	boulevard

c.-à-d.	c'est-à-dire	that is to say
C.C.P.	compte de chèques postaux	postal accounts
Cie	Compagnie	Company
C.R.S.	Compagnies Républicaines de Sécurité	French Riot Police
cv	chevaux-vapeur	horsepower
E.U.	Etats-Unis	United States
exp.	expéditeur	sender
€	euro	euro
F.S.	franc suisse	Swiss franc
M.	Monsieur	Mr.
Mlle	Mademoiselle	Miss
MM.	Messieurs	Gentlemen
Mme	Madame	Mrs.
P.D.G.	Président Directeur Général	Chief Executive Officer
ex.	(par) exemple	for example
p.p.	port payé	postage paid
P.T.T.	Postes et Télécommunications	Post Office & Telecommunications
R.A.T.P.	Régie Autonome des Transports Parisiens	Paris Transport Authority
R.D.	Route Départementale	local road
R.F.	République Française	French Republic
R.N.	Route Nationale	national road
S.A.	Société anonyme	inc.
S.I.	Syndicat d'Initiative	tourist office
S.N.C.F.	Société Nationale des Chemins de Fer Français	French National Railway
s.v.p.	s'il vous plaît	please
TTC	toutes taxes comprises	all taxes included

| TVA | taxe à la valeur ajoutée | sales tax (V.A.T.) |
| U.E.[1] | Union Européenne | European Union |

[1]You may still hear people refer to the C.E.E. (Communauté économique européenne), or the European Economic Community, the former name of the U.E.

3 AT THE AIRPORT

As a tourist, you should proceed through Customs (*La Douane*) as smoothly and rapidly as airport security and the number of arriving passengers will allow. Most of the personal belongings you bring into or out of Europe or Canada are duty-free. However, tobacco products and alcohol above certain amounts are taxed.

When leaving Europe, you may bring up to $400 worth of souvenirs duty-free back to the United States. Residents of the United Kingdom don't pass through Customs when returning from a trip spent wholly in the European Union. Canadian residents who have been out of Canada for more than a week may return with C$500 worth of goods duty-free; if they've been away less than a week but more than 48 hours, they may return with C$200 worth of goods. Australian residents 18 and older may bring home A$400 worth of souvenirs duty-free, and New Zealanders 17 and older may bring home NZ$700 worth of souvenirs.

Customs officials at major airports generally have a working knowledge of English. However, you may find the following phrases useful at the airport. First we present a typical exchange at passport control.

DIALOGUE
Customs and Immigration (Contrôle des Passeports)

Douanière:	Bonjour, Monsieur. Votre passeport, s'il vous plaît.	Boh(n)zhoor, muhsyuh. Vohtr pahspohr, seel voo pleh.
Touriste:	Voici mon passeport.	Vwahsee moh(n) pahspohr.
Douanière:	Vous êtes américain?	Voo zeht amehreeka(n)?
Touriste:	Oui, je suis américain.	Wee, zhuh swee zah-mehreeka(n).
Douanière:	Combien de temps allez-vous rester en France?	Koh(m)byeh(n) duh tah(m) ahlay-voo rehstay ah(n) frah(n)s?
Touriste:	Je vais rester une semaine.	Zhuh veh rehstay ewn suhmehn.

Customs Official:	Hello, sir. Your passport, please.
Tourist:	Here's my passport.
Customs Official:	Are you American?
Tourist:	Yes, I'm American.
Customs Official:	How long will you be in France?
Tourist:	I'll be here for a week.

CLEARING CUSTOMS

What is your nationality?	Quelle est votre nationalité?	Kehl eh vohtr nahsy-ohnahleetay?
I am . . .	Je suis . . .	Zhuh swee . . .
_American (m).	_américain.	_ahmayreeka(n).
_American (f).	_américaine.	_ahmayreekehn.
What's your name?	Comment vous appelez-vous?	Kohmah(n) voo zahplay-voo
My name is . . .	Je m'appelle . . .	Zhuh mahpehl . . .
Where are you staying?	Où est-ce que vous logez?	Oo ehskuh voo lohzhay?
I'm staying at the ____ Hotel.	Je loge à l'hôtel ____.	Zhuh lohzh ah lohtehl ____.
Are you here on vacation?	Vous êtes en vacances?	Voo zeht ah(n) vahkah(n)s?
Yes, I'm on vacation.	Oui, je suis en vacances.	Wee, zhuh swee zah(n) vahkah(n)s.
I'm just passing through.	Je suis de passage.	Zhuh swee duh pahsahzh.
I'm here on a business trip.	Je suis en voyage d'affaires.	Zhuh swee zah(n) vwahyahzh dahfehr.
I'll be here . . .	Je vais rester . . .	Zhuh vay rehstay . . .
_a week.	_une semaine.	_ewn smehn.
_several weeks.	_plusieurs. semaines.	_plewzyuhr smehn.
_a few days.	_quelques jours.	_kehlkuh zhoor.
_until ____.	_jusqu'à ____.	_zhewskah ____.

29

Nothing to declare	Rien à déclarer	Ryeh(n) nah day-klahray
Goods to declare	Articles à déclarer	Ahrteekl ah day-klahray
Do you have anything to declare?	Avez-vous quelque chose à déclarer?	Ahvay-voo kehlkuh shohz ah dayklahray?
I have nothing to declare.	**Je n'ai rien à déclarer.**	**Zhuh neh reeya(n) nah dayklahray.**
Can you open this bag?	Pouvez-vous ouvrir cette valise?	Pooveh-voo oovrrer seht vahleez?
You have to pay duty on these items.	Il faut payer des droits de douane sur ces articles.	Eel foh payay day drwah duh dwahn sewr say zahrteekl.
It's for my own personal use.	C'est pour mon usage personnel.	Seh poor moh(n) new-zahzh pehrsohnehl.
These are gifts.	Ce sont des cadeaux.	Suh soh(n) day kahdoh.
Have a nice stay!	Bon séjour!	Boh(n) sayzhoor!

LUGGAGE AND PORTERS

Porters are usually available at the principal airports and train stations. You may prefer to use the baggage cart to get your luggage to your ground transportation.

I need . . .	**Il me faut . . .**	**Eel muh foh . . .**
_a porter.	_un bagagiste*.	_uh(n) bagazheest.
_a baggage cart.	_un chariot.	_uh(n) sharyoh.
Here's my luggage.	Voici mes bagages.	Vwahsee may bahgahzh.
This is mine.	**C'est à moi.**	**Seh tah mwah.**
Take my bags . . .	**Portez mes bagages . . .**	**Pohrtay may bahgahzh . . .**
_to the taxi.	_jusqu'au taxi.	_zhewskoh taksee.
_to the bus stop.	_jusqu'à l'arrêt de bus.	_zhewskah lareh duh bews.

*An older term, *porteur,* may also be heard.

30

| Be careful, please! | Faites attention, s'il vous plaît! | Feht zahtah(n)syoh(n), seel voo pleh! |
| How much is that? | C'est combien? | Seh koh(m)byeh(n)? |

AIRPORT TRANSPORTATION AND SERVICES

Where is/are . . .	Où est/sont . . .	Oo eh/soh(n) . . .
_the car rental agencies?	_les agences de location de voitures?	_lay zahzhah(n)s duh lohkahsyoh(n) duh vwahtewr?
_the taxis?	_les taxis?	_lay tahksee?
_the duty-free shop?	_le magasin duty-free?	_luh mahgahza(n) dewtee free?
_the bus stop?	_l'arrêt de bus?	_lahray duh bews?
_the bus to the city?	_le bus qui va en ville?	_luh bews kee vah ah(n) veel?
_the information booth?	_le bureau des renseignements?	_luh bewroh duh rah(n)sehnyuhma(n)?
_the ticket counter?	_le comptoir?	_luh koh(m)twahr?
_the luggage check-in?	_l'enregistrement des bagages?	lah(n) rehzheestruhmah(n) day bahgahzh?
_the lost baggage office?	_le bureau des objets trouvés?	_luh bewroh dayzohbzhay troovay?
_the currency exchange?	_le bureau de change?	_luh bewroh duh shah(n)zh?
_the bathroom?	_les toilettes?	_lay twahleht?
_the exit?	_la sortie?	_lah sohrtee?
_the phone?	_le téléphone?	_luh taylayfohn?

FLIGHT ARRANGEMENTS

Is there a direct flight to Brussels?	Y a-t-il un vol direct pour Bruxelles?	Yahteel uh(n) vohl deerehkt poor Brewsehl?
What time does it leave?	A quelle heure part l'avion?	Ah kehl uhr pahr lahvyoh(n)?
I'd like . . .	Je voudrais . . .	Zhuh voodreh . . .

31

_a one-way ticket.	_un aller.	_uh(n) nahlay.
_a round-trip ticket.	_un aller-retour.	_uh(n) nahlay ruhtoor.
_a seat in first class.	_une place en première classe.	_ewn plahs ah(n) pruhmyehr klahs.
_a seat in tourist (coach) class.	_une place en classe économique.	_ewn plahs ah(n) klahs ehkohnohmeek.
_a seat in the no-smoking section.	_une place non-fumeur.	_ewn plahs noh(n)-fumuhr.
_a window seat.	_une place côté fenêtre.	_ewn plahs kohtay fuhnehtr.
_an aisle seat.	_une place côté couloir.	_ewn plahs kohtay koolwahr.
What is the arrival time? (lit., At what time does one arrive?)	A quelle heure est-ce qu'on arrive?	Ah kel uhr ehs koh(n) nahreev?
Do I need to change planes?	Faut-il que je change d'avions?	Fohteel kuh zhuh shah(n)zh dahvyoh(n)?
There's a connection in Geneva.	Il y a une correspondance à Genève.	Eel yah ewn kohreh-spoh(n)dah(n)s ah Zhuhnehv.
When is check-in?	A quelle heure est l'enregistrement?	Ah kel uhr eh lah(n)-rehzheestruhmah(n)?
What is the flight number?	Quel est le numéro du vol?	Kehl eh luh newmay-roh dew vohl?
From what gate does this flight leave?	De quelle porte part ce vol?	Duh kehl pohrt pahr suh vohl?
I'd like to ____ my reservation for flight number 43.	Je voudrais ____ ma réservation pour le vol numéro quarante-trois.	Zhuh voodreh ____ mah rayzehrvah-syoh(n) poor luh vohl newmayroh kahrah(n)t-trwah.
_confirm	_confirmer	_koh(n)feermay
_cancel	_annuler	_ahnewlay
_change	_changer	_shah(n)zhay

I'd like to check these bags.	Je voudrais enregistrer ces bagages.	Zhuh voodreh ah(n)rehzheestray say bahgahzh.
I only have this carry-on.	Je n'ai qu' un bagage à main.	Zhuh nay keh(n) bahgahzh ah meh(n).
How late is take-off going to be?	L'avion va partir avec combien de minutes de retard?	Lahvyoh(n) vah pahrteer ahvehk koh(m)byeh(n) duh meenewt duh ruhtahr?
May I have my boarding pass?	Puis-je avoir ma carte d'embarquement?	Pweezh ahvwahr mah kahrt dehmbahrkmah(n)?
Will they be serving a meal?	Va-t-on servir un repas?	Vahtoh(n) sehrveer uh(n) ruhpah?
I missed my plane.	J'ai manqué mon avion.	Zhay mah(n)kay moh(n) nahvyoh(n).
Will my ticket be good for the next flight?	Est-ce que mon billet sera valable pour le prochain vol?	Ehskuh moh(n) beeyay srah vahlahbl poor luh prohsha(n) vohl?

4 MONEY MATTERS

ABOUT THE CURRENCY

In France and Belgium, the unit of currency is the euro [uh(r)-ROH], which replaced the franc in both countries, and in the rest of the European Monetary Union, in January 2002. Exchange rates fluctuate, of course, but the euro, symbolized €, is often nearly equivalent to the U.S. dollar or half the British pound. The euro is divided into 100 cents.

Coins: 1, 2, 5, 10, 20, and 50 cents; 1 and 2 euros.

Banknotes: 5, 10, 20, 50, 100, 200, and 500 euros.

In Switzerland, the currency remains the Swiss franc, abbreviated SF or CHF, and is divided into 100 centîmes.

Coins: 5, 10, 20, and 50 centîmes; 1, 2, and 5 francs.

Banknotes: 10, 20, 50, 100, 500, and 1,000 francs.

In Canada, the monetary system is similar to that of the United States (dollars and cents). In recent years the Canadian dollar has been worth somewhat less than the U.S. dollar.

DIALOGUE   At the Bank (À la Banque)

Le client:	Pouvez-vous me changer cent dollars?	Pooveh-voo muh shah(n)zhay sah(n) dohlahr?
La caissière:	Certainement, Monsieur. Le cours est à un euro aujourd'hui. Ça vous fait donc cent euros.	Sehrteh(n)mah(n), muhsyuh. Luh koor eh tah ah(n) uhroh ohzho ordwee. Sah voo feh doh(n)k sah(n)tuhroh.
Le client:	Bien. Voici mes chèques de voyage.	Byeh(n). Vwahsee may shehk duh vwahyahzh.
La caissière:	Pourriez-vous les signer, Monsieur.	Pooryeh voo lay seenyay, muhsyuh.
Le client:	Bien sûr. Eh bien, voilà.	Byeh(n) sewr. Ay byeh(n), vwahlah.

| La caissière: | **Et votre passeport, s'il vous plaît.** | Ay vohtruh pahspohr, seel voo pleh. |
| Le client: | **Le voici.** | Luh vwahsee. |

Customer:	Could you change $100 for me?
Teller:	Certainly, sir. The rate is one euro to the dollar today. So that would be one hundred euros.
Customer:	Fine. Here are my traveler's checks.
Teller:	Would you please sign them, sir?
Customer:	Of course. Here they are.
Teller:	And your passport, please.
Customer:	Here it is.

CHANGING MONEY

Banks are generally open from 9 to noon and 2 to 5 although many of the larger banks in major cities remain open during the lunch break. You can change money at banks and at *bureaux de change* [bewroh duh shah(n)zh] (currency exchange offices), which are open beyond normal banking hours. You can also change money at some hotels. You will find the best exchange rates, however, at banks and at ATMs in the Cirrus and Plus networks. Usually three rates are dollars:

1. L'achat [lahshah]—the rate for buying dollars. This is the relevant rate for you since the bank is buying your dollars.

2. La vente [lah vah(n)t]—the rate for selling dollars. The dollar is worth less at this rate. Generally you're better off waiting until you return to the United States to change back your money.

3. Chèques de voyage [shehk duh vwahyahzh]—traveler's check rates, which differ slightly from cash rates.

Remember that at banks, you usually need your passport when exchanging money. At ATMs in France you can use only four-digit PIN numbers (so you may need to change your PIN before departure); transaction fees may be higher than at home. Make sure your credit cards have been programmed for use at ATMs if you want to use them to get cash advances.

Visa and Mastercard are accepted at most hotels, restaurants, and stores. Many establishments don't accept American Express because they are charged a higher fee. Signs indicating which cards are acceptable are usually prominently displayed in the establishment.

Where is the nearest bank?	Où est la banque la plus proche?	Oo eh lah bah(n)k lah plew prohsh?
Is there a currency exchange office nearby?	Y a-t-il un bureau de change près d'ici?	Yahteel uh(n) bewroh duh shah(n)zh preh deesee?
I'd like to change some dollars.	Je voudrais changer des dollars.	Zhuh voodreh shah(n)zhay day dohlahr.
How much is the dollar worth?	Combien vaut le dollar?	Koh(m)byeh(n) voh luh dohlahr?
I'd like to buy euros.	Je voudrais acheter des euros.	Zhuh voo-dreh ah-shuh-teh day zuh-roh.
Can I change traveler's checks?	Est-ce que je peux changer des chèques de voyage?	Ehskuh zhuh puh shah(n)zhay day shehk duh vwahyahzh?
Where do I sign?	Où est-ce que je dois signer?	Oo ehskuh zhuh dwah seenyay?
Can you give me . . .	Pouvez-vous me donner . . .	Pooveh-voo muh dohnay . . .
_large bills?	_l'argent en grosses coupures?	_lahrzhah(n) ah(n) grohs koopewr?
_small bills?	_l'argent en petites coupures?	_lahrzhah(n) ah(n) puhteet koopewr?
_five 5-euro bills?	_cinq billets de cinq euros?	_sa(n) beeyay duh sa(n) kuh-roh?
_some change?	_de la monnaie?	_duh lah mohneh?

PAYING THE BILL

The bill, please.	L'addition, s'il vous plaît.	Lahdeesyoh(n), seel voo pleh.
How much is it?	C'est combien?	Seh koh(m)byeh(n)?
Is service included?	Le service est-il compris?	Luh sehrvees eh teel koh(m)pree?
This is for you.	C'est pour vous.	Seh poor voo.

36

TIPPING

Tipping should be the least of one's problems in France. There's a 15% service charge built into all restaurant and hotel bills and charges at barbers and beauty parlors.

Tipping is optional for cab rides but the French typically round up the fare or give the driver an extra euro. When you call a cab in France or in Belgium, you are charged from the moment it leaves to pick you up. A surcharge is added for luggage transport, airport and railway station pickups, and nighttime pickups. In Paris, there is a €5 minimum charge for any taxi ride.

Airport and railway porters charge a posted fee, but an additional €.50 tip is appreciated. Give hotel porters and bellhops a euro or two. Tip the concierge according to any special services he or she may have performed, such as procuring hard-to-get theater or concert tickets. Room service warrants a tip of about €.50, even though there is already a room service charge. Tipping the room-cleaning staff is entirely optional; if you stay a week, you may leave a euro in the room on the last day.

Tip bus tour guides and museum guides €.50 to a euro. Tip theater ushers €.50.

At bars and in cafés and restaurants, the service charge is always included in the bill. There are no exceptions. Set your mind at ease. Whatever you leave above and beyond is up to you. The French leave no more than small change, maybe one or two euros on an average dinner bill.

An exception to all this may occur in a truly great restaurant with outstanding service, where the captain, waiter, and sommelier (wine steward) go out of their way to turn your meal into a really memorable experience. In that case, any extras will be appreciated. But distribute individually, with *mercis* and handshakes, in the French style. Leaving money on the table is considered rude.

5 GETTING AROUND

EXPLORING ON FOOT

It is hard to dispute the old adage that the best way to get to know a new city is to explore it on foot. Many of the better guide books encourage this by providing self-guided walking tours of the prominent landmarks and neighborhoods in major cities. The following section is designed to help you orient yourself and get directions from natives as you move about the city.

You may notice that in providing street directions, the French rarely talk about numbers of *blocks* (*rue* [rew] or *pâtés de maisons* [pahtay duh mehzoh(n)]). They are much more likely to refer to the distance in meters (*mètres* [mehtr]) or point out landmarks such as traffic lights (*feux de circulation* [fuh duh seerkewlahsyoh(n)]). This is understandable when you consider how irregular and unpredictable street patterns are in many European cities!

FINDING YOUR WAY IN PARIS

If you are staying in Paris for any length of time or if you plan to go anywhere that is not a major tourist attraction, well-known hotel, or restaurant, you might do well to purchase *Fodor's Citypack Paris* or any of the other handy little map-guides to the city. Paris is divided into 20 *arrondissements*, or districts, and Parisian addresses will include the number of the arrondissement. The map-guides include a complete index of street names plus individual arrondissement maps and a map of the entire city. The city maps will also indicate the nearest *métro* station for any location. Some of these guides also feature lists of churches, embassies, hospitals, theaters, parks, cinemas, police stations, gardens, department stores, etc., along with their addresses. These materials can be found at bookstores and street kiosks.

Excuse me, sir/madam/miss.	Pardon, Monsieur/ Madame/ Mademoiselle.	Pahrdoh(n), muhsyuh/ mahdahm/ mahduhmwahzehl.

Where is the Pantheon?	Où est le Panthéon?	Oo eh luh pah(n)tay-oh(n)?
Do you have a map of the city?	Avez-vous un plan de la ville?	Ahvay-voo uh(n) plah(n) duh lah veel?
Could you show me on the map, please?	Montrez-moi sur le plan, s'il vous plaît?	Moh(n)tray-mwah sewr luh plah(n), seel voo pleh?
Can I get there on foot?	Puis-je y aller à pied?	Pweezh ee ahlay ah pyay?
How far is it?	C'est à quelle distance?	Seh tah kehl dees-tah(n)s?
I think I'm lost.	Je crois que je suis perdu(e).	Zhuh krwah kuh zhuh swee pehrdew.
How can I get to this address?	Comment puis-je aller à cette adresse?	Kohmah(n) pwee zhuh ahlay ah seht ahdrehs?
How long does it take on foot?	Combien de temps est-ce que cela prend à pied?	Koh(m)byeh(n) duh tah(m) ehskuh slah prah(n) ah pyay?

Here are a few responses you may get to your questions:

C'est tout droit.	Seh too drwah.	It's straight ahead.
Tournez à gauche (à droite).	Toornay ah gohsh (ah drwaht).	Turn left (right).
C'est là-bas.	Seh lah-bah.	It's down there.
C'est . . .	Seh . . .	It's . . .
_derrière ____	_dehryehr ____	_behind ____
_devant ____	_duhvah(n) ____	_in front of ____
_à côté de ____	_ah kohtay duh ____	_next to ____
_près de ____	_preh duh ____	_near ____
_après ____	_ahpray ____	_after ____
Tournez à gauche après le carrefour.	Toornay ah gohsh ahpreh luh kahrfoor.	Turn left after the intersection.
On ne peut pas y aller à pied.	Oh(n) nuh puh pah zee ahlay ah pyay.	You can't get there on foot.
Vous n'êtes pas sur le bon chemin.	Voo neht pah sewr luh boh(n) shuhma(n).	You are not on the right road.
C'est après les feux.	Seh tahpreh lay fuh.	It's beyond the traffic light.

DIALOGUE   On the Street (Dans la Rue)

Touriste:	**Pardon, Monsieur, pour aller au Musée d'Orsay s'il vous plaît**	Pahrdoh(n), muhsyuh, poor ahlay oh Mewzay dahrsay see voo play?
Parisien:	**Oui, ce n'est pas loin d'ici. Continuez tout droit et le musée sera sur la gauche.**	Wee, suh nay pah lwa(n) deesee. Koh(n)teeneway too drwah ay luh mewzay suhrah suhr lah gohsh.
Touriste:	**Merci. Alors, je peux y aller à pied?**	Mehrsee. Ahlohr, zhuh puh ee ahlay ah pyay?
Parisien:	**Ah oui! Bien sûr! Mais le musée est fermé aujourd'hui. Il est fermé le lundi.**	Ah wee! Byeh(n) sewr! May luh mewzay ay fehr-may ohzhoordwee. Eel ay fehrmay luh luh(n)dee.
Touriste:	**Tant pis. J'irai demain.**	Tah(n) pee. Zheeray duhma(n).
Parisien:	**Alors, bon séjour à Paris!**	Ahlohr, boh(n) sayzhoor ah Pahree!

....

Tourist:	Excuse me, sir, how can I get to the Orsay Museum?
Parisian:	Yes, it's not far from here. Continue straight ahead and the museum will be on the left.
Tourist:	Thanks. So I can walk there?
Parisian:	Yes, of course! But the museum is closed today. It's closed on Mondays.
Tourist:	Too bad. I'll go tomorrow.
Parisian:	Well, have a good stay in Paris!

PUBLIC TRANSPORTATION

Paris is endowed with the greatest public transportation system of any of Europe's major cities. A city-to-suburb network, the RER, connects with the superb, in-city Métro system. It's all the result of a highly subsidized program that keeps everything moving in Paris, and at prices that everyone can afford.

The fare system sounds more complicated than it is. These are the choices: you can buy tickets one at a time, either at a Métro station or on the bus, or in blocks of ten (Métro stations only) by asking for *un carnet* [uh(n) kahrnay]. On a ten-ride basis, the price is cut by about a third. Tickets for the RER, which takes you further out (all the way to Versailles, if you like) cost more depending on how far you travel.

On the Métro, one ticket will get you one ride anywhere on the system, regardless of the number of transfers. By bus, one ticket gets you a ride on one bus. If you change buses, you need another ticket. But for a visitor there are far better schemes. There's the so-called *Formule 1*, which means unlimited rides for one day on all public transportation within city limits at great savings. Then there are tourist passes, called *Paris-visite*, for one, two, three, and five days at reasonable rates.

If you are staying in Paris longer, the biggest money-saver of all is the *Carte orange*. This is the commuter ticket geared to natives on a monthly basis. There is also a *Coupon hebdomadaire* issued by the week—Monday to Sunday—which can be bought by visitors. What you get is unlimited transportation for seven days.

For the *Carte orange* and *Coupon hebdomadaire* you need a passport-type photo; most railway station Métro sections have photo machines for do-it-yourself picture-taking.

With all of these you get a pass, with a slot containing what looks like a regular Métro ticket, except that the magnetic tape is computer-set for constant reuse in Métro turnstiles. *Note: You must put your name and signature on the pass. And you must write the pass number on the ticket.* On buses, simply flash the pass (with ticket in it) at the driver as you get on. Do not stamp, or *composte* [koh(m)-POST], the ticket or it will no longer work in the Métro. Be sure to hold on to your ticket until the end of your trip: You need it to show to a ticket controller if you are asked, and to get out of RER stations.

To make it easier to use the bus and Métro, the entire system is documented in easy-to-understand maps and diagrams.

USING THE MÉTRO

Where's the nearest subway station?

Où est la station de métro la plus proche?

Oo eh lah stahsyoh(n) duh maytroh lah plew prohsh?

What line goes to ____?	Quelle ligne va à ____?	Kehl leenyuh vah ah ____?
Is this the train for ____?	Est-ce bien le métro qui va à ____?	Ehs byeh(n) luh mehtroh kee vah ah ____?
Where do I change to go to ____?	Où faut-il changer pour aller à ____?	Oo fohteel shah(n)zhay poor ah-lay ah ____?
Do I get off here to go to ____?	Est-ce que je descends ici pour aller à ____?	Ehskuh zhuh dehsah(n) zeesee poor ahlay ah ____?

Subway Signs

Guichet	Ticket Window
Tête de train	Head of the Train (the train stops here)

ON THE BUS

What bus do I take to go to ____?	Quel bus dois-je prendre pour aller à ____?	Kehl bews dwahzh prah(n)dr poor ahlay ah ____?
Where is the nearest bus stop?	Où est l'arrêt de bus le plus proche?	Oo eh lahreh duh bews luh plew prohsh?
Does this bus go to ____?	Est-ce que ce bus va à ____?	Ehskuh suh bews vah ah ____?
When is the next bus to ____?	Quand part le prochain bus pour ____?	Kah(n) pahr luh proh-sha(n) bews poor ____?
What is the fare to ____?	Quel est le prix du trajet pour ____?	Kehl eh luh pree dew trahzhay poor ____?
Do you need exact change?	Faut-il avoir la monnaie exacte?	Fohteel ahvwahr lah mohnay ehg-zahkt?
I want to get off at ____.	Je veux descendre à ____.	Zhuh vuh dehsah(n)dr ah ____.
Please tell me when to get off?	Pourriez-vous me dire quand je dois descendre?	Pooryay-voo muh deer kah(n) zhuh dwah dehsah(n)dr?
Do I need to change buses?	Faut-il changer de bus?	Fohteel shah(n)zhay duh bews?

42

Bus Signs

Défense de parler au conducteur	Do Not Talk to the Driver
Arrêt demandé	Stop Requested

TAKING A TAXI

Taxi travel in French-speaking Europe follows the same basic patterns as in the United States. Meters are in use except for certain out-of-city trips. In Paris, make sure you have a metered cab by checking for the lighted sign on the roof of the vehicle. Parisian taxis use a system of differential rates. Rate A, the lowest, is used for trips within Paris on weekdays. Rate B, somewhat higher, applies for in-Paris trips from 8 PM to 6:30 AM on weeknights, all day weekends and holidays, and for nearby suburbs (including airports) on weekdays. Rate C is the highest and is used evenings in the suburbs. Rates are clearly posted and will also indicate supplemental charges for luggage and a fourth adult passenger. When you phone for a taxi, you are charged from the time the taxi leaves to pick you up.

Be warned that Parisian taxi drivers are a stressed-out breed—theirs are the most dangerous vehicles on the road apart from scooters.

Where is the nearest taxi stand?	Où est la station de taxis la plus proche?	Oo eh lah stahsyoh(n) duh tahksee lah plew prohsh?
Are there any taxis around here?	Y a-t-il des taxis par ici?	Yahteel day tahksee pahr eesee?
Taxi!	**Taxi!**	**Tahksee!**
Are you free?	**Êtes-vous libre?**	**Eht-voo leebr?**
Please take me . . .	**S'il vous plaît, conduisez-moi . . .**	**Seel voo pleh, koh(n)dweezay-mwah . . .**
_to the airport.	_à l'aéroport.	_ah lah-ehrohpohr.
_to the train station.	_à la gare.	_ah lah gahr.
_to the bus station.	_à la gare routière	_ah lah gahr rootyehr
_downtown.	_au centre-ville.	_oh sah(n)truh-veel.
_to the Hotel ____.	_à l'hôtel ____.	_ah lohtehl ____.

43

_to this address.	_à cette adresse.	_ah seht ahdrehs.
_to this restaurant.	_à ce restaurant.	_ah suh reh-stohrah(n).
_to this store.	_à ce magasin.	_ah suh mahgahza(n).
How much is it to ____?	C'est combien pour aller à ____?	Seh koh(m)byeh(n) poor ahlay ah ____?
I'm in a hurry!	**Je suis pressé(e)!**	**Zhuh swee prehsay!**
Stop here, please.	**Arrêtez-vous ici, s'il vous plaît.**	**Ahrehtay-voo zeesee seel voo pleh.**
Wait here for me;	Attendez-moi ici;	Ahtah(n)day mwah
I'll be right back.	je reviens tout de suite.	eesee; zhuh ruhvyeh(n) toot sweet.
Could you please drive more slowly!	Conduisez plus lentement, s'il vous plaît!	Koh(n)dweezay plew lah(n)tuhmah(n), seel voo pleh!
How much do I owe you?	**Combien je vous dois?**	**Koh(m)byeh(n) zhuh voo dwah?**
Keep the change.	**Gardez la monnaie.**	**Gahrday lah mohneh.**
Taxi stand	Station de taxis	Stahsyoh(n) duh tahksee

GOING BY TRAIN

As is the case in most European countries, there is a single state-run system in France, which is known as the SNCF (Société Nationale des Chemins de Fer Français, www.sncf.com). The train system in France is a source of pride for the entire country. It is rapid, economical, and reliable—except when there are strikes (three or four times a year). It is also extremely comprehensive, serving small towns and large cities alike.

There are three types of trains: The *TGV* (*train à grande vitesse*) is a high-speed train that cuts traveling time between large and medium-size cities to a minimum; the *TGL* (*train grande ligne*) is a rapid train, though not as fast a the TGV, that stops only at major cities; and the *TER* (*train express régional*) is a local train that stops everywhere.

There are two main types of sleeping accommodations: *Couchette* means bunk-style sleeping in second class (six bunks per compartment, while *wagon-lit* (officially called *Voitures-lits*) means first-class, private accommodations for one or two people.

In first class, good-quality full-course meals are served at an extra charge. In addition, sandwiches, snacks, and soft drinks are available in the *wagon-lit*. It's best to bring your own food for longer journeys, as supplies are limited and prices are high for very mediocre food.

Where is/are . . .	Où est/sont . . .	Oo eh/soh(n) . . .
_the train station?	_la gare?	_lah gahr?
_the ticket window?	_le guichet?	_luh gheeshay?
_the first-class compartments?	_les compartiments de première classe?	_lay koh(m)pahr-teemah(n) duh pruh-myehr klahs?
_the (second-class) sleeping cars?	_les wagons couchettes	_lay vahgoh(n) koosheht
_the first-class sleeping cars?	_les wagon-lits?	_lay vahgoh(n)-lee?
_the no-smoking section?	_le wagon non-fumeur?	_luh vahgoh(n) noh(n)-fewmuhr?
_the smoking section?	_le wagon fumeur?	_luh vahgoh(n) fewmuhr?
_the reservations office?	_le bureau des réservations?	_luh bewroh day ray-zehrvahsyoh(n)?
_the baggage check?	_la consigne manuelle	lah koh(n)seenyuh mahnewehl?
_the baggage lockers?	_la consigne automatique?	_lah koh(n)seenyuh ohtohmahteek?
_the lost and found?	_le bureau des objets trouvés?	_luh bewroh day zohbzhay troovay?
_the platforms?	_les quais?	_lay keh?
I'd like a ticket to Lyons . . .	Je voudrais un billet pour Lyon . . .	Zhuh voodreh zuh(n) beeyay poor Leeoh(n) . . .
_first class.	_première classe.	_pruhmyehr klahs.
_second class.	_deuxième classe.	_duhzyehm klahs.
_one-way.	_aller simple.	_ahlay sa(m)pl.
_round-trip.	_aller-retour.	_ahlay-ruhtoor.

45

_on the next train.	_dans le prochain train.	_dah(n) luh proh-sha(n) tra(n).
I'd like to reserve . . .	Je voudrais réserver . . .	Zhuh voodreh rayzehr-vay . . .
_a bunk on top.	_une couchette supérieure.	_ewn koosheht sew-payryuhr.
_a bunk in the middle.	_une couchette intermédiaire.	ewn koosheht eh(n)tehrmehdyehr.
_a bunk on the bottom.	_une couchette inférieure.	_ewn koosheht eh(n)fehryuhr.
_a bed in the sleeping car.	_une place dans un wagon-lit.	_ewn plahs dah(n) zuh(n) vahgoh(n)-lee.
I'd like to check my bags.	Je voudrais enregistrer mes bagages.	Zhuh voodreh zah(n)rehzheestray may bahgahzh.
Does this train stop in ____?	Ce train s'arrête-t-il à ____?	Suh tra(n) sahrehteel ah ____?
From which platform does it leave?	De quel quai part-il?	Duh kehl keh pahr-teel?
Is the train on time?	Le train est-il à l'heure?	Luh tra(n) ehteel ah luhr?
Is there a change of trains in ____?	Est-ce qu'il y a un changement à ____?	Ehskeel yah uh(n) shahnzhmah(n) ah ____?
I'm going to Dijon; do I need to change trains?	Je vais à Dijon; dois-je changer de train?	Zhuh veh zah Dee-zhoh(n); dwahzh shah(n)zhay duh tra(n)?
Is this seat free?	Cette place, est-elle libre?	Seht plahs, eh tehl leebr?
This seat is occupied.	Cette place est occupée.	Seht plahs eh tohkew-pay.
Could you tell me when we get to Nancy?	Pourriez-vous me dire quand nous arriverons à Nancy?	Pooryay-voo muh deer kah(n) noo zahreevroh(n) ah Nah(n)see?

Train Signs

Entrée	Entrance
Sortie	Exit
Renseignements	Information
i	Information
Salle d'attente	Waiting Room
Bureau des réservations	Reservations Office
Accès aux quais	To the Platforms
Fumeurs	Smoking
Non-fumeurs	Nonsmoking
Enregistrement des bagages	Baggage Check
Service Bagages à domicile	Door-to-door Service

TRAVELING BY BOAT

When is the next boat for ____?	**Quand part le prochain bateau pour ____?**	Kah(n) pahr luh proh-sha(n) bahtoh poor ____?
Where does the boat leave from?	D'où part le bateau?	Doo pahr luh bahtoh?
How long is the trip?	**Combien de temps prend la traversée?**	Koh(m)byeh(n) duh tah(m) prah(n) lah trahvehrsay?
Where does the boat stop?	Où est-ce qu'on fait escale?	Oo ehs koh(n) feh tehskahl?
How much is a seat in . . .	**Combien coûte un billet . . .**	Koh(m)byeh(n) koot uh(n) beeyay . . .
_first class?	_de première classe?	_duh pruhmyehr klahs?
_second class?	_de deuxième classe?	_duh duhzyehm klahs?
_cabin class?	_de cabine?	_duh kahbeen?
I missed the boat.	**J'ai manqué le bateau.**	Zhay mah(n)kay luh bahtoh.
What should I do?	**Qu'est-ce que je dois faire?**	Kehskuh zhuh dwah fehr?

COMMON PUBLIC SIGNS

Below is a list of the various signs you are likely to encounter as you move about in a French-speaking country. Other signs are described above in Using the Métro, On the Bus, and Going by Train. Road signs are included in Chapter 11, On the Road.

A louer	Ah looay	For Rent
Ascenseur	Ahsah(n)suhr	Elevator
Attention	Ahtah(n)syoh(n)	Caution
A vendre	Ah vah(n)dr	For Sale
Caisse	Kehs	Cashier
Chaud	Shoh	Hot
Chemin privé	Shuhma(n) preevay	Private Road
Chien méchant	Shyeh(n) mayshah(n)	Beware of the Dog
Interdit aux chiens	A(n)tehrdee oh shyeh(n)	No Dogs
Dames	Dahm	Women
Danger	Dah(n)zhay	Danger
Danger de mort	Dah(n)zhay duh mohr	Danger of Death
Défense de . . .	Dayfah(n)s duh . . .	Do Not . . .
Défense d'entrer	Dayfah(n)s dah(n)tray	Keep Out
Défense de fumer	Dayfah(n)s duh fewmay	No Smoking
Eau non potable	Oh noh(n) pohtahbl	Do Not Drink the Water
Eau potable	Oh pohtahbl	Drinking Water
Ecole	Aykohl	School
En panne	Ah(n) pehn	Out of Order
Entrée	Ah(n)tray	Entrance
Entrez sans frapper	Ah(n)tray sah(n) frahpay	Enter without Knocking
Fermé	Fehrmay	Closed
Froid	Frwah	Cold
Fumeurs	Fewmuhr	Smoking
Guichet	Gheeshay	Ticket Window
Haute tension	Oht tah(n)syoh(n)	High Voltage

Heures d'ouverture	Uhr doovehrtewr	Business Hours
Hommes	Ohm	Men
Hôpital	Ohpeetahl	Hospital
Horaires	Ohrehr	Schedule
Hors service	Ohr sehrvees	Out of Order
Il est défendu de . . .	Eel eh dayfah(n)dew duh . . .	It Is Forbidden to . . .
Jours fériés	Zhoor fayryay	Holidays
Libre	Leebr	Free, Unoccupied
Messieurs	Maysyuh	Men
Ne pas déranger	Nuh pah dayrah(n)zhay	Do Not Disturb
Ne pas toucher	Nuh pah tooshay	Do Not Touch
Non fumeurs	Noh(n) fewmuhr	No Smoking
Occupé	Ohkewpay	Occupied
Ouvert de . . . à . . .	Oovehr duh . . . ah . . .	Open from . . . to . . .
Passage souterrain	Pahsohzh sootehra(n)	Underground Passage
Peinture fraîche	Pa(n)tewr frehsh	Wet Paint
Poussez	Poosay	Push
Prière de ne pas déranger	Preeyehr duh nuh pah dayrah(n)zhay	Do Not Disturb
Privé	Preevay	Private
Quai	Keh	Track
Renseignements	Rah(n)sehnyuhmah(n)	Information
Réouverture le . . .	Rayoovehrtewr luh . . .	We Will Reopen on . . .
Réservé	Rayzehrvay	Reserved
Salle d'attente	Sahl dahtah(n)t	Waiting Room
Soldes	Sohld	Sales, Discounts
Sonnez	Sohnay	Ring
Sortie	Sohrtee	Exit

Sortie de secours	Sohrtee duh suhkoor	Emergency Exit
Sur rendez-vous	Sewr rah(n)day-voo	By Appointment
Stationnement interdit	Stahsyohnmah(n) a(n)tehrdee	No Parking
Tirez	Teeray	Pull
Toilettes	Twahleht	Restrooms
Voie	Vwah	Platform
WC	Vay Say	Restrooms

ACCOMMODATIONS

One of the joys of traveling in French-speaking Europe is the abundance of clean, comfortable, well-run hotels in a variety of price ranges. There are also lots of choices for accommodations other than the traditional hotel, as described below.

In France, hotels are officially classified in five categories: from one to four stars, plus L for luxury accommodations. The hotel's category is listed at its entrance, and room rates will reflect this classification. Sometimes the stars have more to do with facilities—hair dryers, TVs, etc.—than with comfort. A two-star hotel can be perfectly charming, though not all of them are.

If you do arrive in a city without reservations, your best bet is to check in with the official tourist office (*Office de Tourisme* [ohfees dew tooreesmuh]), often located downtown near the train station. They will help you find a hotel in the price range and location you desire.

In addition to the standard hotel, many other varieties of accommodations are available to the traveler, especially outside Paris. Start with the rural top-of-the-line *Relais et Châteaux* [Ruhlay zay shahtoh] chain—not really a chain, but some 150 independently owned and operated castle hotels and manor houses in various parts of France, banded together in name only for purposes of advertising, promotion, and working through a central reservation system. (In the U.S.: 212/856-0115 or 800/860-4930, and www.relaischateaux.com.)

An alternative is the group *Châteaux et Hôtels de France,* with over 530 properties chosen for their character and personal service. Prices start at less than $80 a night. For more information see www.chateauxhotels.com.

Relais du silence [Ruhlay dew seelah(n)s] (www.silence hotels.com) specialize in country living with guaranteed peace and quiet. *Châteaux et Demeures de Tradition* brings together hotels in châteaux or manors, and restaurants that specialize in regional foods and wines (www.ch-demeures.com). Renting a furnished apartment or country house is probably the best way to experience France. *Gîtes de France* is an extremely well-run national network; keep in mind that prices go up during school holidays. The main office in Paris (59 rue St-Lacore, 75009, 01.49.70.75.75) offers brochures for each region with pictures of the accommodations.

Fermes auberges [Fehrm ohbehrzh] offer no-frills country accommodations. *Gîtes ruraux* [Zheet rewroh] are apartments or small country homes in rural areas, which can be rented by the week or month. Information on all of these can be had from the French Government Tourist Office.

Other low-cost alternatives abound throughout the country. *Chambres d'hôte* [shah(m)bruh doht] are bed-and-breakfast type accommodations offering comfortable rooms at attractive prices and a chance to meet local families and sample their way of life.

And, finally, a good alternative for the long-distance automobile traveler, *motels* [mohtehl] have begun to spring up on main roads in suburban locations and near airports all over the country.

DIALOGUE   At the Front Desk (À la Réception)

Cliente:	**Bonjour, Monsieur. Avez-vous une chambre pour deux personnes pour une nuit?**	Boh(n)zhoor, muhsyuh. Ahvay-voo ewn shah(m)br poor duh pehrsohn poor ewn nwee?
Gérant:	**Un moment, Madame. Je vais voir . . . Oui, j'en ai une au troisième ètage avec un lit à deux places.**	Uh(n) mohmah(n), mahdahm. Zhuh veh voir . . . Wee, zhah(n) nay ewn oh trwahzyehm aytahzh ahvehk uh(n) lee ah duh plahs.
Cliente:	**C'est parfait. Y a-t-il une salle de bain?**	Say pahrfeh. Yahteel ewn sahl duh ba(n)?
Gérant:	**Non, mais il y a des toilettes avec une douche.**	Noh(n), may eel yah day twah-let ahvehk ewn doosh.
Cliente:	**Très bien. Est-ce que je pourrais la voir?**	Treh byeh(n). Ehskuh zhuh poorray lah vwahr?
Gérant:	**Oui, bien sûr. Suivez-moi, Madame.**	Wee, byeh(n) sewr, Sweevay mwah, mahdahm.

Customer:	Hello. Do you have a room for two people for one night?
Manager:	One moment, madam. Let me see . . . Yes, I have one on the fourth floor* with a double bed.
Customer:	Perfect. Does it have a bathroom?
Manager:	No, but it does have a toilet and a shower.
Customer:	Fine. Could I see it?
Manager:	Yes, of course. Follow me, madam.

*Our first floor is the *rez-de-chaussée* [rehduhshohsay] (ground floor) in France. Thus, their *premier étage* [pruhmyeh raytahzh] (first floor) is our second floor, etc.

HOTEL ARRANGEMENTS AND SERVICES

I have a reservation.	J'ai une réservation.	Zhay ewn raysehrvah-syoh(n).
I'd like a room . . .	Je voudrais une chambre . . .	Zhuh voodreh zewn shah(m)br . . .
_for tonight.	_pour ce soir.	_poor suh swahr.
_with one bed.	_à un lit.	_ah uh(n) lee.
_with two beds.	_à deux lits.	_ah duh lee.
_with a double bed.	_avec un grand lit.	_ahvehk uh(n) grah(n) lee.
_with twin beds.	_avec des lits jumeaux.	_ahvehk day lee zhewmoh.
_with a bathroom.	_avec salle de bain.	_ahvehk sahl duh ba(n).
_with a shower.	_avec douche.	_ahvehk doosh.
_with air-conditioning.	_climatisée.	_kleemahteezay.
_with a view.	_avec vue.	_ahvehk vew.
Is there . . .	Y a-t-il . . .	Yahteel . . .
_a toilet?	_des toilettes?	_day twahleht?
_a television?	_la télévision?	_lah taylayveesyoh(n)?
We're going to stay . . .	Nous allons rester . . .	Noo zahloh(n) rehstay . . .

53

_one night.	_une nuit.	_ewn nwee.
_a few days.	_quelques jours.	_kehlkuh zhoor.
_a week.	_une semaine.	_ewn suhmehn.
I'd like to see the room.	Je voudrais voir la chambre.	Zhuh voodreh vwahr lah shah(m)br.
I'll take it.	Je la prends.	Zhuh lah prah(n).
I'm not going to take it.	Je ne vais pas la prendre.	Zhuh nuh vay pah lah prah(n)dr.
Do you have a room that's . . .	Avez-vous une chambre . . .	Ahvay-voo zewn shah(m)br . . .
_quieter?	_plus tranquille?	_plew trah(n)keel?
_bigger?	_plus grande?	_plew grah(n)d?
_less expensive?	_moins chère?	_mwa(n) shehr?
How much is it . . .	Quel est le prix . . .	Kehl eh luh pree . . .
_per night?	_pour une nuit?	poor ewn nwee?
_per week?	_pour une semaine?	poor ewn suhmehn?
_with all meals?	_en pension complète?	_ah(n) pah(n)syoh(n) koh(m)pleht?
_with breakfast?	_avec le petit déjeuner?	_ahvehk luh puhtee dayzhuhnay?
_without breakfast?	_sans le petit déjeuner?	_sah(n) luh puhtee dayzhuhnay?
Where can I park?	Où puis-je me garer?	Oo pweezh muh gahray?
Please have my bags sent up to my room.	Faites monter mes bagages à ma chambre, s'il vous plaît.	Feht moh(n)tay may bahgahzh ah mah shah(m)br seel voo pleh.
Could you put this in your safe?	Pouvez-vous mettre ceci au coffre?	Poovay voo mehtr suhsee oh kohfr?
I'd like to speak with . . .	Je voudrais parler.	Zhuh voodreh pahrlay.
_the manager.	_au directeur.	_oh deerehktuhr.
_the hall porter.	_au portier.	_oh pohrteeyay.
_the maid.	_à la femme de chambre.	_ah lah fahm duh shah(m)br.
_the bellhop.	_au chasseur.	_oh shahsuhr.

54

May I have . . .	Puis-je avoir . . .	Pweezh ahvwahr . . .
_a blanket?	_une couverture?	_ewn koovehrtewr?
_hangers?	_des cintres?	_day sa(n)tr?
_some ice?	_des glaçons?	_day glahsoh(n)?
_a pillow?	_un oreiller?	_uh(n) nohrahay?
_some stationery?	_du papier à lettres?	_dew pahpyay ah lehtr?
_some soap?	_du savon?	_dew sahvoh(n)?
_a towel?	_une serviette?	_ewn sehrvyeht?
_toilet paper?	_du papier hygiénique?	_dew pahpyay eezheeyayneek?
Where is . . .	Où est . . .	Oo eh . . .
_the elevator?	_l'ascenseur?	_lahsah(n)suhr?
_the garage?	_le garage?	_luh gahrahzh?
_the dining room?	_la salle à manger?	_lah sahl ah mah(n)zhay?
_the laundry?	_la blanchisserie?	_lah blah(n)sheesree?
_the beauty salon?	_le salon de coiffure?	_luh sahloh(n) duh kwahfewr?
There's a problem with . . .	Il y a un problème avec . . .	Eel yah uh(n) prohblehm ahvehk . . .
_the key.	_la clé.	_lah klay.
_the heat.	_le chauffage.	_luh shohfahzh.
_room service.	_le service d'étage	_luh sehrvees daytahzh
_the hot water.	_l'eau chaude	_loh shohd.
_the air-conditioner.	_la climatisation	_lah kleemahteezahsyoh(n)
Could you make up the room now?	Pouvez-vous faire la chambre tout de suite?	Poovay-voo fehr lah shah(m)br tood sweet?
I'm in room ____.	"J'ai la chambre ____."	Zhay lah shah(m)br ____.
Can you get me a baby-sitter?	Pouvez-vous me trouver une garde d'enfants?	Poovay-voo muh troovay ewn gahrd dah(n)fah(n)?
We're leaving tomorrow.	Nous partons demain.	Noo pahrtoh(n) duhma(n).

55

Please prepare the bill.	Voulez-vous préparer la note.	Voolay-voo pray-pahray lah noht.
We're leaving at 10 AM	Nous partons à dix heures.	Noo pahrtoh(n) ah dee zuhr.
Could you please call us a taxi?	Pourriez-vous nous appeler un taxi?	Pooreeyay-voo noo zah-play uh(n) tahksee?
Please have my luggage brought downstairs.	Pourriez-vous faire descendre mes bagages?	Pooreeyay-voo fehr day-sah(n)druh may bahgahzh?

The visitor to French-speaking countries will be delighted with the range and variety of food and types of restaurants, though it's not an easy country for vegetarians. One of the glories of France is its regional cuisines, and many unpretentious but high-quality establishments are surprisingly affordable.

Keep in mind that few restaurants, apart from brasseries, serve food outside traditional mealtimes. The quality of restaurant food is high in Switzerland, where cheese and meat fondues are a specialty. Belgium's national dish is *moules-frites* [moohl freet], mussels with French fries, and its beers are legendary. In Quebec you'll find excellent French and Asian restaurants, with very affordable food. Try Montreal bagels, lighter and crispier than their New York counterparts. The following is a partial list of categories of eating establishments.

auberges, Fermes-auberges relais de campagne [Ohbehrzh, Fehrm-ohbehrzh, ruhlay duh koh(n)pahnyuh]	Variations on the theme of country inn, many of these establishments serve excellent traditional food.
bar [bahr]	Bars serve drinks, coffee, and light meals such as omelettes and sandwiches.
bistrot [beestroh]	An unpretentious neighborhood restaurant with simple fare and a limited menu.
brasserie [brahsree]	A large café offering meals and drinks.
cabaret [kahbahray]	A type of supper club featuring entertainment that may include singing, dancing, and political satire.
café [kahfay]	The quintessential French social institution, the place to hang out, refresh oneself, read, write, or people-watch. Cafés serve coffee, teas, infusions, beer, liquor, and wine plus light meals or snacks and soft drinks.

crêperie [krehpree]	May be a stand-up or sit-down restaurant. In any case, the bill of fare is crêpes—thin and tasty pancakes with a variety of meat, vegetable or dessert fillings.
restaurant [rehstohrah(n)]	The range of style, ambiance, culinary specialty, and price category is impressive! Make sure you check the menu in the window to get an idea of what it will cost before you decide to go in.
routier [rootyay]	The closest French equivalent to the diner or truck stop. Don't expect refined atmosphere (or high prices), but the food in many *routiers* is tasty and attractively prepared.
salon de thé [sahloh(n) duh tay]	The French tearoom serves pastries and other desserts along with tea and coffee. Light meals are offered in some *salons*.
snack-bar [snahkbahr]	Also called *buffet-express* [bewfay ehks-prehs], the *snack-bar* is often found near bus and train stations and is just what you think it is!

MEALS AND MEALTIMES

Breakfast (le petit déjeuner [luh ptee dayzhuhnay]) is a light meal in France and is commonly served until about 10 AM If breakfast is included in the price of your hotel room, it may very well be what is called *petit dèjeuner complet* [puhtee dayzhuhnay koh(m)play]. This consists of bread (croissants or French bread in slices) with butter and jam, plus a steaming cup of *café au lait* [kahfay oh lay]. *Café au lait* is quite light, with hot milk mixed in equal amounts with strong coffee. Tea and hot chocolate are often available as well.

If breakfast is *not* included with your hotel room, you will probably find that it is a good deal cheaper at the café around the corner than at the hotel restaurant.

Lunch (le déjeuner [luh dayzhuhnay]) is traditionally the big meal of the day in many regions. Shorter midday breaks have led, in recent years, to lighter, quicker lunches for many working people, though the big Sunday noontime meal *en famille* [ah(n) fahmeey] remains the rule. Lunch is served from noon until 2 or 3. Since some businesses and many public services still close between 12 and 2, you may find that many restaurants fill up rather rapidly at this time.

Dinner (le dîner [luh deenay]) begins later in France than in the United States. Restaurants begin serving between 7 and 8 PM, but most people don't come in until after 8. Evening dining is a leisurely affair, with people lingering over their food and drinks. The formal structure of the French dinner certainly encourages this relaxed pace. The meal may begin with an *apéritif* (ahpayreeteef) such as vermouth, sherry, kir, or a glass of sweet wine. Cocktails are not as common as in the United States as before-dinner drinks but are available at most bars.

The meal proper usually consists of three or four courses, sometimes more in traditional or luxury restaurants. Take the opportunity to taste regional cheeses, often presented on a giant platter or trolley. One can order *à la carte* [ah lah kahrt]. In addition, most restaurants have a fixed-price menu—*menu à prix fixe* [muhnew ah pree feeks]. Often there are several fixed-price menus varying in price and in the number of courses served. Choices are limited in fixed-price menus but they are often an excellent value. When you feel adventurous, you may wish to try the *menu gastronomique* [muhnew gahstrohnohmeek]. This menu features gourmet specialties and rare dishes. *Bon appétit* [boh(n) nahpaytee]!

DIALOGUE At the Restaurant (Au Restaurant)

Serveur:	Qu'est-ce que vous prendrez, Madame?	Kehskuh voo prah(n)dray, mahdahm?
Cliente:	Je ne sais pas. Quelle est la spécialité du chef?	Zhuh nuh seh pah . . . Kehl ay lah spaysyahl-eetay dew shehf?
Serveur:	Je vous recommande ceci.	Zhuh voo ruhkohmah(n)d suhsee.

Cliente:	**Très bien.**	Tray byeh(n).
Serveur:	**Et qu'est-ce que vous désirez boire?**	Ay kehskuh voo day-zeeray bwahr?
Cliente:	**Apportez-moi une bouteille d'eau minérale, s'il vous plaît.**	Ahpohrtay mwah ewn bootehy doh meenay-rahl, seel voo pleh.

Waiter:	May I take your order, Ma'am?
Customer:	I don't know . . . What is the chef's specialty?
Waiter:	I recommend this.
Customer:	Fine.
Waiter:	Something to drink?
Customer:	Please bring me a bottle of mineral water.

GOING TO A RESTAURANT

Do you know a good restaurant nearby?	Connaissez-vous un bon restaurant près d'ici?	Kohnehsay voo uh(n) boh(n) rehstohrah(n) preh deesee?
There are several.	Il y en a plusieurs.	Eel yah(n) nah plewzyuhr.
Is it expensive?	C'est cher?	Seh shehr?
No, it's not expensive.	Non, ce n'est pas cher.	Noh(n), suh nay pah shehr.
No, it's inexpensive.	Non, c'est bon marché.	Noh(n), seh boh(n) mahrshay.
What's the name of the restaurant?	Comment s'appelle le restaurant?	Kohmah(n) sahpehl luh rehstohrah(n)?
It's called Chez Pierre.	Il s'appelle Chez Pierre.	Eel sahpehl Shay Pyehr.
Do you need to make reservations?	Est-ce qu'il faut réserver?	Ehskeel foh rayzehr-vay?
I'd like to reserve a table . . .	Je voudrais réserver une table . . .	Zhuh voodreh rayzehr-vay ewn tahbl . . .
_for two people.	_pour deux personnes.	_poor duh pehrsohn.

_for tomorrow evening.	_pour demain soir.	_poor duhma(n) swahr.
_for eight PM.	_pour huit heures.	_poor weet uhr.
_on the terrace.	_en terrasse.	_ah(n) tehrahs.
_by the window.	_près de la fenêtre.	_preh duh lah fuhnehtr.
_in the no-smoking section.*	_dans la salle non-fumeurs.	_dah(n) lah sahl noh(n)-fewhmuhr.
Sir!/Ma'am!/Miss!	Monsieur!/Madame!/Mademoiselle!	Muhsyuh/Mahdahm Mahduhmwahzehl!
The menu, please.	La carte, s'il vous plaît.	Lah kahrt, seel voo pleh.
What are the special local dishes?	Quelle est la spécialité de la région?	Kehl eh lah spaysyahl-eetay duh la rayzhy-oh(n)?
I'd like a light meal.	Je voudrais un repas léger.	Zhuh voodreh uh(n) ruhpah layzhay.
I'll take the 10-euro menu.	Je prendrai le menu à dix euros.	Zhuh prah(n)dreh luh muhnew ah deez uh(r)-ROH.
Do you have children's meals?	Est-ce qu'il y a des menus enfants?	Ehskeelyah day muhnyoo ah(n)fah(n)?
Are you ready to order?	Avez-vous choisi?	Ahvay-voo shwahzee?
Not yet.	Pas encore.	Pahz ah(n)kohr.
To begin (for starters) . . .	Pour commencer . . .	Poor koh(m)mah(n)say . . .
Next . . .	Ensuite . . .	Ah(n)sweet . . .
Finally . . .	Pour terminer . . .	Poor tehrmeenay . . .
That's all.	C'est tout.	Seh too.
Have you finished?	Vous avez terminé?	Voo zahvay tehrmeenay?

*Note: In France, smoking is more acceptable than in the United States, so no-smoking sections in cafés and restaurants may be inadequate or altogether unavailable.

...e have . . .	Est-ce que nous pourrions avoir . . .	Ehskuh noo pooryoh(n) ahvwahr . . .
...p water?	_une carafe d'eau?	_ewn kahrahf doh?
_silverware?	_des couverts?	_day koovehr?
_a napkin?	_une serviette?	_ewn sehrvyeht?
_a cup?	_une tasse?	_ewn tahs?
_a glass?	_un verre?	_uh(n) vehr?
_a fork?	_une fourchette?	_ewn foorsheht?
_a spoon?	_une cuillère?	_ewn kweeyehr?
_a knife?	_un couteau?	_uh(n) kootoh?
_an ashtray?	_un cendrier?	_uh(n) sah(n)dreeyay?
_a plate?	_une assiette?	_ewn ahsyeht?
_a toothpick?	_un cure-dent?	_uh(n) kewr-dah(n)?
_a saucer?	_une soucoupe?	_ewn sookoop?
_some bread?	_du pain?	_dew pa(n)?
_some butter?	_du beurre?	_dew buhr?
_some salt?	_du sel?	_dew sehl?
_some pepper?	_du poivre?	_dew pwahvr?
_some mustard?	_de la moutarde?	_duh lah mootahrd?
_some lemon?	_du citron?	_dew seetroh(n)?
_some sugar?	_du sucre?	_dew sewkr?
_some ketchup?	_du ketchup?	_dew kehchuhp?
_some mayonnaise?	_de la mayonnaise?	_duh lah mahyohnehz?
_a little more . . . ?	_encore un peu de . . . ?	_ah(n)kohr uh(n) puh duh . . . ?
Where is the bathroom?	Où sont les toilettes?	Oo soh(n) lay twahleht?

APPETIZERS (ENTRÉES)

Appetizers are extremely varied and especially delicious and attractively prepared in French cuisine. Be careful: Appetizers are almost always referred to as entrées, while main courses (known as entrées in the United States) are called *plats* (plah). Appetizers may be either hot or cold and may be prepared with meat, fish, eggs, or vegetables. Often the key to a successful appetizer is the subtle and careful mix of ingredients and spices. Here is a sampler of some of the major types of entrées a traveler may find.

andouille [ah(n)dooy]	grilled and seasoned tripe sausage
artichauts à la vinaigrette [ahrteeshoh ah lah veenehgreht]	artichokes in vinaigrette dressing
bouchée à la reine [booshay ah lah rehn]	creamed sweetbreads and mushrooms in a pastry shell
crudités [krewdeetay]	raw mixed vegetables such as carrots, tomatoes, beets, and celery served with a vinaigrette
escargots de Bourgogne [ehskahrgoh duh boorgeenyohn]	classic preparation of cooked snails served in butter and seasoned with lots of garlic, shallots, and other spices
pâté [pahtay]	very tasty liver purée that is spread on slices of crusty bread. *Pâté de campagne* [pahtay duh kah(m)pahnyuh] mixes several kinds of meats, while *pâté de foie gras* [pahtay duh fwah grah] mixes goose liver with other kinds of meat. If it's served *en croûte* [ah(n) kroot], it is wrapped in a pastry shell.
quenelles [kuhnehl]	pike dumplings in a white sauce
rillettes [reeyeht]	pork mix cooked in its own fat and served as a spread to go on bread
terrine [tehreen]	a type of deep pot in which this kind of pâté is served, hence the pâté itself

EGG DISHES (LES OEUFS)

Eggs are served in a variety of ways as appetizers or light meals. Traditionally, they are not a breakfast staple as they are in the United States. Note: In the singular, we say *un oeuf* [uh(n) nuhf], for *an egg* or *one egg,* but in the plural the *f* is silent—*des oeufs* [day zuh] for *some eggs.*

oeufs en cocotte [uh zah(n) kohkoht]	baked in cups with cream and eaten with a spoon
oeufs en gelée [uh zah(n) zhuhlay]	poached and served cold in a gelled consommé
omelette [ohmleht]	The French variety is oval with a creamy center. There are numerous versions:
	_nature [nahtewr] plain
	_aux fines herbes [oh feen zehrb] with chives, tarragon, and parsley
	_au jambon [oh zhah(m)boh(n)] with ham
	_au fromage [oh frohmahzh] with cheese
piperade [pee-prahd]	a delightful mixture of tomato, onion, and pepper filling found mainly in the Atlantic Pyrénées
quiche [keesh]	an egg or flan tart with a rich filling of cheese, seafood, or poultry. The best-known variety is *quiche lorraine* [keesh lohrehn], which features bacon and gruyère cheese.
soufflé [sooflay]	This well-known French export must be light and fluffy and can be made with cheese, ham, vegetables, or other ingredients

SOUPS (LES SOUPES)

In France, soups are almost never eaten as a meal, but are served as a starter.

bisque	beesk	chowder
_d'écrevisse	_daykruhvees	_crayfish
_de homard	_duh hohmahr	_lobster
bouillabaisse	**booyahbehs**	**Provençal fish stew**
consommé	koh(n)sohmay	broth
_madrilène	_mahdreelehn	_with tomatoes
_printanier	_pra(n)tahnyay	_with vegetables
crème	**krehm**	**cream**
_d'asperges	_dahspehrzh	_of asparagus
_de volaille	_duh vohlahy	_of chicken

garbure	gahrbewr	cabbage soup with meat
petite marmite	puhteet mahrmeet	meat and vegetable soup
potage	pohtahzh	soup
_à l'ail	_ah lahy	_garlic
_parmentier	_pahrmah(n)tyay	_potato
soupe	soop	soup
_aux choux	_oh shoo	_cabbage
_du jour	_dew zhoor	_of the day
_à l'oignon	_ah lohnyoh(n)	_onion
_au pistou	_oh peestoo	_Provençal vegetable
velouté	vuhlootay	cream
_de tomates	_duh tohmaht	_of tomato
_de volaille	_duh vohlahy	_of chicken

FISH AND SEAFOOD (POISSON ET FRUITS DE MER)

Fish may be served as a main course or a second appetizer. Many fish are local and have no equivalents in the United States. Also, familiar favorites such as lobster will look and taste somewhat different. What is really distinctive about French fish is their preparation and the delicate sauces in which they are served.

Qu'est-ce que vous avez comme . . .	Kehskhuh voo zahvay kohm . . .	What do you have in the way of . . .
_poisson?	_pwahsoh(n)?	_fish?
_fruits de mer?	_frwee duh mehr?	_seafood?
l'aiglefin.	lehgluhfa(n).	haddock.
l'anchois.	**lah(n)shwa.**	**anchovies.**
l'anguille.	lah(n)geey.	eel.
le bar.	luh bahr.	bass.
la lotte de mer.	lah loht duh mehr.	angler.
le brochet.	luh brohshay.	pike.

65

le cabillaud.	luh kahbeeyah.	cod (fresh).
le calmar.	luh kahlmahr.	squid.
le crabe.	luh krahb.	crab.
les coquillages.	lay kohkeeyahzh.	shellfish.
les coquilles St. Jacques.	lay kohkeey sa(n) zhahk.	scallops.
les crevettes.	**lay kruhveht.**	**shrimp.**
les écrevisses.	lay zaykruhvees.	crayfish.
le hareng.	luh ahrah(n).	herring.
le homard.	**luh ohmahr.**	**lobster.**
le homard à l'américaine.	luh ohmahr ah lahmayreekehn.	lobster in butter with tomatoes and brandy.
les huîtres.	**lay zweetr.**	**oysters.**
la langouste.	lah lah(n)goost.	spiny lobster.
les langoustines.	lay lah(n)goosteen.	prawns.
le loup.	luh loo.	bass.
le maquereau.	luh mahkroh.	mackerel.
la morue.	lah mohrew.	cod.
les moules.	**lay mool.**	**mussels.**
les palourdes.	lay pahloord.	clams.
la perche.	lah pehrsh.	perch.
le poulpe.	luh poolp.	octopus.
le rouget.	luh roozhay.	red mullet.
les sardines.	lay sahrdeen.	sardines.
le saumon.	**luh sohmoh(n).**	**salmon.**
le saumon fumé.	luh sohmoh(n) fumay.	smoked salmon.
le sole.	luh sohl.	sole.
le thon.	luh toh(n).	tuna.
la truite.	**lah trweet.**	**trout.**
le turbot.	luh tewrboh.	turbot.

Preparation Methods for Fish

au four	oh foor	**baked**
frit	free	**fried**
grillé	greeyay	**grilled**
mariné	mahreenay	**marinated**
poché	pohshay	**poached**
cuit à la vapeur	kwee ah lah vahpuhr	**steamed**

MEAT (LES VIANDES)

l'agneau	lahnyoh	**lamb**
l'andouillette	lah(n)dweeyeht	tripe sausage
le bacon	luh bay-kuhn	bacon
le bifteck	luh beeftehk	**steak**
la blanquette de veau	lah blah(n)keht duh voh	**veal stew**
le boeuf	luh buhf	**beef**
le boudin	luh booda(n)	blood sausage
le carré d'agneau	luh kahray dahnyoh	rack of lamb
le cassoulet	luh kahsoolay	stew with sausage, white beans, and tomatoes
la cervelle	lah sehrvehl	brains
la charcuterie	lah shahrkewtree	coldcuts and pâtés
le châteaubriand	luh shahtohbreeah(n)	porterhouse steak
le cochon de lait	luh kohshoh(n) duh leh	suckling pig
la côte de boeuf	lah koht duh buhf	ribs of beef
les côtelettes	lay kohtleht	cutlets
les côtes	lay koht	chops
les cuisses de grenouille	lay kwees duh gruhn-ooy	frogs' legs
l'entrecôte	lah(n)truhkoht	sirloin steak
l'escalope	lehskahlohp	cutlet
le filet de boeuf	luh feelay duh buhf	fillet of beef

le filet mignon	luh feelay meenyoh(n)	filet mignon
le foie	luh fwah	liver
le gigot d'agneau	luh zheegoh dohnyoh	leg of lamb
le jambon	**luh zhah(m)boh(n)**	**ham**
la langue	lah lah(n)g	tongue
le lard	**luh lahr**	**bacon**
les médaillons de veau	lay maydahyoh(n) duh voh	veal tenderloin
le navarin de mouton	luh nahvahra(n) duh mootoh(n)	lamb stew
le pot-au-feu	luh poh-toh-fuh	boiled beef stew
le ris de veau	luh ree duh voh	sweetbreads (veal)
les rognons	lay rohnyoh(n)	kidneys
le rosbif	luh rohsbeef	roast beef
les saucisses	lay sohsees	small sausages
le saucisson	luh sohseesoh(n)	large slicing sausage
la selle d'agneau	lah sehl dahnyoh	saddle of lamb
le steak	luh stehk	steak
le tournedos	luh toornuhdoh	small beef fillet
les tripes	lay treep	tripe

Methods of Meat Preparation

à l'étouffée	ah laytoofay	stewed
bouilli	booyee	boiled
braisé	**brehzay**	**braised**
frit	free	fried
grillé	**greeyay**	**broiled**
rôti	**rohtee**	**roasted**
sauté	sohtay	sautéed
Je préfère mon steak . . .	**Zhuh prayfehr moh(n) stehk . . .**	**I like my steak . . .**
_bleu.	_bluh.	_very rare.

68

_saignant.	_sehnyah(n).	_rare.
_à point.	_ah pwa(n).	_medium.
_bien cuit.	_byeh(n) kwee.	_well-done.

Note: In general, the French prefer their meats less well-done than Americans. Bear that in mind when selecting one of the above categories.

GAME AND POULTRY (GIBIER ET VOLAILLE)

le blanc de poulet	luh blah(n) duh poolay	chicken breast
la caille	lah kahy	quail
la venaison	lah vuhnehzoh(n)	venison
le canard	**luh kahnahr**	**duck**
le caneton	luh kahntoh(n)	duckling
le chapon	luh shahpoh(n)	capon
le civet de lièvre	lah seeveht duh leeyehvr	hare stew
le coq au vin	luh kohk oh va(n)	chicken in red wine sauce
la dinde	**lah da(n)d**	**turkey**
le faisan	luh fuhzah(n)	pheasant
le lapin	**luh lahpa(n)**	**rabbit**
le lièvre	luh lyehvr	hare
le marcassin	luh mahrkahsa(n)	young wild boar
l'oie	lwah	goose
le perdreau/la perdrix	luh pehrdroh/lah pehrdree	partridge
le pigeonneau	luh peezhohnoh	squab
la poularde	lah poolahrd	pullet
la poule au pot	lah pool oh poh	chicken stew
le poulet	**luh poolay**	**chicken**
le salmis	luh sahlmee	game stewed in wine
le sanglier	luh sa(n)gleeyeh	wild boar
le suprême de volaille	luh sewprehm duh vohlahy	chicken breast cooked in chaudfroid

69

| le vol-au-vent | luh vohl-oh-vah(n) | pastry filled with chicken, meat, or fish prepared in a sauce |

SAUCES AND TYPES OF PREPARATION

The key to the success of so many French dishes is the use of absolutely fresh ingredients and the subtle combinations of flavors in the sauces that accompany the meat, fish, poultry, and vegetables. Below you will find a list of the most common preparations.

ailloli [ahyohli]	mayonnaise and garlic
allemande [ahlmah(n)d]	white sauce with veal stock
à la bonne femme [ah lah bohn fahm]	creamy white sauce with vegetables
américaine [ahmayreekehn]	sauce of white wine, brandy, tomatoes, and spices
béarnaise [bayahrnehz]	sauce of butter, eggs, shallots, tarragon, and wine
béchamel [bayshahmehl]	thick white sauce
bercy [behrsee]	wine sauce with fish stock
beurre blanc [buhr blah(n)]	butter sauce with shallots and wine
beurre noir [buhr nwahr]	browned butter sauce
bigarade [beegahrahd]	orange sauce for duck
blanquette [blah(n)keht]	egg and cream sauce
bordelaise [bohrduhlehz]	the adjective form of Bordeaux; sauce made with Bordeaux wine, mushrooms and shallots
bourguignonne [boorgeenyohn]	sauce made with Burgundy wine
bretonne [bruhtohn]	fish sauce with beans and mushrooms
caen [kah(n)]	made with apple brandy
chantilly [shah(n)teeyee]	sweet, rich whipped cream
chasseur [shahsuhr]	white sauce with mushrooms and parsley

daube [dohb]	stew with beef, red wine, garlic, and onions
diable [dyahbl]	spicy pepper sauce
estragon [ehstrahgoh(n)]	made with tarragon
farci [fahrsee]	stuffed
fenouil [fuhnooy]	made with fennel
financière [feenah(n)syehr]	with Madeira wine, truffles, and mushrooms
fines herbes [feen zehrb]	assortment of chopped herbs
florentine [flohrah(n)teen]	with spinach
forestière [fohrehstyehr]	with wild mushrooms
gratin [grahta(n)]	baked in a dish with cheese
hollandaise [ohlah(n)dehz]	lemony egg and butter sauce
indienne [a(n)dyehn]	with curry spices
jardinière [zhahrdeenyehr]	with French vegetables, "from the garden"
lyonnaise [lyohnehz]	with onions
madère [mahdehr]	with Madeira wine
maître d'hôtel [mehtr dohtehl]	light butter sauce with lemon and parsley
marchand de vin [mahrshah(n) duh va(n)]	red wine sauce with meat stock and shallots
meunière [muhnyehr]	cooked in flour and topped with lemon-butter sauce
mornay [mohrnay]	white wine and cheese sauce
mousseline [moosleen]	creamy Hollandaise sauce
nantua [nah(n)twah]	white sauce with cream, shellfish, and tomatoes
normande [nohrmah(n)d]	with mushrooms and eggs
parmentier [pahrmah(n)tyay]	with potatoes
périgourdine [payreegoordeen]	with truffles (named for the region of Périgord, known for its truffles)
piquante [peekah(n)t]	spicy sauce

71

poivrade [pwahvrahd]		dark sauce with peppers and onions
porto [pohrtoh]		made with port wine
provençale [prohvah(n)sahl]		in the style of Provence, the Mediterranean area around Nice; made with garlic, tomatoes, olives, and anchovies
rémoulade [raymoolahd]		mayonnaise and mustard
velouté [vuhlootay]		thickened chicken stock
véronique [vayrohneek]		with grapes
verte [vɛhrt]		mayonnaise with parsley and watercress
vinaigrette [veenehgreht]		oil, vinegar, and mustard dressing for salads, crudités, and vegetables

VEGETABLES (LES LÉGUMES)

l'artichaut	**lahrteeshoh**	**artichoke**
le fond d'artichaut	luh foh(n) dahrteeshoh	artichoke heart
les asperges	lay zahspehrzh	asparagus
l'aubergine	lohbehrzheen	eggplant
la betterave	lah behtrahv	beets
les carottes	lay kahroht	carrots
le céleri	luh saylree	celery
les cèpes	lay sehp	flap mushrooms
les champignons	**lay shah(m)peenyoh(n)**	**mushrooms**
la chicorée	lah sheekohray	chicory
le chou	luh shoo	cabbage
le chou de Bruxelles	luh shoo duh Brewseh	brussels sprout
le chou-fleur	**luh shoo-fluhr**	**cauliflower**
le concombre	luh koh(n)koh(m)br	cucumber
les cornichons	lay kohrneeshoh(n)	pickles
la courgette	lah koorzheht	zucchini
le cresson	luh krehsoh(n)	watercress

les endives	lay zah(n)deev	endives
les épinards	**lay zaypeenahr**	**spinach**
les fèves	lay fehv	white beans
les flageolets	lay flahzhohlay	green shell beans
les haricots verts	lay ahreekoh vehr	green beans
la laitue	lah laytew	lettuce
les lentilles	lay lah(n)teey	lentils
le maïs	luh mah-ees	corn
les navets	lay nahvay	turnips
les oignons	**lay zohnyoh(n)**	**onions**
les petits pois	lay ptee pwah	peas
le piment	luh peemah(n)	green pepper
le poireau	luh pwaroh	leek
les pommes de terre	**lay pohm duh tehr**	**potatoes**
la tomate	lah tohmaht	tomato

Some Classic Vegetable Dishes

artichauts à la grecque [ahrteeshoh ah lah grehk]	artichokes in herbs and olive oil, served cold
asperges au gratin [ahspehrzh oh grahta(n)]	asparagus in cheese sauce and bread crumbs
aubergine farcie [ohbehrzheen fahrsee]	stuffed and baked eggplant
choucroute garnie [shookroot gahrnee]	sauerkraut, meats, and sausage served hot
chou farci [shoo fahrsee]	stuffed cabbage
épinards à la crème [aypeenahr ah lah krehm]	creamed spinach
légumes panachés [laygewm pahnahshay]	mixed vegetables
macédoine de légumes [mahsaydwahn duh laygewm]	mixed, chopped vegetables
ratatouille [rahtahtooy]	chopped eggplant with tomato, zucchini, onion, and olive oil

HERBS AND SPICES
(FINES HERBES ET ÉPICES)

ail	ahy	garlic
aneth	ahneht	dill
anis	ahnees	anise
basilic	bahzeeleek	basil
cannelle	kahnehl	cinnamon
câpres	kahpruh	capers
cerfeuil	sehrfuhy	chervil
ciboulette	seebooleht	chives
clous de girofle	kloo duh zheerohfl	cloves
cumin	kewma(n)	caraway
échalote	ayshaloht	shallot
estragon	ehstrahgoh(n)	tarragon
gingembre	zha(n)zhah(m)br	ginger
laurier	lohryay	bay leaf
marjolaine	mahrzhohlehn	marjoram
menthe	mah(n)t	mint
noix de muscade	nwah duh mewskahd	nutmeg
origan	ohreegah(n)	oregano
persil	pehrsee	parsley
piment	peemah(n)	pimiento
poivre	pwahvr	pepper
romarin	rohmahra(n)	rosemary
safran	sahfrah(n)	saffron
sauge	sohzh	sage
thym	ta(m)	thyme

POTATOES, PASTA, AND RICE
(POMMES DE TERRE, PÂTES, ET RIZ)

Je voudrais des pommes de terre . . .	Zhuh voodreh day pohm duh tehr . . .	I'd like some potatoes . . .

_à l'anglaise.	_ah lah(n)glehz.	_peeled and boiled.
_lyonnaise.	_leeyohnehz.	_sautéed with onions.
_maître d'hôtel.	_mehtr dohtehl.	_cooked with milk, served with parsley.
_mousseline.	_moosleen.	_mashed, with cream.
_rissolées.	_reesohlay.	_roasted.
_en robe des champs.	_ah(n) rohb day shah(m).	_in their jackets.
_sautées.	_sohtay.	_sautéed.
_soufflées.	_sooflay.	_whipped light and fluffy.
Je voudrais . . .	Zhuh voodray . . .	I'd like . . .
_des chips.	_day sheep.	_potato chips.
_des frites.	_day freet.	_French fries.
_des pommes dauphine.	_day pohm doh feen	_potatoes baked with butter and Swiss cheese.
_de la purée de pommes de terre.	_duh lah pewray duh pohm duh tehr.	_mashed potatoes.
_des pommes vapeur.	_day pohm vahpuhr.	_boiled potatoes.
Je voudrais . . .	Zhuh voodray . . .	I'd like . . .
_des pâtes.	_day paht.	_some pasta.
_des nouilles.	_day nooy.	_some noodles.
_des spaghetti.	_day spahgehtee.	_some spaghetti.
Apportez-moi . . .	Ahpohrtay-mwah . . .	Bring me . . .
_du riz.	_dew ree.	_some rice.
_du riz pilaf.	_dew ree peelahf.	_some rice pilaf.
_du riz cantonnais.	_dew ree kah(n)tohneh.	_some fried rice.
_du risotto à la turque.	_dew reezohtoh ah lah tewrk.	_rice with saffron and tomatoes.
_du riz créole.	_dew ree krayohl.	_rice with tomatoes and peppers.

_du riz à la va-
lencienne.

_dew ree ah lah
vahlah(n)syehn.

_rice with toma-
toes, onions, saf-
fron, and shell-
fish.

SALADS (LES SALADES)

salade de betterave [sahlahd
duh behtrahv]

beet salad

salade de chou [sahlahd duh
shoo]

cole slaw

salade italienne [sahlahd
eetahlyehn]

antipasto

salade niçoise [sahlahd
neeswahz]

string beans, tomatoes, pota-
toes, olives, and hard-boiled
eggs in oil and vinegar

salade romaine à l'es-
tragon [sahlahd rohmehn ah
lehstrahgoh(n)]

romaine lettuce and tarragon

salade russe [sahlahd rews]

diced vegetables

salade de saison [sahlahd duh
sehzoh(n)]

salad of the season

salade de tomates [sahlahd
duh tohmaht]

tomato salad

salade verte [sahlahd vehrt]

mixed green salad

CHEESE (LES FROMAGES)

blue d'auvergne
[bluh dohvehrnyuh]

soft cheese with a sharp flavor

boursin [boorsa(n)]

soft, mild cheese with herbs

brie [bree]

this famous creamy white cheese
can be mild or strong

camembert
[kahmah(m)behr]

the well-known cheese from
Normandy

cantal [kah(n)tahl]

flavor varies with degree of
aging; the older it is, the harder
its texture and the stronger its
flavor

chèvre [shehvr]	goat's milk cheese in many varieties and flavors (try some early in your trip; they take getting used to)
comté [koh(m)tay]	similar to gruyère (see below), but slightly stronger.
demi-sel [duhmee-sehl]	type of cream cheese
emmenthal [ehmah(n)tahl]	what we usually refer to as Swiss cheese (gruyère with the holes)
fromage blanc [frohmahzh blah(n)]	similar to cottage cheese
fromage de chèvre [frohmahzh duh shehvr]	same as *chèvre*, above
fromage de Hollande [frohmahzh duh Ohlah(n)d]	"Dutch cheese," usually gouda
gruyère [grewyehr]	our "Swiss" without the holes
livarot [leevahroh]	soft, fermented, strong-smelling cheese from Normandy
munster [muh(n)stehr]	soft, somewhat sharp Alsatian cheese
petit suisse [puhtee swees]	sprinkle with sugar and eat it for dessert
pont l'évêque [poh(n) layvehk]	smooth cheese from Normandy
port-salut [pohr-sahlew]	a type of *St. Paulin* (see below)
reblochon [ruhbloh-shoh(n)]	mild and soft
roquefort [rohkfohr]	sharp and aromatic, blue-veined, made from ewe's milk
St. Paulin [Sa(n) Pohla(n)]	a mild, smooth cheese

FRUIT (LES FRUITS)

Served after the cheese at a French meal, fruit is often a dessert selection.

Qu'est-ce que vous avez comme fruits?	Kehskuh voo zahvay kohm frwee?	What kinds of fruit do you have?
Je prendrai . . .	**Zhuh prah(n)dreh . . .**	**I'll have . . .**
_un abricot.	_uh(n) nahbreekoh.	_an apricot.
_de l'ananas.	_duh lahnahnas.	_some pineapple.
_une banane.	**_ewn bahnahn.**	**_a banana.**
_un brugnon.	_uh(n) brewnyoh(n).	_a nectarine.
_des cassis.	_day kahsees.	_some black currants.
_des cerises.	_day sreez.	_some cherries.
_un citron.	_uh(n) seetroh(n).	_a lemon.
_un citron vert.	_uh(n) seetroh(n) vehr.	_a lime.
_des dattes.	_day daht.	_some dates.
_des figues.	_day feeg.	_some figs.
_des fraises.	**_day frehz.**	**_some strawberries.**
_des framboises.	_day frah(m)bwahz.	_some raspberries.
_des fruits secs	_day frwee sehk.	_some dried fruit.
_des groseilles.	_day grohzehy.	_some red currants.
_une mandarine.	_ewn mah(n)dahreen.	_a tangerine.
_du melon.	_dew muhloh(n).	_some melon.
_des mûres.	_day mewr.	_some mulberries.
_des myrtilles.	_day meerteey.	_some blueberries.
_une orange.	_ewn ohrah(n)zh.	_an orange.
_un pamplemousse.	**_uh(n) pah(n)pluhmoos.**	**_a grapefruit.**
_de la pastèque.	_duh lah pahstehk.	_some watermelon.

_une pêche.	_ewn pehsh.	_a peach.
_une poire.	_ewn pwahr.	_a pear.
_une pomme.	**_ewn pohm.**	**_an apple.**
_des pruneaux.	_day prewnoh.	_some prunes.
_des prunes.	_day prewn.	_some plums.
_du raisin blanc.	_dew rayza(n) blah(n).	_white grapes.
_du raisin noir.	_dew rayza(n) nwahr.	_black grapes.
_des raisins secs.	_day rayza(n) sehk.	_raisins.

NUTS (LES NOIX)

des noix	day nwah	walnuts
des amandes	day zahmah(n)d	almonds
des pistaches	day peestash	pistachios
des châtaignes	day shahtehn	chestnuts
des noisettes	day nwahzeht	hazelnuts
des noix d'acajou	day nwah dahkahzhoo	cashews
des cacahuètes	day kahkahweht	peanuts

DESSERTS (LES DESSERTS)

un baba au rhum [uh(n) bahbah oh ruhm]	yeasted cake in rum
une bombe [ewn boh(m)b]	ice cream concoction with fruit and whipped cream
une coupe glacée [ewn koop glahsay]	ice cream and whipped cream
une crème caramel [ewn krehm kahrahmehl]	caramel pudding
des crêpes suzette [day krehp sewzeht]	crêpes served flaming in an orange-flavored brandy sauce

Note: *Crêpes* (thin pancakes) are dessert items when *sucrées*, or sweet. Other dessert crêpes are made with fruit or chocolate sauce.

un flan [uh(n) flah(n)]	custard with a caramel sauce
un gâteau [uh(n) gahtoh]	cake or cakelike desserts
une glace [ewn glahs]	ice cream _à la vanille [ah lah vahneey] vanilla _au chocolat [oh shohkohlah] chocolate _à la fraise [ah lah frehz] strawberry _napolitaine [nahpohleetehn] combined with ices _panachée [pahnahshay] mixed flavors
une macédoine de fruits [ewn mah-saydwahn duh frwee]	fruit cup served with liqueur
une mousse [ewn moos]	light custardlike dessert made with eggs and whipped cream
une mousse au chocolat [ewn moos oh shohkohlah]	chocolate mousse
une omelette norvégienne [ewn ohmleht nohrvayzhy-ehn]	baked alaska
une pâtisserie [ewn pahteesree]	general term for pastry (or pastry shop); popular pastries include: _un éclair [uh(n) nayklehr] filled with custard and topped with a swab of chocolate or vanilla frosting _un millefeuille [uh(n) meel-fuhy] "a thousand leaves" or layers of crisp, light, buttery pastry dough
une pêche melba [ewn pehsh mehlbah]	vanilla ice cream topped with peaches and raspberry syrup
une poire belle-hélène [ewn pwahr behl-aylehn]	pears and vanilla ice cream with chocolate sauce
une pomme bonne femme [ewn pohm bohn fahm]	baked apple

un sorbet [uh(n) sohrbay]	sherbet
un soufflé [uh(n) sooflay]	egg yolks, beaten egg whites, and a fruity flavoring
une tarte aux pommes [ewn tahrt oh pohm]	apple pie

NONALCOHOLIC BEVERAGES (BOISSONS SANS ALCOOL)

Garçon,	Gahrsoh(n),	Waiter, bring
apportez-moi . . .	ahpohrtay-mwah . . .	me . . .
un café	uh(n) kahfay	a cup of coffee
_au lait.	_oh leh.	_with milk.
_crème.	_krehm.	_with cream.
_décaféiné.	_daykahfayeenay.	_decaffeinated.
_express.	_ehksprehs.	_espresso.
_noir.	_nwahr.	_black.
_soluble.	_sohlewbl.	_instant.
du cidre.	dew seedr.	some cider.
une citronnade.	ewn seetrohnahd.	a lemonade.
un citron pressé.	uh(n) seetroh(n) preh-say.	a "do-it-yourself" lemonade.
un déca.	uh(n) daykah.	a decaf.
de l'eau	duh loh	some ____ water.
_fraîche.	_frehsh.	_cold.
_avec des glaçons.	_ahvehk day glahsoh(n).	_ice
_minérale ga- zeuse.	_meenayrahl gahzuhz.	_carbonated min- eral
_minérale non- gazeuse.	_meenayrahl noh(n)- gahzuhz.	_noncarbonated mineral
une infusion.	ewn a(n)fewzyoh(n).	an infusion (herbal tea).
une camomille.	ewn kahmohmeel.	a chamomile.
une verveine.	ewn vehrvehn.	a verbena.

un jus	uh(n) zhew	a ____ juice.
_de fruits.	_duh frwee.	_fruit
_d'orange.	**_dohrah(n)zh.**	_orange
_de pample- mousse.	_duh pah(m)pluh- moos.	_grapefruit
_de pomme.	_duh pohm.	_apple
_de tomate.	_duh tohmaht.	_tomato
une limonade.	ewn leemohnahd.	fizzy lemonade.
un soda.	uh(n) sohdah.	a soda.
un thé	**uh(n) tay**	a cup of tea
_citron.	_seetroh(n).	_with lemon.
_glacé.	_glahsay.	_iced.
_au lait.	_oh leh.	_with milk.
_sucré.	_sewkray.	_with sugar.

ALCOHOLIC BEVERAGES (BOISSONS ALCOOLISÉES)

Apéritifs

The *apéritif* [ahpayreeteef] is taken leisurely before dinner as an appetite stimulant. The stronger cocktail, used as an aid to "unwind," is less common.

byrrh [beer]	dry red wine with herbs
Dubonnet [Dewbohnay]	slightly sweet wine, comes in *rouge* (roozh—red) or *blanc* (blah(n)—white)
Kir [keer]	white wine with sweet black currant liquer or raspberry liquer
Kir Royal [keer royahl]	same as above, but with champagne instead of white wine
Pernod [Pehrnoh]	green, anisette-flavored (lico-rice) liqueur
Ricard [Reekahr]	another licorice-flavored drink
Saint-Raphaël [Sa(n) rahfah-ehl]	wine and brandy-based drink

sherry [shehree]	amber wine from Spain; comes in degrees of sweetness
vermouth [vehrmoot]	red or white wine with herbs and bitters
vermouth-cassis [vehrmoot-kahsees]	vermouth and sweet black currant liqueur

Phrases for Ordering Drinks

straight	sec	sehk
on the rocks	avec des glaçons	ahvehk day glahsoh(n)
with water	à l'eau	ah loh

Beer (La Bière)

I'd like a ____ beer.	Je voudrais une bière . . .	Zhuh voodray zewn byehr . . .
_bottled	_en bouteille.	_ah(n) booteh.
_local	_du pays.	_dew payee.
_draft	_pression.	_prehsyoh(n)
_light	_blonde.	_bloh(n)d.
_dark	_brune.	_brewn.
Bring me a beer.	Apportez-moi un demi. (lit., a half-liter)	Ahpohrtay-mwah uh(n) duhmee.

Wine (Les Vins)

France is one of the great wine-producing countries of the world, with a 2,000-year-old tradition and thousands of distinctive wines to its credit. Virtually every region of the country with favorable climate and soil conditions produces some wine, but the vineyards of greatest renown are found in Burgundy, the Bordeaux area, Champagne, the Loire Valley, the Rhône Valley, and Alsace. An up-and-coming wine region is the Languedoc-Roussillon.

Quality control is an elaborate and rigorous procedure carried out by an agency of the State. Only wines that meet a strict set of criteria receive the title *Appellation d'origine contrôlée* [ah-puhlasyoh(n) dohreezheen koh(n)trohlay], which you will see printed on the label.

Ordering Wine

What wine do you recommend?	Quel vin me recommandez-vous?	Kehl va(n) muh ruhkohmah(n)day-voo?
Where does this wine come from?	D'où vient ce vin?	Doo vyeh(n) suh vah(n)?
I'd like . . .	Je voudrais . . .	Zhuh voodreh . . .
_a bottle of . . .	_une bouteille de . . .	_ewn bootehy duh . . .
_red wine.	_vin rouge.	_va(n) roozh.
_rosé wine.	_vin rosé.	_va(n) rohzay.
_white wine.	_vin blanc.	_va(n) blah(n).
_sparkling wine.	_vin mousseux.	_va(n) moosuh.
_robust wine.	_vin corsé.	_va(n) kohrsay.
_sweet wine.	_vin doux.	_va(n) doo.
_dry wine.	_vin sec.	_va(n) sehk.
_light wine.	_vin léger.	_va(n) layzhay.
_a half bottle.	_une demi-bouteille.	_ewn duhmee-bootehy.
_a carafe.	_une carafe.	_ewn kahrahf.
_a glass.	_un verre.	_uh(n) vehr.
_a liter.	_un litre.	_uh(n) leetr.
_another bottle.	_une autre bouteille.	_ewn ohtr bootehy.
_a local wine.	_un vin du pays.	_uh(n) va(n) dew payee.
_to taste some . . .	_goûter un peu de . . .	_gootay uh(n) puh duh . . .
_to see the wine list.	_voir la carte des vins.	_vwahr lah kahrt day va(n).

After-Dinner Drinks (Cognacs et Liqueurs)

Here is a brief rundown of some of the more prominent after-dinner specialties.

cognac [kohnyahk]   the king of brandies, a wine-distilled drink from the region of Charentes. Courvoisier, Hennessy, Martel, and Remy-Martin are four distinct types of cognac.

| eau-de-vie [oh-duh-vee] | distilled fruit brandies, som.. what stronger in taste. Popu.. *eaux-de-vie* include calvados, framboise, kirsch, and Poire William. |
| liqueur [leekuhr] | often sweetened and may be colored as well; some of the more well-known liqueurs include Bénédictine, Chambord, Chartreuse, Cointreau, crème de cassis, crème de menthe, and Grand Marnier. |

SPECIAL DIETS

I'm on a diet.	Je suis au régime.	Zhuh swee zoh ray-zheem.
I'm on a special diet.	Je suis un régime spécial.	Zhuh swee ray-zheem spaysyahl.
Do you have vegetarian dishes?	**Est-ce que vous avez des plats végétariens?**	**Ehskuh voo zahvay day plah vayzhay-tahrya(n)?**
I'm allergic to ____.	Je suis allergique à ____.	Zhuh swee zahlehrzheek ah ____.
I can't eat . . .	Je n'ai pas le droit . . .	Zhuh nay pah luh drwah
_salt.	_au sel.	_oh sehl.
_fat.	_au gras.	_oh grah.
_sugar.	_au sucre.	_oh sewkr.
_flour.	_à la farine.	_ah lah fahreen.
I'm diabetic.	Je suis diabétique.	Zhuh swee deeyahbay-teek.
I'm looking for a kosher restaurant.	**Je cherche un restaurant casher.**	**Zhuh shehrsh uh(n) rehstohrah(n) kah-shehr.**
I don't eat pork.	Je ne mange pas de porc.	Zhuh nuh mah(n)zh pah duh pohr.
I want to lose/gain weight.	Je veux maigrir/grossir.	Zhuh vuh mehgreer/grohseer.

85

READING THE MENU

Many restaurant menus feature English translations for the convenience of visitors from other countries. The following list of common menu terms should prove useful where translations are not provided.

attente, 30 min.	ahtahnt trahnt meenewt	30 minutes for preparation
au choix . . .	oh shwah . . .	choice of . . .
boisson comprise	bwahsoh(n) koh(m)preez	drink included
en saison	ah(n) sayzohn	in season
en sus	ah(n) sews	extra charge
garniture au choix	gahrneetewr oh shwah	choice of vegetable
menu à 15 euros	muhnew ah ka(n)z uhroh	15-euro menu
menu touristique	muhnew tooreesteek	tourist menu (usually lower cost but fewer choices)
plat du jour	plah dew zhoor	special of the day
pour deux personnes	poor duh pehrsohn	for two people
selon arrivage	suhloh(n) ahreevahzh	when available
servi de 7h à 11h	sehrvee duh seht uhrah ohnz uhr	served from 7–11 AM
service compris	sehrvees koh(m)pree	service included
service non-compris	sehrvees noh(n)-koh(m)pree	service not included
supplément pour changement de garniture	sewplaymah(n) poor shah(n)zhmah(n) duh gahrneetewr	extra charge for change of vegetable
toutes nos viandes sont servies avec une garniture	toot noh vyahnd soh(n) sehrvee ahvek ewn gahrneetewr	all our meat dishes come with a vegetable
TTC (toutes taxes comprises)	toot tahks koh(m)preez	all taxes included

THE BILL (L'ADDITION)

Since all French restaurants are required by law to post their menus where they can be seen before entering, the cost of the meal should come as no surprise. Further, French restaurants always include the gratuity, tax, and sometimes a house wine in the price of the meal. Credit cards are accepted almost everywhere in Europe. The French tip a few extra euros when the food or service was especially good.

Sir!/Ma'am!/Miss! **The check, please.**	Monsieur!/Madame! Mademoiselle! **L'addition, s'il vous plaît.**	Muhsyuh!/ Mahdmwahzehl! **Lah-deesyoh(n), seel voo pleh.**
What is this amount for?	Que représente cette somme?	Kuh ruhprayzah(n)t seht sohm?
Excuse me, I believe there is an error here.	Excusez-moi, je crois qu'il y a une erreur ici.	Ehkskewzay-mwah, zhuh krawh keel yah ewn ehruhr eesee.
Do you accept . . .	Est-ce que vous acceptez . . .	Ehskuh voo zahksehp-tay . . .
_this credit card?	_cette carte de crédit?	_seht kahrt duh kray-dee?
_travelers checks?	_les chèques de voyage?	_lay shehk duh vwahyahzh?
This is for you.	C'est pour vous.	Seh poor voo.
The meal was excellent.	Le repas était excellent.	Luh ruhpah aytay ehksehlah(n).

COMPLAINTS (RÉCLAMATIONS)

There must be some mistake.	Je crois qu'il y a une erreur.	Zhuh krwah keel yah ewn ehruhr.
I didn't order this.	Je n'ai pas commandé cela.	Zhuh neh pah kohmah(n)day suhlah.
Could I change this?	Est-ce que vous pourriez me changer ceci?	Ehskuh voo pooryay muh shah(n)zhay suh-see?
This is too . . .	C'est trop . . .	Seh troh . . .
_rare (bloody).	_saignant.	_sehnyah(n).

_well-done.	_cuit.	_kwee.
_salty.	_salé.	_sahlay.
_bitter.	_amer.	_ahmehr.
_sweet.	_sucré.	_sewkray.
This isn't clean.	Ce n'est pas propre.	Suh neh pah prohpr.
There's (a knife) missing.	Il manque (un couteau).	Eel mah(n)k (uh[n] kootoh).
This is cold.	C'est froid.	Seh frwah.
May I see the headwaiter, please?	Je voudrais parler au maître-d'hôtel, s'il vous plaît.	Zhuh voodreh pahrlay oh mehtr-dohtehl, seel voo pleh.

SOCIALIZING   8

Meeting people, making new friends and acquaintances, discovering a new culture, and sharing your own through personal relationships are some of the most memorable experiences to be enjoyed through travel. People in French-speaking Europe generally take more time than Americans to establish personal relationships. Their formality may lead you to perceive them as somewhat reserved or distant. Conversely, Europeans often see Americans as overly familiar or superficial. With good will, patience, and a sense of humor on both sides, these cultural differences can be a source of stimulation and enrichment and heighten your enjoyment of international travel.

Some organizations can help you meet French people. Try the *American Club of Paris* (34 ave. de New York, 75016 Paris; tel. 01.47.23.64.36), and check for listings in *France-USA Contacts* (*FUSAC*), a free English-language magazine available at American restaurants in Paris and from FUSAC offices in Paris (26 rue Bénard, 75014 Paris; tel. 01.56.53.54.54) and New York (48 W. 12th St., New York, NY 10011; tel. 212/929-2929). It's also online at www.fusac.com.

WICE—originally a women's association, but open to men—offers conversation exchange classes (20 bd. du Montparnasse, 75015; tel. 01.45.66.75.50).

DIALOGUE   Introductions (Des Présentations)

Julie Johnson:	Bonjour, Monsieur. Permettez-moi de me présenter. Je m'appelle Julie Johnson.	Boh(n)zhoor, muhsyuh. Pehrmehtay-mwah duh muh prayzah(n)tay. Zhuh mahpehl Julie Johnson.
Pierre Jacquot:	Enchanté, Madame. Je suis Pierre Jacquot.	Ah(n)shah(n)tay, mahdahm. Zhuh swee Pyehr Zhakoh.
Julie Johnson:	Très heureuse.	Treh zuhruhz.
Pierre Jacquot:	Vous êtes en vacances ici à Nice?	Voo zeht ah(n) vahkah(n)s eesee ah Nees?

Julie Johnson:	**Oui, je vais rester ici encore une semaine.**	Wee, zhuh veh rehstay eesee ah(n)kohr ewn suhmehn.
Pierre Jacquot:	**Alors, bonne fin de séjour. Au revoir, Madame.**	Ahlohr, bohn fa(n) duh say-zhoor. Oh ruhvwahr, mahdahm.
Julie Johnson:	**Merci. Au revoir, Monsieur.**	Mehrsee. Oh ruhvwahr, muhsyuh.

Julie Johnson:	Hello! Allow me to introduce myself. My name is Julie Johnson.
Pierre Jacquot:	Pleased to meet you. I'm Pierre Jacquot.
Julie Johnson:	Nice meeting you.
Pierre Jacquot:	Are you here in Nice on vacation?
Julie Johnson:	Yes. I'll be here another week.
Pierre Jacquot:	Have a good stay. Good-bye now.
Julie Johnson:	Thank you. Good-bye.

Note: The French use the titles "Monsieur" and "Madame" in speaking to acquaintances who are not close friends. In English, we would probably use first names or no form of address at all.

FIRST CONVERSATION

I'd like to introduce you to ____.	Je voudrais vous présenter à ____.	Zhuh voodreh voo prayzah(n)tay ah ____.
Pleased to meet you.	Enchanté(e).	Ah(n)shah(n)tay.
Allow me to introduce myself.	**Permettez-moi de me présenter.**	Pehrmehtay-mwah duh muh prayzah(n)tay.
What's your name?	Comment vous appelez-vous?	Kohmah(n) voo zahplay-voo?
My name is . . .	Je m'appelle . . .	Zhuh mahpehl . . .
I am . . .	Je suis . . .	Zhuh swee . . .
This is . . .	Voici . . .	Vwahsee . . .
_my husband.	_mon mari.	_moh(n) mahree.
_my wife.	_ma femme.	_mah fam.

_my colleague.	_mon/ma collègue.	_moh(n)/mah kohlehg.
_my friend.	_mon ami(e).	_moh(n) nahmee.
How are you?	Comment allez-vous?	Kohmah(n) talay-voo?
Fine, thanks, and you?	Très bien, merci, et vous?	Treh byeh(n), mehrsee, ay voo?
How's it going?	Ça va?	Sah vah?
It's going well, thank you.	Ça va merci.	Sah vah, mehrsee.
Where do you live?	Où est-ce que vous habitez?	Oo ehskuh voo zahbeetay?
I live in New York.	J'habite à New York.	Zhahbeet ah Noo Yohrk.
How do you like France?	Qu'est-ce que vous pensez de la France?	Kehskuh voo pah(n)say duh lah Frah(n)s?
I like France very much.	J'adore la France.	Zhahdohr lah Frah(n)s.
I just arrived.	Je viens d'arriver.	Zhuh vyeh(n) dahreevay.
I'm not sure yet.	Je ne sais pas encore.	Zhuh nuh seh pah zah(n)kohr.
I like the people very much.	J'aime beaucoup les gens.	Zhehm bohkoo lay zhah(n).
I like the landscape.	J'aime les paysages.	Zhehm luh payeezahzh.
Everything is so . . .	Tout est si . . .	Too teh see . . .
_interesting.	_intéressant.	_a(n)tayrehsah(n).
_different.	_différent.	_deefayrah(n).
That's . . .	C'est . . .	Seh . . .
_strange.	_bizarre.	_beezahr.
_stupid.	_stupide.	_stewpeed.
_wonderful.	_merveilleux.	_mehrvehyuh.
_sad.	_triste.	_treest.
_beautiful.	_beau.	_boh.

WHERE ARE YOU FROM?

Where are you from?	D'où venez-vous?	Doo vuhnay-voo?
I come from Belgium.	Je viens de Belgique.	Zhuh vya(n) duh Behlzheek.

Note: To express the idea of *from* ____, use *de* before a feminine country, *du* before a masculine country, *d'* before a country or continent beginning with a vowel, and *des* with a country that is plural (like the United States).

I come . . .	Je viens . . .	Zhuh vya(n) . . .
_from France.	_de France.	_duh Frah(n)s.
_from Portugal.	_du Portugal.	_dew Pohrtewgahl.
_from Ireland.	_d'Irlande.	_deerlah(n)d.
_from the United States.	_des Etats-Unis.	_day zaytah-zewnee.

Note: For *in* or *to*, use *en* before a feminine country, continents, and masculine countries beginning with a vowel. For other masculine countries, *to* or *in* is rendered by *au*. Plural countries take *aux*.

I'm going . . .	Je vais . . .	Zhuh veh . . .
_to France.	_en France.	_ah(n) Frah(n)s.
_to Portugal.	_au Portugal.	_oh Pohrtewgahl.
_to Israel.	_en Israël.	_ah(n) neezra-ehl.
_to the United States.	_aux Etats-Unis.	_oh zaytah-zewnee.

Also note that for cities, use *de* alone to express *from*—*je viens de Paris* [zhuh vyeh(n) duh Pahree]—and use *à* alone to express *to*—*je vais à Paris* [zhuh vay zah Pahree].

CONTINENTS AND COUNTRIES

Africa	l'Afrique	lahfreek
Asia	l'Asie	lahzee
Australia	l'Australie	lohstrahlee
Europe	l'Europe	luhrohp
North America	l'Amérique du Nord	lahmayreek dew nohr

South America	l'Amérique du Sud	lahmayreek dew sewd
Algeria	l'Algérie (f)	lahlzhayree
Algerian	algérien(ne)	ahlzhayrya(n)/yehn
Argentina	l'Argentine (f)	lahrzhah(n)teen
Argentinian	argentin(e)	ahrzhah(n)ta(n)/teen
Austria	l'Autriche (f)	lohtreesh
Austrian	autrichien(ne)	ohtreeshya(n)/yehn
Belgium	la Belgique	lah Behlzheek
Belgian	belge	behlzh
Brazil	le Brésil	luh Brayzeel
Brazilian	brésilien(ne)	brayzeelya(n)/yehn
Canada	le Canada	luh Kahnahdah
Canadian	canadien(ne)	kahnahdya(n)/yehn
China	la Chine	lah Sheen
Chinese	chinois(e)	sheenwah/wahz
Czech Republic	la République Tchèque	lah raypewbleek tshehk
Czech	tchèque	tshehk
Denmark	le Danemark	luh Dahnmahrk
Danish	danois(e)	dahnwah/wahz
England	l'Angleterre (f)	lah(n)gluhtehr
English	anglais(e)	ah(n)glay/glehz
Finland	la Finlande	lah Fa(n)lah(n)d
Finnish	finlandais(e)	fa(n)lah(n)day/dehz
France	la France	lah Frah(n)s
French	français(e)	frah(n)say/sehz
Germany	l'Allemagne	lahlmahnyuh
German	allemand(e)	ahlmah(n)/mah(n)d
Great Britain	la Grande Bretagne	lah Grah(n)d Bruhtahnyuh
British	britannique	breetahneek

Greece	la Grèce	lah Grehs
Greek	grec(que)	grehk
India	l'Inde (f)	la(n)d
Indian	indien(ne)	a(n)dya(n)/yehn
Ireland	l'Irlande (f)	leerlah(n)d
Irish	irlandais(e)	eerlah(n)day/dehz
Israel	l'Israël (m)	leezrah-ehl
Israeli	israélien(ne)	eezrahaylya(n)/yehn
Italy	l'Italie (f)	leetahlee
Italian	italien(ne)	eetalya(n)/yehn
Japan	le Japon	luh Zhahpoh(n)
Japanese	japonais(e)	zhahpohnay/nehz
Korea	la Corée	lah Kohray
Korean	coréen(ne)	kohraya(n)/yehn
Luxembourg	le Luxembourg	luh Lewksah(n)boor
Luxembourger (-ian)	luxembourgeois(e)	lewksah(n)boorzhwah/ zhwahz
Mexico	le Mexique	luh Mehkseek
Mexican	mexicain(e)	mehkseeka(n)/kehn
Morocco	Le Maroc	luh Mahrohk
Moroccan	marocain(e)	mahrohka(n)/kehn
Netherlands	les Pays-Bas (m)	lay Payee-Bah
Dutch	néerlandais(e)	nayehrlah(n)deh/dehz
New Zealand	la Nouvelle Zélande	lah Noovehl Zay- lah(n)d
New Zealander	néo-zélandais(e)	nayoh-zaylah(n)deh/dehz
Norway	la Norvège	lah Nohrvehzh
Norwegian	norvégien(ne)	nohrvayzhya(n)/yehn
Poland	Pologne	Pohlohnyuh
Polish	polonais(e)	pohlohneh(z)
Portugal	le Portugal	luh Pohrtewgahl

Portuguese	portugais(e)	pohrtewgeh/gehz
Russia	la Russie	lah Rewsee
Russian	russe	rews
Scotland	l'Ecosse (f)	laykohs
Scottish	écossais(e)	aykohseh/sehz
Spain	l'Espagne (f)	lehspahnyuh
Spanish	espagnol(e)	ehspahnyohl
Sweden	la Suède	lah Swehd
Swedish	suédois(e)	swaydwah/dwahz
Switzerland	la Suisse	lah Swees
Swiss	suisse	swees
Thailand	la Thaïlande	lah Tah-eelah(n)d
Thai	thaïlandais	tah-eelah(n)deh/dehz
Turkey	la Turquie	lah Tewrkee
Turkish	turc(que)	tewrk
United States	les Etats-Unis (m)	lay zaytah-zewnee
American	américain(e)	ahmayreeka(n)/kehn

WHAT DO YOU DO?

What do you do?	Que faites-vous?	Kuh feht voo?
What's your profession?	**Quelle est votre profession?**	**Kehl eh vohtr prohfeh-syoh(n)?**
I'm a . . .	Je suis . . .	Zhuh swee . . .
_businessman.	_homme d'affaires.	_zohm dahfehr.
_businesswoman.	_femme d'affaires.	_fahm dahfehr.
_doctor.	_médecin.	_maydsa(n).
_lawyer	_avocat(e).	_ahvohkah(t).
I'm retired.	Je suis à la retraite.	Zhuh swee zah lah ruhtreht.

OCCUPATIONS

accountant	comptable	koh(m)tahbl
architect	architecte	ahrsheetehkt
artist	artiste	ahrteest
baker	boulanger	boolah(n)zhay
butcher	boucher	booshay
cardiologist	cardiologue	kahrdeeohlohg
carpenter	charpentier	shahrpah(n)tyay
chef	chef	shehf
clerk	clerc	klehr
cook	cuisinier (cuisinière)	kweezeenyay(-yehr)
dentist	dentiste	dah(n)teest
doctor	médecin	maydsa(n)
electrician	électricien	aylehktreesyeh(n)
engineer	ingénieur	a(n)zhaynyuhr
lawyer	avocat	ahvohkah
locksmith	serrurier	sehrewryay
maid	employé(e) de maison	ehmplohyay duh maysohn
neurologist	neurologue	nuhrohlohg
nurse	infirmier (infirmière)	a(n)fehrmyay(-yehr)
ophthalmologist	ophtamologiste	ohftahmohlohg
optician	opticien(ne)	ohpteesyeh(n)/yehn
painter	peintre	pa(n)tr
plumber	plombier (plombière)	plohmbyay(-yehr)
salesperson	vendeur(-euse)	vah(n)duhr(-duhz)
sculptor	sculpteur	skewltuhr
shopkeeper	commerçant(-e)	kohmehrsah(n) (-sah(n)t)
waiter	serveur	sehrvuhr
waitress	serveuse	sehrvuhz
writer	écrivain	aykreeva(n)

MAKING FRIENDS

May I offer you a drink?	Puis-je vous offrir à boire?	Pweezh voo zohfreer ah bwahr?
Would you like to get a drink?	**Voulez-vous prendre un verre?**	**Voolay-voo prah(n)dr uh(n) vehr?**
With pleasure.	Avec plaisir.	Ahvehk plehzeer.
No, thanks.	Merci.*	Mehrsee.
Would you like to come with us to a café?	Est-ce que vous aimeriez nous accompagner au café?	Ehskuh voo zehmuhryay noo zahkoh(m)panyay oh kahfay?
Gladly.	Volontiers.	Vohloh(n)tyay.
May I bring a friend?	Est-ce que je peux emmener un ami (une amie)?	Ehskuh zhuh puh ah(m)mnay uh(n) nah-mee (ewn ahmee)?
Do you mind if I smoke?	Ça vous dérange si je fume?	Sah voo dayrah(n)zh see zhuh fewm?
Not at all.	Pas du tout.	Pah dew too.
Yes, a bit.	Oui, un peu.	Wee, uh(n) puh.
May I telephone you?	**Est-ce que je peux vous téléphoner?**	**Ehskuh zhuh puh voo taylayfohnay?**
What's your phone number?	Quel est votre numéro de téléphone?	Kehl eh vohtr newmay-roh duh taylayfohn?
What is your address?	Quelle est votre adresse?	Kehl eh vohtr ahdrehs?
Can I give you a ride?	Est-ce que je peux vous déposer quelque part?	Ehskuh zhuh puh voo daypohzay kehlkuh pahr?
Are you married?	**Etes-vous marié(e)?**	**Eht-voo mahryay?**
No, but I have a girlfriend/boyfriend.	Non, mais j'ai une petite amie/un petit ami.	Noh(n), may zhay ewn pteet ahmee/uh(n) ptee tahmee.
I'm single.	Je suis célibataire.	Zhuh swee say-leebahtehr.

*Note: The French often decline an offer by saying "merci," always accompanied by a slight shake of the head.

97

I'm a widow(er).	Je suis veuve (veuf).	Zhuh swee vuhv (vuhf).
I'm divorced.	Je suis divorcé(e).	Zhuh swee deevohrsay.
I'm traveling with a friend.	Je voyage avec un ami (une amie).	Zhuh vwahyahzh ahvehk uh(n) nahmee (ewn ahmee).
I'm alone.	Je suis seul(e).	Zhuh swee suhl.
You should come visit us.	Vous devriez venir nous voir.	Voo duhvreeay vuhneer noo vwahr.
You're so kind!	Vous êtes si gentil(s)!	Voo zeht see zhah(n)teey!
Are you free . . .	**Etes-vous libre . . .**	**Eht voo leebr . . .**
_this evening?	**_ce soir?**	**_suh swahr?**
_tomorrow?	**_demain?**	**_duhma(n)?**
I'll wait for you here.	Je vous attends ici.	Zhuh voo zahtah(n) eesee.
I'll pick you up in the hotel lobby.	Je viendrai vous chercher à l'hôtel.	Zhuh vyeh(n)dray voo shehrshay ah lohtehl.
It's getting late.	Il se fait tard.	Eel suh fay tahr.
It's time to get back.	Il est temps de rentrer.	Eel eh tah(m) duh rah(n)tray.
We're leaving tomorrow.	Nous partons demain.	Noo pahrtoh(n) duhma(n).
Thanks for everything.	**Merci pour tout.**	**Mehrsee poor too.**
I had a very good time.	Je me suis très bien amusé(e).	Zhuh muh swee treh byeh(n) nahmewzay.
We're going to miss you.	Vous allez nous manquer.	Voo zahlay noo mah(n)kay.
It was nice to have met you.	Je suis très heureux (heureuse) d'avoir fait votre connaissance.	Zhuh swee treh zuhruh (zuhruhz) dahvwahr fay vohtruh kohnay-sah(n)s.
Give my best to . . .	Mes amitiés à . . .	May zahmeetyay ah . . .

98

THE FAMILY

I'm traveling with my family.	Je voyage avec ma famille.	Zhuh vwahyahzh ahvehk mah fahmeey.
I have . . .	J'ai . . .	Zheh . . .
_a husband.	_un mari.	_uh(n) mahree.
_a wife.	_une femme.	_ewn fahm.
_a daughter.	_une fille.	_ewn feey.
_a son.	_un fils.	_uh(n) fees.
_two daughters.	_deux filles.	_duh feey.
_two sons.	_deux fils.	_duh fees.
_a father.	_un père.	_uh(n) pehr.
_a mother.	_une mère.	_ewn mehr.
_a grandfather.	_un grand-père.	_uh(n) grah(n)-pehr.
_a grandmother.	_une grand-mère.	_ewn grah(n)-mehr.
_a grandson.	_un petit fils.	_uh(n) ptee fees.
_a granddaughter.	_une petite fille.	_ewn pteet feey.
_a cousin (m).	_un cousin.	_uh(n) kooza(n).
_a cousin (f).	_une cousine.	_ewn koozeen.
_an aunt.	_une tante.	_ewn tah(n)t.
_an uncle.	_un oncle.	_uh(n) noh(n)kl.
_a sister.	_une soeur.	_ewn suhr.
_a brother.	_un frère.	_uh(n) frehr.
_in-laws.	_des beaux-parents.	_day boh-pahrah(n).
_a father-in-law.	_un beau-père.	_uh(n) boh-pehr.
_a mother-in-law.	_une belle-mère.	_ewn behl-mehr.
_a sister-in-law.	_une belle-soeur.	_ewn behl-suhr.
_a brother-in-law.	_un beau-frère.	_uh(n) boh-frehr.
My eldest son . . .	Mon fils aîné . . .	Moh(n) fees ehnay . . .
My eldest daughter . . .	Ma fille aînée . . .	Mah feey ehnay . . .
My youngest son . . .	Mon fils cadet . . .	Moh(n) fees kah-day . . .

99

My youngest daughter . . .	Ma fille cadette . . .	Mah feey kahdeht . . .
How old are your children?	Quel âge ont vos enfants?	Kehl ahzh oh(n) voh zah(n)fah(n)?
My children are very young.	Mes enfants sont très jeunes.	May zah(n)fah(n) soh(n) treh zhuhn.
Peter is three years older than Paul.	Peter a trois ans de plus que Paul.	Peter ah trwah zah(n) duh plews kuh Paul.

IN THE HOME

Make yourself at home.	**Faites comme chez vous.**	Feht kohm shay voo.
You may sit here.	Asseyez-vous ici.	Ahsehyay-voo zeesee.
What a pretty house!	Quelle jolie maison!	Kehl zhohlee mehzoh(n)!
I really like this neighborhood.	J'aime beaucoup ce quartier.	Zhehm bohkoo suh kahrtyay.
At our house . . .	Chez nous . . .	Shay noo . . .
At your house . . .	Chez vous . . .	Shay voo . . .
At my house . . .	Chez moi . . .	Shay mwah . . .
At home (i.e., in the States) we like baseball.	Chez nous, on aime le baseball.	Shay noo, oh(n) nehm luh baysbohl.
At your place (i.e., in France) people like soccer.	Chez vous, on aime le football.	Shay voo, oh(n) nehm luh footbohl.
Here is . . .	Voici . . .	Vwahsee . . .
_the kitchen.	_la cuisine.	_lah kweezeen.
_the living room.	_le salon.	_luh sahloh(n)
_the dining room.	_la salle à manger.	_lah sahl ah mah(n)zhay.
_the bedroom.	_la chambre.	_lah shah(m)br.
_the attic.	_le grenier.	_luh gruhnyay.

Note: *Chez* is an innocent-looking little word that has a wide range of meanings. As shown above, when combined with a personal pronoun, it often refers to one's dwelling: *chez moi* means (at) my house. In a different context, *chez moi* might mean "in my town," "in my country," etc.

_the cellar.	_la cave.	_lah kahv.
_the closet.	_l'armoire.	_lahrmwahr.
_the couch.	**_le canapé.**	**_luh kahnahpay.**
_the rug.	_le tapis.	_luh tahpee.
_the carpeting.	_la moquette.	_lah mohkeht.
_the appliances.	_les appareils ménagers.	_lay zahpahrehy may-nahzhay.
_the armchair.	_le fauteuil.	_luh fahtuhy.
_the table.	**_la table.**	**_lah tahbl.**
_the chair.	**_la chaise.**	**_lah shehz.**
_the ceiling.	_le plafond.	_luh plahfoh(n).
_the floor.	_le plancher.	_luh plah(n)shay.
It's . . .	C'est . . .	Seh . . .
_a house.	_une maison.	_ewn mehzoh(n).
_an apartment.	_un appartement.	_uh(n) nahpahrtuhmah(n).
_a villa.	_une villa.	_ewn veelah.
_a condominium.	_une copropriété.	_ewn kohprohpreeyaytay.
_a second home.	_une résidence secondaire.	_ewn rayzeedah(n)s suhkoh(n)dehr.
Can I get you a drink?	Puis-je vous offrir un verre?	Pweezh voo zohfreer uh(n) vehr?
Thanks for having invited us to your home.	Merci de nous avoir invités chez vous.	Mehrsee duh noo zahvwahr a(n)veetay shay voo.
You must come and visit us.	Il faut venir nous voir.	Eel foh vuhneer noo vwahr.

TALKING ABOUT LANGUAGE

Do you speak . . .	**Parlez-vous . . .**	**Pahrlay voo . . .**
_English?	**_anglais?**	**_zah(n)gleh?**
_Spanish?	_espagnol?	_zehspahnyohl?
_German?	_allemand?	_zahlmah(n)?

I only speak English.	Je parle seulement anglais.	Zhuh pahrl suhlmah(n) ah(n)gleh.
I speak a little French.	Je parle un peu français.	Zhuh pahrl uh(n) puh frah(n)seh.
My French is so bad!	Mon français est si mauvais!	Moh(n) frah(n)seh eh see mohveh!
That is not true.	Ce n'est pas vrai.	Suh nay pah vray.
Your French is excellent.	Votre français est excellent.	Vohtruh frah(n)say ay tehksehlah(n).
I really want to learn French.	Je tiens à apprendre le français.	Zhuh tyeh(n) ah ahprah(n)dr luh frah(n)seh.
Speak slowly.	Parlez lentement.	Pahrlay lah(n)tuhmah(n).
Could you repeat that?	Répétez, s'il vous plaît.	Raypaytay, seel voo pleh.
I don't understand.	Je ne comprends pas.	Zhuh nuh koh(m)prah(n) pah.
How do you write that?	Comment ça s'écrit?	Kohmah(n) sah say-kree?
How do you say "spoon" in French?	Comment dit-on "spoon" en français?	Kohmah(n) dee-toh(n) "spoon" ah(n) frah(n)seh?
Is there anyone who speaks English here?	Y a-t-il quelqu'un ici qui parle anglais?	Yah teel kehlkuh(n) ee-see kee pahrl ah(n)gleh?
Could you translate this for me?	Pouvez-vous me traduire ceci?	Poovay-voo muh trahdweer suhsee?
Can you understand me?	Me comprenez-vous?	Muh koh(m)pruhnay-voo?

LANGUAGES

Arabic	l'arabe	lahrahb
Chinese	le chinois	luh sheenwah
English	l'anglais	lah(n)gleh
French	le français	luh frah(n)seh
German	l'allemand	lahlmah(n)

Japanese	le japonais	luh zhahpohneh
Portuguese	le portugais	luh pohrtewgeh
Russian	le russe	luh rews
Spanish	l'espagnol	lehspahnyohl

Note: The definite article is used with names of languages but commonly omitted after the verb *parler* (to speak).

9 PERSONAL CARE

AT THE BARBERSHOP/HAIR SALON

Is there a barbershop/hair salon nearby?	Est-ce qu'il y a un coiffeur/un salon de beauté près d'ici?	Ehskeel yah uh(n) kwahfuhr/uh(n) sahloh(n) duh bohtay preh deesee?
Do I need an appointment?	Est-ce que je dois prendre rendez-vous?	Ehskuh zhuh dwah prah(n)dr rah(n)day-voo?
Can I get an appointment for today?	Puis-je prendre rendez-vous pour aujourd'hui?	Pweezh prah(n)dr rah(n)day-voo poor ohzhoordwee?
I need a haircut.	J'ai besoin d'une coupe.	Zhay buhzwa(n) dewn koop.
Please leave it long here.	Laissez-les longs ici, s'il vous plaît.	Lehsay-lay loh(n) eesee, seel voo pleh.
Please cut it short.	Je les veux courts, s'il vous plaît.	Zhuh lay vuh koor, seel voo pleh.
Not too short!	Pas trop court!	Pah troh koor!
Cut a bit more off . . .	Coupez un peu plus . . .	Koopay uh(n) puh plews . . .
_here.	_ici.	_eesee.
_in front.	_devant.	_duhvah(n).
_on the side.	_sur les côtés.	_sewr lay kohtay.
_the neck.	_sur la nuque.	_sewr lah newk.
_the back.	_derrière.	_dehryehr.
_the top.	_dessus.	_dehsew.
It's fine like that.	C'est bien comme ça.	Seh byeh(n) kohm sah.
I'd like . . .	Je voudrais . . .	Zhuh voodreh . . .
_a razor cut.	_une coupe au rasoir.	_ewn koop oh rahzwahr.
_a shampoo.	_un shampooing.	_uh(n) shah(m)pwa(n).
_a set.	_une mise en plis.	_ewn meez ah(n) plee.

_a permanent.	_une permanente.	_ewn pehr-mahnah(n)t.
_a manicure.	**_une manucure.**	**_ewn mahnewkewr.**
_a touch-up.	_une retouche.	_ewn ruhtoosh.
_a facial.	_un massage facial.	_uh(n) mahsahzh fah-syahl.
_a blow dry.	_un brushing.	_uh(n) bruhsheeng.
_a color rinse.	_un shampooing colorant.	_uh(n) shah(m)pwa(n) kohlohrah(n).
Make the part . . .	Faites la raie . . .	Feht lah reh . . .
_on the right.	_à droite.	_ah drwaht.
_on the left.	_à gauche.	_ah gohsh.
_down the middle.	_au milieu.	oh meelyuh.
No hairspray, please.	Pas de laque, s'il vous plaît.	Pah duh lahk, seel voo pleh.
Could I see a color chart?	Puis-je voir les nuances de teintes?	Pwee-zh vwahr lay nuwah(n)s duh ta(n)t?
I'd prefer . . .	Je préférerais . . .	Zhuh prayfehruhray . . .
_a lighter shade.	_une teinte plus claire.	_ewn ta(n)t plew klehr.
_a darker shade.	_une teinte plus foncée.	_ewn ta(n)t plew foh(n)say.
I prefer . . .	Je préfère . . .	Zhuh prayfehr . . .
_light blond.	_blond (clair).	_bloh(n) (klehr).
_brunette.	_brun.	_bruh(n).
I'd like a shave.	Je voudrais me faire raser.	Zhuh voodray muh fehr rahzay.
Trim my . . .	Rafraîchissez-moi . . .	Rahfrehsheesay mwah . . .
_mustache.	_la moustache.	_lah moostahsh.
_beard.	_la barbe.	_lah bahrb.

105

LAUNDRY AND DRY CLEANING

Where is the nearest . . .	Où est ____ la plus proche?	Oo eh ____ lah plew prohsh?
_laundry?	_la blanchisserie	_lah blah(n)sheesree
_dry cleaner?	_le pressing	_luh prehseeng
_laundromat?	_la laverie automatique	_lah lahvree ohtohmahteek
I have some clothes to be . . .	J'ai des vêtements à . . .	Zheh day vehtmah(n) ah . . .
_washed.	_laver.	_lahvay.
_dry cleaned.	_nettoyer à sec.	_nehtwahyay ah sehk.
_ironed.	_repasser.	_ruhpahsay.
_mended.	_réparer.	_raypahray.
I need them . . .	Il me les faut . . .	Eel muh lay foh . . .
_tomorrow.	_demain.	_duhma(n).
_the day after tomorrow.	_après-demain.	_ahpreh-duhma(n).
_in a week.	_dans une semaine.	_dah(n) zewn suhmehn.
When will they be ready?	Quand seront-ils prêts?	Kah(n) suhroh(n)teel preh?
I'm leaving tomorrow.	Je pars demain.	Zhuh pahr duhma(n).
This isn't mine.	Ce n'est pas à moi.	Suh neh pah zah mwah.
There is a shirt missing.	Il manque une chemise.	Eel mah(n)k ewn shuhmeez.
Can you get this stain out?	**Pouvez-vous faire partir cette tache?**	**Poovay-voo fehr pahr-teer seht tahsh?**
Can you sew on this button?	Pouvez-vous me recoudre ce bouton?	Poovay-voo muh ruhkoodr suh bootoh(n)?
I have . . .	J'ai . . .	Zheh . . .
_two shirts.	_deux chemises.	_duh shuhmeez.
_five underpants.	_cinq slips.	_sa(n) sleep.

_a suit.	_un complet.	_uh(n) koh(m)play.
_eight pairs of socks.	_huit paires de chaussettes.	_whee pehr duh shohseht.
_several handkerchiefs.	_plusieurs mouchoirs.	_plewzyuhr mooshwahr.
_two ties.	_deux cravates.	_duh krahvaht.
_a sweater.	_un pull.	_uh(n) pool.
_two pairs of pants.	_deux pantalons.	_duh pah(n)tahloh(n).
_a bathing suit.	_un maillot de bain.	_uh(n) mahyoh duh ba(n).
_three blouses.	_trois chemisiers.	_trwah shuhmeezeeay.

10 HEALTH CARE

It is a good idea to check with your health insurance company to find out what accident and illness expenses overseas are covered by your current policy.

Many doctors in France, Switzerland, Belgium, and Quebec speak English, especially in larger cities. American embassies or consulates can help you locate English-speaking doctors. The telephone number of the American embassy in Paris is 01.43.12.22.22. Paris is home to the well-respected American Hospital (tel. 01.46.41.25.25), with a mostly bilingual staff, in the suburb of Nevilly.

DIALOGUE   At The Doctor's (Chez le Médecin)

Médecin:	Qu'est-ce que vous avez, Madame?	Kehskuh voo zahvay, mahdahm?
Touriste:	Je ne sais pas exactement . . . Je ne me sens pas bien. J'ai mal à la tête.	Zhuh nuh seh pah ehgzahktuhmah(n) . . . Zhuh nuh muh sah(n) pah byeh(n). Zheh mahl ah lah teht.
Médecin:	Avez-vous des nausées?	Ahvay-voo day nohzay?
Touriste:	Oui, j'ai vomi ce matin.	Wee, zheh vohmeeh suh mahta(n).
Médecin:	Depuis quand êtes-vous malade?	Duhpwee kah(n) eht voo mahlahd?
Touriste:	Depuis dimanche; c'est-à-dire, depuis trois jours.	Duhpwee deemah(n)sh; seht-ah-deer, duhpwee trwah zhoor.
Doctor:	What's the matter?	
Tourist:	I don't know exactly . . . I'm not feeling well. I have a headache.	
Doctor:	Are you nauseated?	
Tourist:	Yes. I threw up this morning.	

Doctor:	How long have you been ill?
Tourist:	Since Sunday; that is for three days.

FINDING A DOCTOR

Could you call me a doctor?	Pouvez-vous m'appeler un médecin?	Poovay-voo mahplay uh(n) maydsa(n)?
Where is the doctor's office?	Où est le cabinet du médecin?	Oo eh luh kahbeenay dew maydsa(n)?
I need a doctor who speaks English.	**J'ai besoin d'un médecin qui parle anglais.**	**Zheh buhzwa(n) duh(n) maydsa(n) kee pahrl ah(n)gleh.**
When can I see the doctor?	Quand pourrais-je voir le médecin?	Kah(n) poorehzh vwahr luh maydsa(n)?
Could the doctor see me here?	Le médecin peut-il venir me voir ici?	Luh maydsa(n) puhteel vuhneer muh vwahr eesee?
Can I have an appointment . . .	**Puis-je avoir un rendez-vous . . .**	**Pweezh ahvwahr uh(n) rah(n)day-voo . . .**
_for today?	_pour aujourd'hui?	_poor ohzhoordwee?
_for tomorrow?	_pour demain?	_poor duhma(n)?
_as soon as possible?	_dès que possible?	_day kuh pohseebl?
What are the doctor's visiting hours?	Quelles sont les heures de visite du médecin?	Kehl soh(n) lay zuhr duh veezeet dew maydsa(n)?
I need . . .	**Il me faut . . .**	**Eel muh foh . . .**
_a general practitioner.	_un généraliste.	_uh(n) zhaynayrahleest.
_a pediatrician.	_un pédiatre.	_uh(n) paydyahtr.
_a gynecologist.	**_un gynécologue.**	**_uh(n) zheenaykohlohg.**
_an eye doctor.	_un oculiste.	_uh(n) nohkewleest.

TALKING TO THE DOCTOR

I don't feel well.	**Je ne me sens pas bien.**	**Zhuh nuh muh sah(n) pah byeh(n).**

I'm sick.	Je suis malade.	Zhuh swee mahlahd.
I don't know what I've got.	Je ne sais pas ce que j'ai.	Zhuh nuh say pah suh kuh zheh.
I have a fever.	**J'ai de la fièvre.**	**Zheh duh lah fyehvr.**
I don't have a temperature.	Je n'ai pas de fièvre.	Zhuh neh pah duh fyehvr.
I'm nauseated.	**J'ai des nausées.**	**Zheh day nohzay.**
I'm feeling dizzy.	J'ai des vertiges.	Zheh day vehrteezh.
I can't sleep.	Je ne peux pas dormir.	Zhuh nuh puh pah dohrmeer.
I threw up.	J'ai vomi.	Zheh vohmee.
I'm constipated.	Je suis constipé(e).	Zhuh swee koh(n)steepay.
I have a cough.	Je tousse.	Zhuh toos.
I have swelling.	Je suis enflé(e).	Zhuh swee zah(n)flay.
I have . . .	**J'ai . . .**	**Zheh . . .**
_asthma.	_de l'asthme.	_duh lahsm.
_been bitten.	_été mordu(e).	_aytay mohrdew.
_bruises.	_des contusions.	_day koh(n)tew-zyoh(n).
_a burn.	_une brûlure.	_ewn brewlewr.
_something in my eye.	_quelque chose dans l'oeil.	_kehlkuh shohz dah(n) luhy.
_a cold.	_un rhume.	_uh(n) rewm.
_cramps.	_des crampes.	_day krah(m)p.
_a cut.	_une coupure.	_ewn koopewr.
_diarrhea.	_la diarrhée.	_lah dyahray.
_a headache.	_mal à la tête.	_mahl ah lah teht.
_a lump.	_une grosseur.	_ewn grohsuhr.
_rheumatism.	_des rheumatismes.	_day rhewmahteezm.
_a sore throat.	**_mal à la gorge.**	**_mahl ah lah gohrzh.**
_a sting.	**_une piqûre.**	**_ewn peekewr.**
_a stomachache.	_mal à l'estomac.	_mahl ah lehstohmah.

_sunstroke.	_une insolation.	_ewn a(n)sohlah-syoh(n).
_an upset stomach.	_une indigestion.	_ewn a(n)deezhehsty-oh(n).
My ____ hurt(s).	J'ai mal . . .	Zheh mahl . . .
_head	_à la tête.	_ah lah teht.
_stomach	_à l'estomac.	_ah lehstohmah.
_neck	_au cou.	_oh koo.
_feet	_aux pieds.	_oh pyay.
I'm allergic to penicillin.	Je suis allergique à la pénicilline.	Zhuh swee ahlehrzheek ah lah pehneeseeleen.
Here is the medicine I take.	Voici le médicament que je prends.	Vwahsee luh maydee-kahmah(n) kuh zhuh prah(n).
I've had this pain for two days.	J'ai cette douleur depuis deux jours.	Zheh seht dooluhr duhpwee duh zhoor.
I had a heart attack four years ago.	J'ai eu une crise cardiaque il y a quatre ans.	Zheh ew ewn kreez kahrdyahk eel yah kahtr ah(n).
I'm four months pregnant.	Je suis enceinte de quatre mois.	Zhuh swee zah(n)sa(n)t duh kahtr mwah.
I have menstrual cramps.	J'ai des règles douleureuses.	Zheh day rehgl dooluhruhz.

Parts of the Body

ankle (left/right)	la cheville (gauche/droite)	lah shuhveey (gohsh/drwaht)
appendix	l'appendice	lahpa(n)dees
arm	le bras	luh brah
artery	l'artère	lahrtehr
back	le dos	luh doh
bladder	la vessie	lah vehsee
bone	l'os	lohs
bowels	les intestins	lay za(n)tehsta(n)
breast	le sein	luh sa(n)

111

buttocks	les fesses	lay fehs
calf	le mollet	luh mohlay
chest	la poitrine	lah pwahtreen
ear	**l'oreille**	**lohrehy**
an eye	un oeil	uh(n) nuhy
eyes	**les yeux**	**lay zyuh**
face	le visage	luh veezahzh
finger	**le doigt**	**luh dwah**
foot	le pied	luh pyay
forehead	le front	luh froh(n)
gland	la glande	lah glah(n)d
hair	les cheveux	lay shuhvuh
hand	la main	lah ma(n)
head	**la tête**	**lah teht**
heart	le coeur	luh kuhr
hip	la hanche	lah ah(n)sh
jaw	la mâchoire	lah mahshwahr
joint	l'articulation	lahrteekewlahsyoh(n)
kidneys	les reins	lay ra(n)
knee	le genou	luh zhuhnoo
leg	**la jambe**	**lah zhah(m)b**
lip	la lèvre	lah lehvr
liver	le foie	luh fwah
lungs	les poumons	lay poomoh(n)
mouth	la bouche	lah boosh
muscle	le muscle	luh mewskl
nail	l'ongle	loh(n)gl
neck	**le cou**	**luh koo**
nose	le nez	luh nay
penis	le pénis	luh paynees
ribs	les côtes	lay koht
shoulder	l'épaule	laypohl

skin	la peau	lah poh
spine	la colonne vertébrale	lah kohlohn vehrtay-brahl
stomach	**l'estomac**	**lehstohmah**
teeth	les dents	lay dah(n)
thigh	la cuisse	lah kwees
throat	la gorge	lah gohrzh
thumb	le pouce	luh poos
toe	l'orteil	lohrtehy
tongue	la langue	lah lah(n)g
tonsils	les amygdales	lay zahmeedahl
vagina	le vagin	luh vahzha(n)
vein	la veine	lah vehn
wrist	le poignet	luh pwahnyay

What the Doctor Says

Déshabillez-vous.	Dayzahbeeyay-voo.	Get undressed.
Déshabillez-vous jusqu'à la ceinture.	Dayzahbeeyay-voo zhewskah lah sa(n)tewr.	Undress to the waist.
Etendez-vous ici.	Aytah(n)day-voo z'eesee.	Lie down here.
Ouvrez la bouche.	Oovray lah boosh.	Open your mouth.
Toussez!	Toosay!	Cough!
Respirez à fond.	Rehspeeray ah foh(n).	Breathe deeply.
Montrez-moi où vous avez mal.	Moh(n)tray-mwah oo voo zahvay mahl.	Show me where it hurts.
Tirez la langue.	Teeray lah lah(n)g.	Stick out your tongue.
Rehabillez-vous.	Rayahbeeyay-voo.	Get dressed.
Depuis quand éprouvez-vous ces douleurs?	Duhpwee kah(n) ay-prouvay voo say dooluhr?	How long have you had these pains?
C'est . . .	Seh . . .	It's . . .
_déboité.	_daybwahtay.	_dislocated.

113

_cassé.	_kahsay.	_broken.
_foulé.	_foolay.	_sprained.
_grave.	_grahv.	_serious.
_infecté.	_a(n)fehktay.	_infected.
Ce n'est pas grave.	**Suh neh pah grahv.**	**It's not serious.**
Il faut vous faire . . .	**Eel foh voo fehr . . .**	**You'll need to get . . .**
_une radio.	_ewn rahdyoh.	_an X ray.
_une piqûre.	_ewn peekewr.	_an injection.
Je vais vous donner un calmant.	Zhuh veh voo dohnay uh(n) kahlmah(n).	I'm going to give you a painkiller.
Vous devriez . . . _aller à l'hôpital.	Voo duhvreeay . . . _ahlay ah lohpeetahl.	You need to . . . _go to the hospital.
_voir un spécialiste.	_vwahr uh(n) spaysyahleest.	_see a specialist.
Je vais prendre votre . . .	**Zhuh vay prah(n)dr vohtr . . .**	**I'm going to take your . . .**
_température.	_tah(m)payrahtewr.	_temperature.
_tension.	_tah(n)syoh(n).	_blood pressure.
Vous avez . . .	**Voo zahvay . . .**	**You have . . .**
_une appendicite.	_ewn ahpa(n)deeseet.	_appendicitis.
_une fracture.	_ewn frahktewr.	_a broken bone.
_une gastrite.	_ewn gahstreet.	_gastritis.
_la grippe.	**_lah greep.**	**_the flu.**
_une intoxication alimentaire.	_ewn a(n)tohkseekahsyoh(n) ahleemah(n)tehr.	_food poisoning.
_une maladie vénérienne.	_ewn mahlahdee vaynayryehn.	_veneral disease.
_une cystite.	_ewn seesteet.	_cystitis.
_une pneumonie.	_ewn pnuhmohnee.	_pneumonia.
_la rougeole.	_lah roozhohl.	_measles.
_le sida.	_luh seedah.	_AIDS.

114

Il me faut un pré-lèvement de . . .	Eel muh foh uh(n) praylehvmah(n) duh . . .	I need a sample of . . .
_votre sang.	_vohtr sah(n).	_your blood.
_vos selles.	_voh sehl.	_your stool.
_votre urine.	_vohtr ewreen	_your urine.

Patient Questions

Is it serious?	C'est grave?	Seh grahv?
Is it contagious?	C'est contagieux?	Seh koh(n)tahzhyuh?
How long should I stay in bed?	Jusqu'à quand dois-je rester couché(e)?	Zhewskah kah(n) dwahzh rehstay kooshay?
What exactly is wrong with me?	**Qu'est-ce que j'ai exactement?**	**Kehskuh zhay ehg-zahk-tuh-mah(n)?**
How frequently do I take this medication?	**Combien de fois par jour dois-je prendre ce médicament?**	**Koh(m)bya(n) duh fwah pahr zhoor dwahzh prah(n)dr suh maydeekah-mah(n)?**
Do I need to see you again?	Est-ce que je dois revenir vous voir?	Ehskuh zhuh dwah ruhvuhneer voo vwahr?
When can I start traveling again?	Quand est-ce que je pourrai poursuivre mon voyage?	Kah(n) tehskuh zhuh pooray poorsweevr moh(n) vwahyahzh?
Can you give me a prescription for . . .	Pourriez-vous me prescrire . . .	Pooryay-voo muh prehskreer . . .
_a painkiller.	_un calmant.	_uh(n) kahlmah(n).
_a tranquilizer.	_un tranquilisant.	_uh(n) trah(n)kee-leezah(n).
_sleeping pills.	_des somnifères.	_day sohmneefehr.
Are these pills or suppositories?	Ce sont des pillules ou des suppositoires?	Suh soh(n) day peelewl oo day sewpoh-zeetwahr?
Can I have a bill for my insurance?	Puis-je avoir une facture pour mon assurance?	Pweezh ahvwahr ewn fahkchewr poor mohn ahsewrah(n)s?

| Could you fill out this medical form? | Pourriez-vous remplir cette feuille de maladie? | Pooryay-voo rah(m)pleer seht fuhy duh mahlahdee? |

AT THE HOSPITAL

Where is the nearest hospital?	Où est l'hôpital le plus proche?	Oo eh lohpeetahl leh plew prohsh?
Call an ambulance!	Appelez une ambulance!	Ahpehlay ewn ah(m)bewlah(n)s!
Help me!	Aidez-moi!	Ehday-mwah!
Get me to a hospital!	**Emmenez-moi à l'hôpital!**	Ah(m)mnay-mwah ah lohpeetahl!
I need first aid.	**J'ai besoin de soins d'urgence.**	zheh buhzwa(n) duh swah(n) dewrzhah(n)s.
I was in an accident.	**J'ai eu un accident.**	Zheh ew uhn akseedah(n).
I cut . . .	Je me suis coupé . . .	Zhuh muh swee koopay . . .
_my hand.	_la main.	_lah ma(n).
_my leg.	_la jambe.	_lah zhah(m)b.
_my face.	_le visage.	_luh veezahzh.
I can't move . . .	**Je ne peux pas bouger . . .**	Zhuh nuh puh pah boozhay . . .
_my finger.	_le doigt.	_luh dwah.
_my leg.	**_la jambe.**	_lah zhah(m)b.
_my neck.	_le cou.	_luh koo.
He/she hurt his/her head.	Il/(elle) s'est blessé(e) à la tête.	Eel/(ehl) seh blehsay ah lah teht.
His ankle is . . .	Sa cheville est . . .	Sah shveey eh . . .
_broken.	_cassée.	_kahsay.
_twisted.	_tordue.	_tohrdew.
_swollen.	_enflée.	_ah(n)flay.
She's bleeding heavily.	Elle saigne abondamment.	Ehl sehnyuh ahboh(n)-dahmah(n).
He's unconscious.	Il s'est évanoui.	Eel seh tayvahnwee.
He/she burned himself/herself.	Il (elle) s'est brûlé(e).	Eel (ehl) seh brewlay.

116

I ate something poisonous. (I got food poisoning.)	J'ai eu une intoxication alimentaire.	Zhay ew ewn a(n)tohkseekahsyoh(n) ahleemah(n)tehr.
When can I leave?	Quand pourrai-je partir?	Kah(n) poorayzh pahrteer?
When will the doctor come?	Quand est-ce que le médecin va passer?	Kah(n) tehskuh luh maydsa(n) vah pahsay?
I can't . . .	Je ne peux pas . . .	Zhuh nuh puh pah . . .
_eat.	_manger.	_mah(n)zhay.
_drink.	_boire.	_bwahr.
_sleep.	_dormir.	_dohrmeer.
Where's the nurse?	Où est l'infirmière?	Oo eh la(n)feermyehr?
What are the visiting hours?	Quelles sont les heures de visite?	Kehl soh(n) lay zuhr duh veezeet?

THE DENTIST

Do you know a dentist?	**Connaissez-vous un dentiste?**	**Kohnehsay-voo uh(n) dah(n)teest?**
It's an emergency.	C'est une urgence.	Seh tewn ewrzhah(n)s.
I'm in a lot of pain.	**J'ai très mal.**	**Zheh treh mahl.**
My gums are bleeding.	Mes gencives saignent.	May zhah(n)seev sehnyuh.
I've lost a filling.	**J'ai perdu un plombage.**	**Zheh pehrdew uh(n) ploh(m)bahzh.**
I broke a tooth.	Je me suis cassé une dent.	Zhuh muh swee kahsay ewn dah(n).
This tooth hurts.	Cette dent me fait mal.	Seht dah(n) muh feh mahl.
I don't want to have it extracted.	Je ne veux pas la faire extraire.	Zhuh nuh vuh pah lah fehr ehkstrehr.
Can you fill it . . .	Pouvez-vous l'obturer . . .	Poovay-voo lohbtewray . . .
_with gold?	_avec de l'or?	_ahvehk duh lohr?
_with silver?	_avec de l'argent?	_ahvehk duh lahrzhah(n)?

117

_temporarily?	_provisoirement?	_prohveezwahrmah(n)?
I want a local anesthetic.	Je veux une anesthésie locale.	Zhuh vuh zewn ahnehstayzee lohkahl.
____ is broken.	____ est cassé(e)	____ eh kahsay.
_My denture	_Mon dentier	_Moh(n) dah(n)tyay
_My bridge	_Mon bridge	_Moh(n) breedzh
_My crown	_Ma couronne	_Mah koorohn
Can you fix it?	Pouvez-vous le/la réparer?	Poovay-voo luh/lah raypahray?
How much do I owe?	Combien vous dois-je?	Koh(m)byeh(n) voo dwahzh?

What the Dentist Says

Vous avez . . .	Voo zahvay . . .	You have . . .
_une infection.	_ewn a(n)fehksyoh(n).	_an infection.
_une dent carriée.	_ewn dah(n) kahryay.	_a decayed tooth.
_un abcès.	_uh(n) ahbseh.	_an abscess.
Ça vous fait mal?	Sah voo feh mahl?	Does that hurt?
Il faut extraire cette dent.	Eel foh ehkstrehr seht dah(n).	That tooth must come out.
Vous devrez revenir . . .	Voo dehvray ruhvneer . . .	You'll need to come back . . .
_demain.	_duhma(n).	_tomorrow.
_dans quelques jours.	_dah(n) kehlkuh zhoor.	_in a few days.
_la semaine prochaine.	_lah smehn prohshehn.	_next week.

THE OPTICIAN

If you wear glasses or contact lenses, it's a good idea to bring an extra pair and to have your prescription with you in case of loss.

I broke . . .	J'ai cassé . . .	Zheh kahsay . . .
_a lens.	_un verre.	_uh(n) vehr.
_the frame.	_la monture.	_lah moh(n)tewr.

I lost . . .	J'ai perdu . . .	Zheh pehrdew . . .
_my glasses.	_mes lunettes.	_may lewneht.
_a contact lens.	_un verre de contact.	_uh(n) vehr duh koh(n)tahkt.
Can they be replaced right away?	Est-ce qu'il est possible de les remplacer tout de suite?	Ehs keel eh pohseebl duh lay rah(m)plahsay tood sweet?
I'd like soft/hard contact lenses.	Je voudrais des verres de contact souples/durs.	Zhuh voodreh day vehr duh koh(n)tahkt soopl/dewr.
Here's the prescription.	Voilà l'ordonnance.	Vwahlah lohr-dohnah(n)s.
When can I come and get them?	Quand pourrai-je venir les chercher?	Kah(n) poorehzh vuh-neer lay shehrshay?
I need sunglasses.	Il me faut des lunettes de soleil.	Eel muh foh day lewneht duh sohlehy.

AT THE PHARMACY

You can recognize a pharmacy by the green cross in the window or on a sign extending from the building. The address of the all-night pharmacy is posted on the door or window of every pharmacy in town. The typical French pharmacy is more specialized than its counterpart in the United States, dealing primarily with prescription and over-the-counter drugs and other health products. You will find household and toilet products at the *supermarché* [sewpehrmahrshay] or the *hypermarché* [eep-ehrmahrshay] and in *parfumeries* [pahrfewmuhree] and *parapharmaciès* [pahrahfahrmahsee]. In Canada, you'll find drugstores that sell household goods, cosmetics, etc., like those in the United States.

Is there an all-night pharmacy near here?	Y a-t-il une pharmacie de garde près d'ici?	Yah teel ewn fahrmah-see duh gahrd preh deesee?
I need something for . . .	Il me faut quelque chose contre . . .	Eel muh foh kehlkuh shohz koh(n)tr . . .
_a cold.	_le rhume.	_luh rewm.
_constipation.	_la constipation.	_lah koh(n)steepah-syoh(n).

_a cough.	_la toux.	_lah too.
_diarrhea.	**_la diarrhée.**	_lah dyahray.
_fever.	_la fièvre.	_lah fyehvr.
_hay fever.	_le rhume des foins.	_luh rewm day fwa(n).
_headache.	_le mal de tête.	_luh mahl duh teht.
_insect bites.	_les piqûres d'insectes.	_lay peekewr da(n)sehkt.
_sunburn.	_les coups de soleil.	_lay koo duh sohlay.
_travel (motion) sickness.	_le mal des transports.	_luh mahl day trah(n)spohr.
_an upset stomach.	**_por une indigestion.**	_poor ewn a(n)dee-zhehstyoh(n).
I'd like . . .	Je voudrais . . .	Zhuh voodreh . . .
_some alcohol.	_de l'alcool.	_duh lahlkohl.
_an analgesic.	_un analgésique.	_uh(n) nahnahlzhay-zeek.
_an antiseptic.	_un antiseptique.	_uh(n) nah(n)teesehp-teek.
_some aspirin.	_de l'aspirine.	_duh lahspeereen.
_a bandage.	_une bande.	_ewn bah(n)d.
_some Band-Aids™.	_des pansements.	_day pah(n)smah(n).
_some contact lens solution.	_un produit pour les verres de contact.	_uh(n) prohdwee poor lay vehr duh koh(n)tahkt.
_some contraceptives.	_des contra-ceptifs.	_day koh(n)trahsehp-teef.
_some cotton.	_du coton hydrophile.	_dew kohtoh(n) eedrohfeel.
_some cough drops.	_des pastilles contre la toux.	_day pahsteey koh(n)tr lah too.
_a disinfectant.	_un désinfectant.	_uh(n) dayza(n)-fehktah(n).
_some ear drops.	_des gouttes pour les oreilles.	_day goot poor lay zohrehy.
_some eye drops.	_des gouttes pour les yeux.	_day goot poor lay zyuh.

_some gauze.	_de la gaze.	_duh lah gahz.
_an insect spray.	_un spray contre les piqûres d'insectes.	_uh(n) spray koh(n)truh lay peekuhr da(n)sehkt.
_a laxative.	_un laxatif.	_uh(n) lahksahteef.
_some nose drops.	_des gouttes nasales.	_day goot nahzahl.
_some pills.	_des pilules.	_day peelewl.
_some sanitary napkins.	_des serviettes hygiéniques.	_day sehrvyeht eezhyayneek.
_some sleeping pills.	_des somnifères.	_day sohmneefehr.
_some suppositories.	_des supposi-toires.	_day sewpoh-zeetwahr.
_some tablets.	_des comprimés.	_day koh(m)preemay.
_some tampons.	_des tampons.	_day tah(m)poh(n).
_a thermometer.	_un thermomètre.	_uh(n) tehrmohmehtr
_some vitamins.	_des vitamines.	_day veetahmeen.
It's urgent!	C'est urgent!	Seh tewrzhah(n)!

11 ON THE ROAD

CAR RENTALS

France has an excellent system of superhighways (*autoroutes* [ohtohroot]) that offer rapid, convenient access between major cities. Tolls can be high, though. If you don't want to pay them, use the slower *routes nationales* [root nahsyohnahl]. Some roadside stops (aires de repos [ehr duh ruhpoh]) are very well developed, with restaurants, supermarkets, hotels, and cafés.

You may use your currently valid American driver's license to rent a car in Europe. If you are renting for a month or more, an International Driver's License may be required and anyway it's always a good idea. They are available at a nominal charge from the American and Canadian Automobile Associations and, in the United Kingdom, from the Automobile Association or the Royal Automobile Club.

Most of the major automobile rental companies have branches in France, Belgium, and Switzerland, including Hertz and Avis. Fly-drive packages not only allow you to have a confirmed reservation before you leave home but offer some attractive deals as well. Beware the advertised low daily rate; it is for the smallest subcompact (which may not be available) and does not usually include taxes or insurance.

If you are planning to rent a car for three weeks or longer, there is a way to get around the high rates of auto rentals. The alternative is leasing, technically known as the "Financed Purchase-Repurchase Plan." You will be provided with a brand-new, factory-fresh car, with no extra charges for collision coverage, and no TVA (value-added tax) to pay. There are some real bargains on smaller Renaults. The minimum rental (lease) is 17 days. The longer you keep the car, the cheaper the per-day and per-week rate, on an unlimited mileage basis. Arrangements need to be made 30 days in advance. For information, contact Renault, Inc. (6 E. 46th St., New York, NY 10017; tel. 212/532-1221; www.renaultusa.com).

DIALOGUE   At the Car-Rental Agency
(À l'Agence de Location de Voitures)

Client:	**Bonjour. Je voudrais louer une voiture pas trop chère.**	Boh(n)zhoor. Zhuh voo-dreh looway ewn vwahtewr pah troh shehr.
Employée:	**Très bien, Monsieur. Il nous reste une Renault Clio climatisée.**	Treh byeh(n), muhsyuh. Eel noo rehst ewn Renoh Cleeoh kleemahteezay.
Client:	**Est-ce que je pourrais l'avoir pour trois jours?**	Ehskuh zhuh pooreh lahvwahr poor trwah zhoor?
Employée:	**Certainement, Monsieur. Et le kilométrage illimité est compris dans le prix.**	Sehrta(n)mah(n), muhsyuh. Ay luh keelohmuhtrahzh eeleemeetay ay koh(m)pree dah(n) luh pree.
Client:	**D'accord, c'est parfait. Je la prends.**	Dakohr, say pahrfay. Zhuh lah prah(n).
Employée:	**Très bien. Votre passeport et votre permis de conduire, s'il vous plaît.**	Treh byeh(n). Vohtr pahspohr ay vohtr pehrmee duh koh(n)dweer, seel voo pleh.

....

Customer: Hello. I'd like to rent an inexpensive car.

Employee: Very well, sir. We still have a Renault Clio with air-conditioning left.

Customer: Could I have it for three days?

Employee: Certainly, sir. And unlimited mileage is included in the price.

Customer: Perfect! I'll take it.

Employee: Very good, sir. Passport and driver's license, please.

Is there a car rental agency in this town?	Y a-t-il une agence de location de voitures dans cette ville?	Yahteel ewn ahzhah(n)s duh lohkahsyoh(n) duh vwahtewr dah(n) seht veel?

I'd like to rent . . .	Je voudrais louer . . .	Zhuh voodreh looay . . .
_a small car.	_une petite voiture.	_ewn puhteet vwahtewr.
_a midsize car.	_une voiture moyenne.	_ewn vwahtewr mwahyehn.
_a large car.	_une grande voiture.	_ewn grah(n)d vwahtewr.
_the least expensive car.	_la voiture la moins chère.	_lah vwahtewr lah mwa(n) shehr.
_a car with automatic transmission.	_une voiture automatique.	_ewn vwahtewr ohtohmahteek.
Do you have unlimited mileage?	Ya-t-il le kilométrage illimité?	Yahteel luh keelohmehtrazh eeleemeetay?
I'd like full insurance coverage.	Je voudrais une assurance tous risques.	Zhuh voodreh ewn ahsew-rah(n)s too reesk.
What's the rate . . .	C'est combien le tarif . . .	Say koh(m)byehn luh tahreef . . .
_per day?	_à la journée?	_ah lah zhoornay?
_per week?	_à la semaine?	_ah lah smehn?
_per kilometer?	_au kilomètre?	_oh keelohmehtr?
Do you accept this credit card?	Acceptez-vous cette carte de crédit?	Ahksehptay-voo seht kahrt duh kraydee?
Do you need my driver's license?	Avez-vous besoin de mon permis de conduire?	Ahvay-voo buhzwa(n) duh moh(n) pehrmee duh koh(n)dweer?
Can I rent it here and return it in ____?	Puis-je la louer ici et la rendre à ____?	Pweezh lah looay ee-see ay lah rah(n)dr oh ____?

DRIVING

Get a good road map (Michelin's is the best), and prepare your itinerary in advance, allowing for plenty of time to sightsee along the way.

Parking is a nightmare in Paris and is often difficult in large towns. Parking lots (*parking* [pahrkeeng]), meters (*parcmètres* [pahrkmehtrs]), and pay and display ticket machines (*horodateurs* [orohdahturs]) are commonplace (be sure to have a supply of coins). Before you park, check the signs, as rules vary. Parking on the street is free in Paris during the month of August, the only month when you're likely to find a parking spot.

Excuse me, how do I get to ____?	Pardon, comment va-t-on à ____?	Pahrdoh(n), kohmah(n) vahtoh(n) ah ____?
Is this the road to ____?	Est-ce bien la route pour ____?	Ehs byeh(n) lah root poor ____?
How far is it to ____?	Nous sommes à quelle distance de ____?	Noo sohm zah kehl deestah(n)s duh ____?
Where can I get a road map of ____?	Où puis-je trouver une carte routière de ____?	Oo pweezh troovay ewn kahrt roo-tyehr duh ____?
Do I . . .	Est-ce que je dois . . .	Ehskuh zhuh dwah . . .
_go straight?	_aller tout droit?	_ahlay too drwah?
_turn right?	_tourner à droite?	_toornay ah drwaht?
_turn left?	_tourner à gauche?	_toornay ah gohsh?
_make a U-turn?	_faire demi-tour?	_fehr duhmee-toor?
I want to go to ____; what do I do at the next intersection?	Je veux aller à ____; qu'est-ce que je dois faire au prochain carrefour?	Zhuh vuh zahlay ah ____; kehskuh zhuh dwah fehr oh proh-sha(n) kahrfoor?
Where can I park?	Où puis-je me garer?	Oo pweezh muh gahray?
Is there a parking lot nearby?	Y a-t-il un parking près d'ici?	Yahteel uh(n) pahrkeeng preh deesee?

DISTANCES AND LIQUID MEASURES

As you may know, distances in French-speaking countries are expressed in kilometers and liquid measures (gas and oil, for example) in liters. Unless you are a whiz at mental calculating, the switch from one system to another can be hard to get used to. The following conversion formulas and charts should help.

DISTANCE CONVERSIONS		LIQUID MEASURE CONVERSIONS	
1 kilometer (km.) = .62 miles		1 liter (l) = .26 gallon	
1 mile = 1.61 km.		1 gallon = 3.78 liters	
Kilometers	**Miles**	**Liters**	**Gallons**
1	0.62	10	2.6
5	3.1	15	4.0
8	5.0	20	5.3
10	6.2	30	7.9
15	9.3	40	10.6
20	12.4	50	13.2
50	31.0	60	15.8
75	46.6	70	18.5
100	62.1		

THE SERVICE STATION

Where is the nearest service station?	Où est la station-service la plus proche?	Oo eh lah stahsyah(n)-sehrvees lah plew prohsh?
Fill it with . . .	Faites le plein . . .	Feht luh pla(n) . . .
_unleaded 95.	_de Sans Plomb 95.	_duh sah(n) plohm kahtr-va(n) ka(n)z.
_unleaded 98.	_de Sans Plomb 98.	_duh sah(n) plohm kahtr-va(n) dee-zweet.
_super.	_de super.	_duh sewpehr.
_diesel.	_de gas-oil.	_duh gahz-wahl.
Give me 20 litres of unleaded 98.	Donnez-moi vingt litres de Sans Plomb 98.	Dohnay-mwah va(n) leetr duh sah(n) plohm kahtr-va(n) dee-zweet.

126

Give me 20 euros of unleaded 98.	Donnez-moi pour 20 euros de Sans Plomb 98.	Dohnay-mwah poor va(n) uhroh duh sah(n) plohm kahtr-va(n) dee-zweet.
Please check . . .	**Voulez-vous bien vérifier . . .**	**Voolay-voo byeh(n) vayreefyay . . .**
_the battery.	_la batterie.	_lah bahtree.
_the brake fluid.	_le liquide de freins.	_luh leekeed duh fra(n).
_the carburetor.	_le carburateur.	_luh kahrbewrahtuhr.
_the tire pressure.	_la pression des pneus.	_lah prehsyoh(n) day pnuh.
_the water.	_l'eau.	_loh.
____ need(s) to be changed.	Il faut changer . . .	Eel foh shah(n)-zhay . . .
_The spark plugs.	_les bougies.	_les boozhee.
_The tire.	_le pneu.	_luh pnuh.
The oil needs to be changed.	**Il faut faire la vidange.**	**Eel foh fehr lah veedah(n)zh.**
My car has broken down.	**Ma voiture est en panne.**	**Mah vwahtewr eh tah(n) pahn.**
Can you repair it?	**Pouvez-vous la réparer?**	**Poovay-voo lah ray-pahray?**
Do you have the part?	Avez-vous la pièce de rechange?	Ahvay-voo lah pyehs duh ruhshah(n)zh?
I've run out of gas.	Je suis en panne d'essence.	Zhuh swee zah(n) pahn dehsah(n)s.
It won't start.	Elle ne démarre pas.	Ehl nuh daymahr pah.
I have a flat tire.	J'ai un pneu crevé.	Zheh uh(n) pnuh kruh-vay.
The battery's dead.	La batterie est à plat.	Lah bahtree eh tah plah.
Can you check the battery?	Pourriez-vous vérifier la batterie?	Pooryay-voo vay-reefyay lah bahtree?
It's overheating.	Le moteur chauffe.	Luh mohtuhr shohf.

127

Can you tow me?	Pouvez-vous la remorquer?	Poovay-voo lah ruhmohrkay.
I have a problem with . . .	J'ai un problème avec . . .	Zheh uh(n) prohblehm ahvehk . . .
_the carburetor.	_le carburateur.	_luh kahrbewrahtuhr.
_the directional signal.	_le clignotant.	_luh kleenyohtah(n).
_the gears.	_les vitesses.	_lay veetehs.
_the brakes.	_les freins.	_lay fra(n).
_the headlights.	_les phares.	_lay fahr.
_the ignition.	_l'allumage.	_lahlewmahzh.
_the radiator.	_le radiateur.	_luh rahdyahtuhr.
_the starter.	_le démarreur.	_luh daymahruhr.
_the transmission.	_la transmission.	_lah trah(n)smee-syoh(n).
I have no tools.	Je n'ai pas d'outils.	Zhuh neh pah dooteey.
Do you have . . .	Avez-vous . . .	Ahvay voo . . .
_a flashlight?	_une lampe de poche?	_ewn lah(m)p duh pohsh?
_a jack?	_un cric?	_uh(n) kreek?
_pliers?	_des pinces?	_day pa(n)s?
_a screwdriver?	_un tournevis?	_uh(n) toornuhvees?
How long will it take?	Combien de temps faut-il compter?	Koh(m)byeh(n) duh tah(m) foh teel koh(m)tay?
I need it today.	Il me la faut aujourd'hui.	Eel muh lah foh ohzhoordwee.

ROAD SIGNS

Accotement non stabilisé	Soft Shoulders
Allumez vos feux.	Headlights On
Autoroute	Highway
Camping interdit	No Camping
Cédez le passage	Yield Right of Way

Centre ville	Downtown
Chantier	Construction
Chaussée défoncée/déformée	Bad Surface
Chaussée glissante	Slippery Road
Chaussée rétrécie	Road Narrows
Chute de pierres	Falling Rocks
Circuit touristique	Scenic Route
Défense d'entrer	No Trespassing
Descente dangereuse	Caution: Steep Hill
Déviation	Detour
Douane	Customs
Feux de circulation	Traffic Light Ahead
File de droite	Right Lane
File de gauche	Left Lane
Impasse/Voie sans issue	Dead End
Interdit aux piétons	No Pedestrians
Respectez les distances de sécurité	No Tailgating
Parking	Parking Lot
Passage à niveau	Railroad Crossing
Passage piétons	Pedestrian Crossing
Péage	Toll
Poids lourds	Trucks
Priorité à droite	Yield to the Right
Propriété privée	Private Property
Ralentir	Slow
Rappel 70	Reminder: Speed Limit Is 70 km/h
Réservé aux autobus	Buses Only
Sens unique	One-Way
Serrez à droite	Keep Right
Sortie d'autoroute	Highway Exit
Sortie de camions	Caution: Truck Exit
Stationnement interdit	No Parking

Stationnement jours impairs	Parking Permitted Odd Days of Month
Stationnement jours pairs	Parking Permitted Even Days of Month
Toutes directions	Through Traffic
Travaux	Construction
Verglas	Icy Road
Virages	Caution: Curves
Voie sans issue	No Through Way

NO ENTRY FOR
MOTOR VEHICLES

DANGEROUS
INTERSECTION
AHEAD

STOP

NO ENTRY

MINIMUM SPEED
(km/hr)

SPEED LIMIT
(km/hr)

DIRECTION TO BE
FOLLOWED (at the
next intersection)

OVERHEAD
CLEARANCE
(meters)

ROTARY

NO PASSING

END OF
NO PASSING ZONE

END OF
RESTRICTION

NO LEFT TURN

NO U-TURN

NO PARKING

ONE WAY

DEAD END

PARKING

SUPERHIGHWAY

YIELD

GAS

DANGER AHEAD

DANGEROUS DESCENT

BUMPS

ROAD NARROWS

LEVEL (RAILROAD) CROSSING

TWO-WAY TRAFFIC

SLIPPERY ROAD

CAUTION— SHARP CURVE

PEDESTRIAN CROSSING

132

DIALOGUE   On the Telephone (Au Téléphone)

Mme. Robert:	**Allô.**	Ahloh.
Jean Guyon:	**Allô. Ici Jean Guyon.**	Ahloh. Eesee Zhah(n) Gheeyoh(n).
Mme. Robert:	**Bonjour, Monsieur. Je voudrais parler à M. Roger, s'il vous plaît.**	Boh(n)zhoor, muhsyuh. Zhuh voodreh pahrlay ah Muhsyuh Rohzhay, seel voo pleh.
Jean Guyon:	**Ne quittez pas . . . Je suis désolé, mais il n'est pas là.**	Nuh keetay pah . . . Zhuh swee dayzahlay, meh eel neh pah lah.
Mme. Robert:	**Quand sera-t-il de retour?**	Kah(n) suhrah teel duh ruhtoor?
Jean Guyon:	**Vers quinze heures.**	Vehr ka(n)z uhr.
Mme. Robert:	**Alors, pourriez-vous lui dire de me rappeler? C'est de la part de Mme. Robert.**	Ahlohr, pooryay-voo lwee deer duh muh rahpehlay. Seh duh lah pahr duh Mahdahm Rohbehr.
Jean Guyon:	**Très bien. Je lui transmettrai le message. Au revoir, Madame.**	Treh byeh(n). Zhuh lwee transmeetreh luh mehsahzh. Ow rvwahr, mahdahm.
Mme. Robert:	**Merci. Au revoir, Monsieur.**	Mehrsee. Oh rvwahr, muhsyuh.

....

Mrs. Robert:	Hello?
Jean Guyon:	Hello. Jean Guyon speaking.
Mrs. Robert:	Hello. I'd like to speak with Mr. Roger, please.
Jean Guyon:	Hold the line . . . I'm sorry, but he's not here.
Mrs. Robert:	When will he be back?
Jean Guyon:	Around three PM.

Mrs. Robert:	Well, could you tell him to return my call? This is Mrs. Robert.
Jean Guyon:	Very well. I'll give him the message. Good-bye.
Mrs. Robert:	Thanks. Good-bye.

TELEPHONES

The French telephone system is modern and efficient. A local call costs about €.09 (€.23 for one minute to the U.S.) for every three minutes. Telephone booths are gradually disappearing, as nearly everyone has a cell phone, or *portable* [pohr-TAH-bluh]; the remaining ones are found at post offices, Métro stations, and cafés. Most French pay phones are operated by telephone cards, or *télécartes* [taylaykahrts]. You can buy a telephone card at a post office, or *tabac* [tahbah]. A card entitles you to so many *units* (not calls). So, if you want to make only one or two calls, you might not want to buy a card—you can still use coins in café phones. However, phones accepting telephone cards are much easier to find.

The first two digits of each French phone number are area codes: 01 for Paris and Ile-de-France; 02 for the northwest; 03 for the northeast; 04 for the southeast; and 05 for the southwest. When you are in France, always dial the ten-digit number. But drop the zero when you are calling France from a foreign country.

International calls can be placed from any phone booth, and international operators will be able to assist you in English. To call direct to the United States, dial 001 plus the area code and number. When calling France from the United States, dial 011 plus 33 plus the number, minus the initial zero. The main cell phone networks in France are SFR, Bouygues, and Itineris. Itineris is run by France Telecom and has the best network.

Where can I make a phone call?	Où puis-je téléphoner?	Oo pweezh taylayfoh-nay?
Is there a phone booth here?	Y a-t-il une cabine téléphonique ici?	Yahteel ewn kahbeen taylayfohneek eesee?
Do you have a phone directory?	Avez-vous un annuaire télé-phonique?	Ahvay-voo zuh(n) nahnwehr taylay-fohneek?

What do I dial to call the United States?	Quel numéro faut-il composer pour appeler les Etats-Unis?	Kehl newmayroh fohteel koh(m)pohzay poor ahpehlay lay zaytah zewnee?
I'd like to call . . .	Je voudrais téléphoner . . .	Zhuh voodreh taylayfohnay . . .
_overseas.	_à l'étranger.	_ah laytrah(n)zhay.
My number is . . .	Mon numéro est . . .	Moh(n) newmayroh eh . . .
How do I get information?	Que fait-on pour avoir les renseignements?	Kuh fehtoh(n) poor ahwwahr lay rah(n)sehnymah(n)?
I was cut off.	J'ai été coupé(e).	Zhay koopay.
To whom am I speaking?	Qui est à l'appareil?	Kee eh tah lahpahray?
Speak more slowly, please.	Parlez plus lentement, s'il vous plaît.	Pahrlay plew lah(n)tuhmah(n), seel voo pleh.
Could you telephone for me?	Pouvez-vous téléphoner pour moi?	Poovay-voo taylayfohnay poor mwah?
I'd like to speak to . . .	Je voudrais parler à . . .	Zhuh voodreh pahrlay ah . . .
Please leave this message:	Pouvez-vous lui transmettre ce message?	Poovay-vous lwee trah(n)smehtr suh mehsahzh?

What You May Hear

C'est de la part de qui?	Seh duh lah pahr duh kee?	Who's calling?
Ne quittez pas.	Nuh keetay pah.	Hold the line.
Ça ne répond pas.	Sah nuh raypoh(n) pah.	They don't answer.
Vous vous êtes trompé de numéro.	Voo voo zeht troh(m)pay duh newmayroh.	You have the wrong number.
Puis-je prendre un message?	Pweezh prah(n)dr uh(n) mehsahzh?	May I take a message?

Pourriez-vous rappeler plus tard?	Pooryay-voo rahplay plew tahr?	Could you call back later?
La ligne est occupée.	Lah leenyeh tohkew-pay.	The line is busy.
On vous demande au téléphone.	Oh(n) voo duhmah(n)d oh taylayfohn.	You have a call.
Quel numéro demandez-vous?	Kehl newmayroh duhmah(n)day-voo?	What number do you want?

THE POST OFFICE

Hours are usually 8 AM to 7 PM, although the main post office in Paris (52 rue du Louvre, 75001) does not close. On weekends, the post office usually opens Saturday mornings only. In Paris post offices, be prepared to wait in line. Stamps can be purchased at the post office or the tobacco shop (*bureau de tabac*).

As for getting mail sent to Paris, your best bet is American Express, 11 rue Scribe, right next to the Opéra. Service is free to card members and customers (you qualify if you use their traveler's checks).

I'm looking for the post office.	**Je cherche un bureau de poste.**	Zhuh shehrsh uh(n) bewroh duh pohst.
Where's the nearest mailbox?	Où est la boîte aux lettres la plus proche?	Oo eh lah bwaht oh lehtr lah plew prohsh?
I'd like to mail a letter.	Je voudrais poster une lettre.	Zhuh voodreh pohstay ewn lehtr.
How much is it to send . . .	**C'est combien pour envoyer . . .**	Seh koh(m)byeh(n) poor ah(n)vwahyay . . .
_a letter (to the United States)?	_une lettre (aux Etats-Unis)?	_ewn lehtr (oh zaytah-zewnee)?
_a postcard?	_une carte postale?	_ewn kahrt pohstahl?
_a registered letter?	_une lettre recommandée?	_ewn lehtr ruhkohmah(n)day?
_this package?	_ce colis?	_suh kohlee?
_a letter by Chronopost International™	_une lettre en Chronopost International™	_ewn lehtr ah(n) krohnohpahst entehrnahseeohnahl

Where can I buy . . .	Où puis-je acheter . . .	Oo pwee-zhuh ahshtay . . .
_stamps?	_des timbres?	_day ta(m)br?
_money orders?	_des mandats-cash?	_day mah(n)dah-kash?
I need to send this package general delivery.	J'ai besoin d'envoyer ce colis en poste restante.	Zheh buh sweh(n) dah(n)vwahyay suh kohlee ah(n) pohst rehstah(n).
Is there mail for me?	Y a-t-il du courrier pour moi?	Yahteel dew kooryay poor mwah?
I need stamps for . . .	Il me faut des timbres pour . . .	Eel muh foh day ta(m)br poor . . .
_five postcards to the United States.	_cinq cartes postales pour les Etats-Unis.	_sa(n) kahrt pohstahl poor lay zahtay-zewnee.

E-MAIL AND THE INTERNET

There are Internet cafés in all major cities and in many small towns as well. Large hotels typically offer Internet access for a fee. In Paris, look for the low-cost, Internet café chain Easy Everything. For store locations, visit www.easyeverything.com, before you leave.

Where is the computer?	Où est l'ordinateur?	oo eh lohrdeenahtuhr
I need to send an e-mail.	J'ai besoin d'envoyer un e-mail.	zheh buhsweh(n) dah(n)vqahyay uh neemayl
Can I get get on the Internet?	Puis-je me connecter à l'Internet?	pwee zhuh muh kohnektay ah leh(n)tehrneht
Do you have a Web site?	Avez-vous un site sur l'Internet?	ahveh voo uh(n) seet sewr leh(n)tehrneht

FAXES AND TELEGRAMS

There is usually a special window at the post office for sending telegrams.

Which window is it for telegrams/faxes?	C'est quel guichet pour les télégrammes/fax?	Seh kehl gheeshay poor lay taylay-grahm/fahks?
May I send a telegram/fax?	Puis-je envoyer un télégramme/fax?	Pweezh ah(n)vwah-yay u(h)n taylay-grahm/fahkes?
I need to send a fax.	J'ai besoin d'envoyer un fax.	zheh buhsweh[n] dah[n]vwahyay uh[n] fahks
What do I dial to start?	Quel numéro faut-il composer pour commencer?	Kehl newmayroh foh-teel koh(m)poh-zay poor kohmoh(n)-say?
Is there a fax for me?	Y a-t-il un fax pour moi?	ee yah teel uh[n] fahks poormwah

THE MEDIA

In Paris, you can get newspapers and magazines from all over the world. The British Time Out Group has a Paris-based operation that publishes a free quarterly *Time Out* magazine, an annual restaurant guide, and an English section in the weekly French magazine *Pariscope*. It is perfect for the American who wants to be *au courant* [oh coorah(n)] or *branché* [brah(n)shay], in the know, in Paris. Watching French television is a good way to practice your ability to understand what is said to you. Many hotels offer English-language television by satellite.

Books and Newspapers (Livres et Journaux)

Do you have . . .	Avez-vous des . . .	Ahvay voo day . . .
_newspapers in English?	_journaux en anglais?	_zhoornoh zah(n) nah(n)glay?
_magazines in English?	_revues en anglais?	_ruhvew zah(n) nah(n)glay?
_books in English?	_livres en anglais?	_leevr zah(n) nah(n)glay?

Radio and Television (Radio et Télévision)

Is there a(n) ____ station?	Est-ce qu'il y a une station . . .	Ehs keel yah ewn stah syoh(n) . . .
_English-speaking	_en anglais?	_ah(n) nah(n)glay?

_music	_musicale?	_moozeekahl?
_news	_d'informations?	_da(n)fohrmahsyoh(n)?
_weather	_météo(rologique)?	_maytayoh(rohlohzheek)?
What is	Quelle est	Kehl eh
_the number on the dial?	_la fréquence?	_lah fraykah(n)s?
_the television channel?	_la chaîne?	_lah shehn?
What time is the program?	À quelle heure commence l'émission?	Ah kehl uhr kohmah(n)s laymee-syoh(n)?
Is there an English-speaking TV channel?	Est-ce qu'il y a une chaîne en anglais?	Eskeel yah ewn shehn ah(n) nah(n)gleh?
Do you have a TV guide?	Est-ce que vous avez un programme télé?	Ehskuh voo zahvay uh(n) prohgrahm taylay?
Do they have international news in English?	Ya-t-il des informations internationales en anglais?	Yahteel day za(n)fohrmahsyoh(n) a(n)tehrnahsyohnahl ah(n) nah(n)gleh?
When is the weather forecast?	A quelle heure est la météo?	Ah kehl uhr ay lah maytayoh?

13 SIGHTSEEING

Before your trip, we recommend reading about the countries you plan to visit. In addition to guidebooks, your travel agent or national tourist office can give you information that will help you plan a sightseeing itinerary. The Internet is also useful for research. You'll find a plethora of links to the Web sites of local tourist offices, publications, attractions, and booking services on www.fodors.com. Once you reach your destination, ask at your hotel for a map of the city. You may also be able to obtain information about bus tours, activities, and places of interest to visit.

DIALOGUE   At the Museum (Au Musée)

Sheila:	**Vous savez je m'intéresse beaucoup à l'histoire de l'art.**	Voo sahvay zhuh ma(n)tayrehs bohkoo ah leestwahr duh lahr.
Pierre:	**Moi aussi! Quelle période préférez-vous?**	Mwah ohsee! Kehl payreeyohd pray-fayray-voo?
Sheila:	**J'adore les impressionnistes. Tenez! Regardez! Voilà un tableau impressionniste. Qui en est le peintre?**	Zhahdohr lay za(m)prehsyohneest. Tuhnay! Ruhgahrday! Vwahlah uh(n) tahbloh a(m)prehsyohneest. Kee ah(n) neh luh pa(n)tr?
Pierre:	**C'est un tableau de Monet.**	Say tuh(n) tahbloh duh Mohnay.
Sheila:	**Ah, oui. En quelle année l'a-t-il terminé?**	Ah, wee. Ah(n) kehl ahnay lahteel tehrmeenay?
Pierre:	**Attendez un moment. Je vais voir . . . en 1898.**	Ahtah(n)day zuh(n) mohmah(n). Zhuh vay vwahr . . . ah(n) meel weet sah(n), kahtruh-va(n)deez-weet.

Sheila:	You know, I'm very interested in art history.
Pierre:	Me too! What period do you like the best?
Sheila:	I love the Impressionists. Look! There's an Impressionist painting. Who's the painter?
Pierre:	It's a painting by Monet.
Sheila:	Oh, yes. What year did he complete it?
Pierre:	Just a moment. I'll look . . . in 1898.

FINDING THE SIGHTS

What is there to see in town?	Quelles sont les curiosités de la ville?	Kehl soh(n) lay kewry-ohzeetay duh lah veel?
How far is it from here?	C'est à quelle distance d'ici?	Seh tah kehl deestah(n)s deesee?
Where is the tourism office?	**Où se trouve l'office du tourisme?**	**Oo suh troov lohfees dew tooreezm?**
Can you tell me about . . .	Pouvez-vous me renseigner sur . . .	Poovay-voo muh rah(n)sehnyay sewr . . .
_guided tours?	_les visites guidées?	_lay veezeet ghee-day?
_excursions?	_les excursions?	_lay zehkskewr-syoh(n)?
Are there English-speaking guides?	Y a-t-il des guides qui parlent anglais?	Yahteel day gheed kee pahrl ah(n)gleh?
We'd like a guide . . .	Nous voudrions un guide . . .	Noo voodreeoh(n) zuh(n) gheed . . .
_for a day.	_pour une journée.	_poor ewn zhoornay.
_for an afternoon.	_pour un après-midi.	_poor uh(n) nahpray-meedee.
When does the excursion begin?	A quelle heure commence l'excursion?	Ah kehl uhr kohmah(n)s lehkskewr-syoh(n)?

141

Is breakfast (lunch, dinner) included?	Est-ce que le petit déjeuner (le déjeuner, le dîner) est compris?	Ehskuh luh ptee day-zhuhnay (luh dayzhuh-nay, luh deenay) eh koh(m)pree?
How much is the excursion, everything included?	À combien revient l'excursion tout compris?	Ah koh(m)byeh(n) ruh-vyeh(n) lehkskewr-syoh(n) too koh(m)pree?
When do we return to the hotel?	À quelle heure revient-on à l'hôtel?	Ah kehl uhr ruhvya(n)-toh(n) ah lohtehl?
Where do the tours start from?	D'où partent les visites?	Doo pahrt lay veezeet?
I'd like to see . . .	**J'aimerais voir . . .**	**Zhehmreh vwahr . . .**
_the aquarium.	_l'aquarium.	_lahkwahryuhm.
_the art galleries.	**_les galéries d'art.**	**_lay gahlree dahr.**
_the botanical gardens.	_le jardin botanique.	_luh zhahrda(n) bohtahneek.
_the business district.	_le quartier des affaires.	_luh kahrtyay day zahfehr.
_the castle.	**_le château.**	**_luh shahtoh.**
_the catacombs.	_les catacombes.	_lay kahtahkoh(m)b.
_the cathedral.	**_la cathédrale.**	**_lah kahtaydrahl.**
_the caves.	_les grottes.	_lay groht.
_the cemetery.	_le cimetière.	_luh seemtyehr.
_the central square.	_la place principale.	_lah plahs pra(n)-seepahl.
_the chapel.	_la chapelle.	_lah shahpehl.
_the church.	_l'église.	_laygleez.
_the citadel.	_la citadelle.	_lah seetahdehl.
_the convent.	_le couvent.	_luh koovah(n).
_the courthouse.	_le palais de justice.	_luh pahleh duh zhewstees.
_downtown.	_le centre ville.	_luh sah(n)truh veel.
_the exhibition center.	_le centre des expositions.	_luh sah(n)tr dayzehks-pohzeesyoh(n).

142

_the factories.	_les usines.	_lay zewzeen.
_the flea market.	**_le marché aux puces.**	_luh mahrshay oh pewss.
_the fortress.	_la forteresse.	_lah fohrtuhrehs.
_the fountains.	_les fontaines.	_lay foh(n)tehn.
_the grave of ____.	_la tombe de ____.	_lah toh(m)b duh ____.
_the harbor.	_le port.	_luh pohr.
_historic sites.	_les sites historiques.	_lay seet eestohreek.
_the library.	_la bibliothèque.	_lah beebleeohtehk.
_the market.	**_le marché.**	_luh mahrshay.
_the monastery.	_le monastère.	_luh mohnahstehr.
_the mosque.	_la mosquée.	_lah mohskay.
_the museums.	_les musées.	_lay mewzay.
_the old city.	_la vieille ville.	_lah vyay veel.
_the opera house.	_l'opéra.	_lohpayrah.
_the park.	_le parc.	_luh pohrk.
_the planetarium.	_le planétarium.	_luh plahnaytahry-uhm.
_the public garden.	_le jardin public.	_luh zhahrda(n) pewbleek.
_the royal palace.	**_le palais royal.**	**_luh pahlay rwahyahl.**
_the ruins.	_les ruines.	_lay rween.
_the shopping district.	_le quartier commerçant.	_luh kahrtyay kohmehrsah(n).
_the stadium.	_le stade.	_luh stahd.
_the statue of ____.	_la statue de ____.	_lah stahtew duh ____.
_the stock exchange.	_la bourse.	_lah boors.
_the synagogue.	_la synagogue.	_lah seenahgohg.
_the tower.	_la tour.	_lah toor.
_the town hall.	_l'hôtel de ville.	_lohtehl duh veel.
_the university.	_l'université.	_lewneevehrseetay.
_the zoo.	_le zoo.	_luh zoh.

143

Would you take our picture?	Voudriez-vous nous prendre en photo?	Voodreeyay-voo noo prah(n)dr ah(n) fohtoh?
One more shot!	Encore une!	Ah(n)kohr ewn!
Smile!	Souriez!	Sooryay!

PARIS FOR FREE

Like many other great cities the world over, Paris offers an exciting array of cultural and recreational attractions that are absolutely free of charge. The following list is merely a sampling; consult the newspapers and weekly city guides, or *Time Out* magazine, for additional ideas.

Bastille Day   If you are fortunate enough to be in Paris on July 14, don't miss the big parade on the Champs-Élysées. Later on there is a choice of spectacular fireworks displays at Montmartre, le Parc Montsouris, and le Palais de Chaillot. The evening before the national holiday, dancing takes place in firehouses in neighborhoods all over the city and at the Bastille.

Festival du Cinéma en Plein Air   Free movies (French and American) are shown on a big screen outdoors at the Parc de la Villette Tuesday through Sunday in the summer. There are also free concerts in the park. Check one of the city guides for listings and times.

La Fête de la Musique   Held annually on June 21, this festival celebrates the summer solstice with an explosion of all types of music, performed in the streets, cafés, and public spaces throughout Paris. The Palais-Royal, Bastille, and other areas host music until the sun comes up.

AT THE MUSEUM

When does the museum open (close)?	A quelle heure ouvre (ferme) le musée?	Ah kehl uhr oovr (fehrm) luh mewzay?
How much is it . . .	Quel est le tarif . . .	Kehl eh luh tahreef . . .
_for an adult?	_pour un adulte?	_poor uh(n) nahdewlt?

_for a child?	_pour un enfant?	_poor uh(n) nah(n)-fah(n)?
_for seniors?	_pour les personnes âgées?	_poor lay pehrsohn zahzhay?
Do you have a guidebook in English?	Avez-vous un guide en anglais?	Ahvay-voo uh(n) geed ah(n) nah(n)gleh?
May I take pictures?	Puis-je prendre des photos?	Pweezh prah(n)dr day fohtoh?
Where can I get reproductions?	Où puis-je acheter des reproductions?	Oo pweezh ahshtay day ruhprohdewk-syoh(n)?
I'm interested . . .	Je m'intéresse . . .	Zhuh ma(n)tayrehs . . .
_in antiques.	_aux antiquités.	_oh zah(n)teekeetay.
_in anthropology.	_à l'anthropologie.	_ah lah(n)trohpohl-ohzhee.
_in archaeology.	_à l'archéologie.	_ah lahrkay-ohlohzhee.
_in ____ art.	_à l'art . . .	_ah lahr . . .
classical	classique	klahseek
medieval	médiéval	maydyayvahl
modern	moderne	mohdehrn
Renaissance	de la Renaissance	duh lah Ruhnaysah(n)s
surrealistic	surréaliste	sewrayahleest
_in ceramics.	_à la céramique.	_ah lah sayrahmeek.
_in fine arts.	_aux beaux-arts.	_oh boh-zahr.
_in furniture.	_aux meubles.	_oh muhbl.
_in geography.	_à la géographie.	_ah lah zhayohgrah-fee.
_in geology.	_à la géologie.	_ah lah zhay-ohlohzhee.
_in handicrafts.	_à l'artisanat.	_ah lahrteezahnah.
_in history.	_à l'histoire.	_ah leestwahr.
_in natural history.	_à l'histoire naturelle.	_ah leestwahr nah-tewrehl.
_in pottery.	_à la poterie.	_ah lah pohtree.

145

| _in sculpture. | _à la sculpture. | _ah lah skewltewr. |
| _in zoology. | _à la zoologie. | _ah lah zoh-ohlohzhee. |

Saving Money on Paris Museums

For €12.20 (one day), €24.32 (3 days), or €36.59 (5 days), you may purchase a card (*la carte Sésame*), which provides entry to more than sixty museums and monuments in the Paris area. The card also entitles you to a small discount on items such as books and catalogs sold in museum shops. The card may be purchased at any of the participating museums (the Louvre, the Rodin museum, etc.) and at some Métro stations.

IN THE COUNTRY

| Can you tell me how to get to ____? | Pouvez-vous m'indiquer le chemin pour ____? | Poovay-voo ma(n)-deekay luh shma(n) poor ____? |
| Where are the most beautiful land-scapes? | Où sont les plus beaux paysages? | Oo soh(n) lay plew boh payeezahzh? |

Word List

bridge	le pont	luh poh(n)
cliff	la falaise	lah fahlehz
farm	la ferme	lah fehrm
field	le champ	luh shah(m)
flowers	les fleurs	lay fluhr
foliage	le feuillage	luh fuhyahzh
forest	la forêt	lah fohreh
garden	le jardin	luh zhahrda(n)
gorge	la gorge	lah gohrzh
hill	la colline	lah kohleen
inn	l'auberge	lohbehrzh
lake	le lac	luh lahk
ledge	la corniche	lah kohrneesh

meadow	le pré	luh pray
mountain	la montagne	lah moh(n)tahnyuh
mountain pass	le col	luh kohl
national park	**le parc national**	**luh pahrk nahsyohnahl**
peak	le sommet	luh sohmay
pond	l'étang	laytah(n)
river	**le fleuve,**	**luh fluhv,**
	la rivière	**lah reevyehr**
road	la route	lah root
scenic route	le circuit	luh seerkwee toorees-
	touristique	teek
sea	**la mer**	**lah mehr**
spring	la source	lah soors
stream	le ruisseau	luh rweesoh
swamp	le marais	luh mahreh
valley	la vallée	lah vahlay
village	le village	luh veelahzh
vineyard	**le vignoble**	**luh veenyohbl**
waterfall	la cascade	lah kahskahd

RELIGIOUS SERVICES

Since France is predominantly Roman Catholic, churches and cathedrals abound all over the country. Most of the great cathedrals that are part of the traveler's circuit are also fully functioning churches and can be more fully appreciated by attending one of the regular masses. A schedule of services is posted on the main entrance of each church.

In Paris and other large cities, Protestant churches, mosques, and synagogues can be located easily by looking in the yellow pages under *Eglises* or asking at the local *Syndicat d'initiative* (tourist office). Entry into mosques is usually restricted to Muslims. At the Mosquée de Paris (2, bis pl. du Puits de l'Ermite; tel. 01.45.35.16.23) you can have mint tea and cakes in the courtyard or treat yourself to a *hammam* (Moroccan steam bath).

The old Jewish quarter in the Marais has many synagogues worth visiting.

I'd like to see . . .	Je voudrais voir . . .	Zhuh voodreh vwahr . . .
_a Catholic church	_une église catholique.	_ewn aygleez kahtoh-leek.
_a mosque.	_une mosquée.	_ewn mohskay.
_a Protestant church.	_une église protestante.	_ewn aygleez Proh-tehstah(n)t.
_a synagogue.	_une synagogue.	_ewn seenahgohg.
When does the mass (service) begin?	A quelle heure commence la messe (le culte)?	Ah kehl uhr kohmah(n)s lah mehs (luh kewlt)?
I'm looking for an English-speaking . . .	Je cherche un ____ qui parle anglais.	Zhuh shehrsh uh(n) ____ kee pahrl ah(n)gleh.
_minister.	_pasteur	_pahstuhr
_priest.	_prêtre	_prehtr
_rabbi.	_rabbin	_rahba(n)

Stores generally open between 9 and 10 AM, and close for the day between 6 and 7 PM Monday through Saturday. Many stores, especially food shops, still close for an hour or two at lunchtime, so check the *heures d'ouverture* [uhr doovehrtewr] (business hours) sign on the door if you plan on shopping around midday. Department stores remain open throughout the day.

Sunday hours vary quite a bit, with most stores closed for the day and others open for at least a few hours. Most food stores remain open on Sunday until noon. For clothes- and gift-shopping on a Sunday in Paris, the best places to go are the Marais district and the Carrousel du Louvre, a mall and food court located underground beneath the museum. Some shops close one other day during the week, most frequently on Monday.

The big city-wide sales in Paris take place in mid-January and in July and much of August. Then, windows everywhere proclaim *Soldes* [sohld] (sales) and *Liquidation* [leekeedahsyoh(n)] (clearance sales).

DIALOGUE   At the Men's Clothing Store (Au Magasin de Vêtements pour Hommes)

Cliente:	Bonjour, Monsieur. Je voudrais une chemise pour mon mari.	Boh(n)zhoor, muhsyuh. Zhuh voodreh ewn shuh-meez poor moh(n) mahree.
Vendeur:	Bonjour, Madame. Nous avons un grand choix de chemises . . . Aimez-vous ce style?	Boh(n)zhoor, mahdahm. Noo zahvoh(n) uh(n) grah(n) shwah duh shuh-meez . . . Ehmay-voo suh steel?
Cliente:	Oui, mais je n'aime pas la couleur. L'avez-vous en bleu?	Wee, meh zhuh nehm pah lah kooluhr. Lahvay-voo ah(n) bluh?
Vendeur:	Oui. Connaissez-vous sa taille?	Wee. Kohnehsay-voo sah tahy?

Cliente:	**Oui. Quarante, je crois.**	Wee. Kahrah(n)t, zhuh krwah.
Vendeur:	**Eh bien, voilà.**	Ay byeh(n), vwahlah.
Cliente:	**Parfait! Pourriez-vous l'emballer, s'il vous plaît?**	Pahrfeh! Poor yay-voo lah(m)bahlay, seel voo pleh?

....

Customer:	Hello. I'd like a shirt for my husband.
Salesman:	Hello. We have a large selection of shirts . . . Do you like this style?
Customer:	Yes, but I don't care for the color. Do you have it in blue?
Salesman:	Yes. Do you know his size?
Customer:	Yes. I think it's a 40.*
Salesman:	Here it is.
Customer:	Perfect! Could you wrap it for me, please?

TYPES OF STORES

I'm looking for . . .	Je cherche . . .	Zhuh shehrsh . . .
_an antique shop.	_un antiquaire.	_uh(n) nah(n)teekehr.
_an art gallery.	_une galerie d'art.	_ewn gahlree dahr.
_an automatic cash machine.	_un guichet automatique.	_uh(n) gheeshay ohtohmahteek.
_a bakery.	_une boulangerie.	_ewn boolah(n)zhree.
_a bank.	_une banque.	_ewn bah(n)k.
_a barbershop.	_un coiffeur.	_uh(n) kwahfuhr.
_a beauty parlor.	_un salon de beauté.	_uh(n) sahloh(n) duh bohtay.
_a bookstore.	_une librairie.	_ewn leebrehree.
_a butcher shop.	_une boucherie.	_ewn booshree.
_a camera store.	_un magasin de photos.	_uh(n) mahgahza(n) duh fohtoh.

*See clothing size conversion charts (page 161) for translating American to French sizes.

_a candy store.	_une confiserie.	_ewn koh(n)feezree.
_a cheese and dairy store.	_une crémerie.	_ewn krehmehree.
_a clothing store for men/women/ children.	_un magasin de vêtements pour hommes/ femmes/ enfants.	_uh(n) mahgahza(n) duh vehtmah(n) poor ohm/fahm/ ah(n)fah(n).
_a delicatessen.	_une charcuterie.	_ewn shahrkewtree.
_a dentist.	_un dentiste.	_uh(n) dah(n)teest.
_a department store.	**_un grand magasin.**	**_uh(n) grah(n) mahgahza(n).**
_a discount store.	Examples of inexpensive variety store chains include Monoprix [Mohnohpree], Prisunic [Preezewneek], and Uniprix [Ewneepree].	
_a drugstore.	_une pharmacie.	_ewn fahrmahsee.
_a drycleaner.	_un pressing.	_uh(n) prehsing.
_a fish store.	_une poisson- nerie.	_ewn pwahsohnree.
_a flower shop.	_une fleuriste.	_ewn fluhreest.
_a furniture store.	_un magasin d'ameublement.	_uh(n) mahgahza(n) dahmuhbluhmah(n).
_a grocery.	_une épicerie/un magasin d'alimentation.	_ewn aypeesree/uh(n) mahgahza(n) dah- leemah(n)tahsyah(n).
_a hardware store.	_une quincaillerie.	_ewn ka(n)kahyuhree.
_a health food store.	_un magasin de produits diététiques.	_uh(n) mahgahza(n) teek. duh prohdwee deeyaytayteek.
_a jeweler.	_une bijouterie.	_ewn beezhootree.
_a laundromat.	_une laverie automatique.	_ewn lahvree ohtohmahteek.
_a leather goods store.	_une maro- quinerie.	_ewn mahrohkeenree.
_a library.	_une biblio- thèque.	_ewn beebleeyohtehk.
_a laundry.	_une blanchisserie.	_ewn blah(n)sheesree.

_a liquor store.	_un magasin de vins et spiritueux.	_uh(n) mahgahza(n) duh va(n) ay speereetwuh.
_a market.	_un marché.	_uh(n) mahrshay.
_a newsstand.	_un kiosque à journaux.	_uh(n) kyohsk ah zhoornoh.
_an optician.	_un opticien.	_uh(n) nohpteesya(n).
_a pastry shop.	_une pâtisserie.	_ewn pahteesree.
_a photographer.	_un photographe.	_uh(n) fohtohgrahf.
_a police station.	_un poste de police.	_uh(n) pohst duh poh-lees.
_a post office.	_un bureau de poste.	_uh(n) bewroh duh pohst.
_a produce shop.	_un magasin de primeurs.	_uh(n) mahgahza(n) duh preemuhr.
_a record store.	_un magasin de disques.	_uh(n) mahgahza(n) duh deesk.
_a shoemaker.	_un cordonnier.	_uh(n) kohrdohnyay.
_a shoe store.	_un magasin de chaussures.	_uh(n) mahgahza(n) duh shohsewr.
_a shopping center.	_un centre commercial.	_uh(n) sah(n)tr kohmehrsyahl.
_a souvenir shop.	_un magasin de souvenirs.	_uh(n) mahgahza(n) duh soovneer.
_a sporting goods store.	_un magasin d'articles de sport.	_uh(n) mahgahza(n) dahrteekl duh spohr.
_a stationer.	_une papeterie.	_ewn pahpehtree.
_a supermarket.	_un supermarché.	_uh(n) sewpehr-mahrshay.
_a tailor.	_un tailleur.	_uh(n) tahyuhr.
_a tobacconist.	_un bureau de tabac.	_uh(n) bewroh duh tahbah.
_a toy shop.	_un magasin de jouets.	_uh(n) mahgahza(n) duh zhooay.

_a travel agency.	_une agence de voyage.	_ewn ahzhah(n)s duh vwahyahzh.
_a veterinarian.	_un vétérinaire.	_uh(n) vaytayreenehr.
_a watchmaker-jeweler.	_une horlogerie-bijouterie.	_ewn ohrlohzhree-beezhootree.

SOUVENIR AND GIFT SHOPPING

France is a shopper's paradise, especially for luxury items such as perfume, lace, handbags, designer clothes, crystal, pottery, kitchen utensils, art prints, and tablecloths. Every region of the country also specializes in fine crafts that often can be purchased directly from the producer. Look for signs indicating a nearby *atelier d'artisanat* (artisan workshop).

For those who prefer or need to do most of their shopping in one location, the best bet would be the *grands magasins* (malls) in Paris. Two of the foremost are *Les Galeries Lafayette* and *Le Printemps,* side by side behind the Opéra. They stock just about anything you might want to buy in Paris. Note that American visitors are entitled to a refund of the TVA, or *taxe sur la valeur ajoutée* (value-added tax), on purchases of €183 or more at any single store. The discount is 12%. You must have your passport with you in the store for the forms to be filled out. Present the completed forms at the airport customs counter prior to checking your luggage. You may have to show your merchandise to the officers. Forms will be stamped, processed, and mailed to the store. A refund will be sent to you a few weeks later or credited to your charge card account.

Belgium is known for its linen, diamond markets, lace products, glassware, and crystal. Be sure not to overlook the many gourmet food items, especially Belgian chocolate, condiments, and candy.

Switzerland is known for high-quality watches and clocks, as well as fondue sets, ceramics, embroidery, wood products, chocolate, and cheeses.

In Canada, you'll find crafts and distinctive foods, like authentic maple syrup.

GENERAL SHOPPING EXPRESSIONS

Where can I find ____?	Où puis-je trouver ____?	Oo pweezh troovay ____?
When do you close?	A quelle heure fermez-vous?	Ah kehl uhr fehrmay-voo?
Can you help me?	**Pouvez-vous m'aider?**	**Poovay-voo mehday?**
I'm just browsing.	Je regarde.	Zhuh ruh-gahrd.
Can you show me . . .	Pouvez-vous me montrer . . .	Poovay-voo muh moh(n)tray . . .
_this?	_ceci?	_suhsee?
_that?	_cela?	_suhlah?
_the one in the window?	_celui de la vitrine?	_suhlwee duh lah vee-treen?
_something less expensive?	_quelque chose de moins cher?	_kehlkuh shohz duh mwa(n) shehr?
_something better?	_quelque chose de mieux?	_kehlkuh shohz duh myew?
_something darker?	_quelque chose de plus foncé?	_kehlkuh shohz duh plew foh(n)say?
_something lighter? (color)	_quelque chose de plus clair?	_kehlkuh shohz duh plew klehr?
_something lighter? (weight)	_quelque chose de plus léger?	_kehlkuh shohz duh plew layzhay?
_something bigger/ smaller?	_quelque chose de plus grand/ petit?	_kehlkuh shohz duh plew grah(n)/puh-tee?
_a different color?	**_une autre couleur?**	**_ewn ohtr kooluhr?**
_a different style?	_un autre style?	_uh(n) nohtr steel?
I'd like a gift for . . .	Je voudrais un cadeau pour . . .	Zhuh voodreh uh(n) kahdoh poor . . .
_an adult.	_un adulte.	_uh(n) nahduhlt.
_a child.	_un enfant.	_uh(n) nah(n)fah(n).
_a girl of seventeen.	_une jeune fille de dix-sept ans.	_ewn zhuhn feey duh dee-seht ah(n).

_a boy of fifteen.	_un garçon de quinze ans.	_uh(n) gahrsoh(n) duh ka(n)z ah(n).
I prefer something . . .	Je préfère quelque chose . . .	Zhuh prayfehr kehlkuh shohz . . .
_locally made.	_de fabrication locale.	_duh fahbreekah-syoh(n) lohkahl.
_handmade.	_fait main.	_feh ma(n).
_more practical.	_de plus pratique.	_duh plew prahteek.
_more typical.	_de plus typique de la région.	_duh plew teepeek duh lah rehzhyo(n).
Show me your selection . . .	Montrez-moi votre choix . . .	Moh(n)tray-mwah vohtr shwah . . .
_of antiques.	_d'antiquités.	_dah(n)teekeetay.
_of cut crystal.	_de cristal taillé.	_duh kreestahl tahyay.
_of jewelry.	_de bijoux.	_duh beezhoo.
_of lace.	_de dentelle.	_duh dah(n)tehl.
_of leather goods.	_d'objets en cuir.	_dohbzhay ah(n) kweer.
_of perfume.	_de parfums.	_duh pahrfuh(m).
How much is this . . .	Combien coûte ceci . . .	Koh(m)byeh(n) koot suhsee . . .
_in dollars?	_en dollars?	_ah(n) dohlahr?
_in euros?	_en euros?	_ah(n) uhroh?
Can you write down the price (for me)?	Pouvez-vous m'écrire le prix?	Poovay voo maykreer luh pree?
I don't want to spend more than ____ dollars/euros.	Je ne veux pas dépenser plus de ____ dollars/euros.	Zhuh nuh vuh pah daypah(n)say plew duh ____ dohlahr/uhroh.
I'll take it.	Je le prends.	Zhuh luh prah(n).
I'll take two.	J'en prends deux.	Zhah(n) prah(n) duh.
Can I pay . . .	Puis-je payer . . .	Pweezh payay . . .
_in dollars?	_en dollars?	_ah(n) dohlahr?
_with traveler's checks?	_avec des chèques de voyage?	_ahvehk day shehk duh vwahyahzh?

155

_with a credit card?	_avec une carte de crédit?	_ahvehk ewn kahrt duh kraydee?
Can you . . .	**Pouvez-vous . . .**	**Poovay-voo . . .**
_order it?	_le commander?	_luh kohmah(n)day?
_send it to me?	**_me l'envoyer?**	**_muh lah(n)vwahyay?**
_deliver it to this address?	_le livrer à cette adresse?	_luh leevray ah seht ahdrehs?
What is the value-added tax?	Quelle est la TVA?	Kehl eh lah tay vay ah?
I'd like my money back.	Je voudrais me faire rembourser.	Zhuh voodreh muh fehr rah(m)boorsay.
Here's my receipt.	Voici le reçu.	Vwahsee luh ruhsew.
May I exchange this?	Puis-je échanger ceci?	Pweezh ayshah(n)zhay suhsee?
May I have a bag?	**Puis-je avoir un sac, s'il vous plaît.**	**Pweezh ah-vwahr uh(n) sahk, seel voo pleh.**
That will be all.	Ce sera tout.	Suh suhrah too.
It's a gift; can you wrap it?	C'est pour offrir; pouvez-vous l'emballer?	Seh poor ohfreer; poovay-voo lah(m)-bahlay?

CLOTHING

I'd like to buy . . .	Je voudrais acheter . . .	Zhuh voodreh zahsh-tay . . .
_a bathrobe.	_un peignoir de bain.	_uh(n) pehnwahr duh ba(n).
_a bathing cap.	_un bonnet de bain.	_uh(n) bohnay de ba(n).
_a bathing suit.	**_un maillot de bain.**	**_uh(n) mahyoh duh ba(n).**
_a belt.	_une ceinture.	_ewn sa(n)tewr.
_a blouse.	**_un chemisier.**	**_uh(n) shuhmeezyay.**
_a bra.	_un soutien-gorge.	_uh(n) sootya(n)-gohrzh.
_a cap.	_une casquette.	_ewn kahskeht.

_a coat.	_un manteau.	_uh(n) mah(n)toh.
_a dress.	_une robe.	_ewn rohb.
_a dressing gown.	_un peignoir.	_uh(n) pehnwahr.
_an evening dress.	_une robe de soir.	_ewn rohb duh swahr.
_gloves.	_des gants.	_day gah(n).
_a handbag/ pocketbook.	_un sac à main.	_uh(n) sahk ah ma(n).
_a handkerchief.	_un mouchoir.	_uh(n) mooshwahr.
_a hat.	_un chapeau.	_uh(n) shahpoh.
_a jacket.	_une veste.	_ewn vehst.
_jeans.	**_un jean.**	**_uh(n) dzheen.**
_an overcoat.	_un pardessus.	_uh(n) pahrduhsew.
_overalls.	_une salopette.	_ewn sahlohpeht.
_panties.	_des culottes.	_day kooloht.
_pants.	**_un pantalon.**	**_uh(n) pahntahloh(n).**
_pantyhose.	_un collant.	_uh(n) kohlah(n).
_pajamas.	_un pyjama.	_uh(n) peezhahmah.
_a raincoat.	_un imper- méable.	_uh(n) na(n)pehrmayahbl.
_a scarf.	_un foulard.	_uh(n) foolahr.
_a long-sleeved shirt.	_une chemise à manches longues.	_ewn shuhmeez ah mah(n)sh loh(n)g.
_a short-sleeved shirt.	_une chemisette.	_ewn shuhmeezeht.
_a sleeveless shirt.	_une chemise sans manches.	_ewn shuhmeez sah(n) mah(n)sh.
_shoes (a pair).	_une paire de chaussures.	_ewn pehr duh shohsewr.
_shorts.	_un short.	_uh(n) shohrt.
_a skirt.	_une jupe.	_ewn zhewp.
_a slip.	_un jupon.	_uh(n) zhewpoh(n).
_socks.	_des chaussettes.	_day shohseht.
_a sports jacket.	_une veste de sport.	_ewn vehst duh spohr.

_stockings.	_des bas.	_day bah.
_a suit (man's).	_un costume.	_uh(n) kohstewm.
_a suit (woman's).	_un tailleur.	_uh(n) tahyuhr.
_suspenders.	_des bretelles.	_day bruhtehl.
_a sweater.	_un pullover.	_uh(n) pewlohvehr.
_a tie.	**_une cravate.**	**_ewn krahvaht.**
_tights.	_un collant.	_uh(n) kohlah(n).
_a turtleneck sweater.	_un pullover à col roulé.	_uh(n) pewlohvehr ah kohl roolay.
_a V-neck sweater.	_un pullover à col en V.	_uh(n) pewlohveh ah kohl ah(n) vay.
_an umbrella.	_un parapluie.	_uh(n) pahrahplwee.
_an undershirt.	_un maillot de corps.	_uh(n) mahyoh duh kohr.
_underwear.	_des sous-vêtements.	_day soo-vehtmah(n).
_a vest.	_un gilet.	_uh(n) zheelay.
Can I try it on?	Puis-je l'essayer?	Pweezh lehsayay?
Do you do alterations?	Faites-vous des retouches?	Feht-voo day ruhtoosh?
Do you have a skirt that's . . .	Avez-vous une jupe . . .	Ahvay voo ewn zhewp . . .
_longer?	_plus longue?	_plew loh(n)gh?
_shorter?	_plus courte?	_plew koort?
_bigger?	_plus grande?	_plew grah(n)d?
_smaller?	_plus petite?	_plew puhteet?
I wear size 42.	Je fais du quarante-deux.	Zhuh fay dew kahrah(n)t-duh.

Colors and Patterns

I think you would look nice in . . .	Je vous voir très bien en . . .	Zhuh voo vwah(r) tray byeh(n) ah(n) . . .
_beige.	_beige.	_behzh.
_black.	_noir.	_nwahr.
_blue.	_bleu.	_bluh.

_brown.	_marron.	_mahroh(n).
_gray.	_gris.	_gree.
_green.	**_vert.**	**_vehr.**
_orange.	_orange.	_ohrah(n)zh.
_pink.	_rose.	_rohz.
_purple.	_violet.	_vyohlay.
_red.	**_rouge.**	**_roozh.**
_white.	**_blanc.**	**_blah(n).**
_yellow.	**_jaune.**	**_zhohn.**
I prefer something . . .	Je préfère quelque chose . . .	Zhuh prayfehr kehlkuh shohz . . .
_lighter.	_de plus clair.	_duh plew klehr.
_darker.	_de plus foncé.	_duh plew foh(n)say.
_in a solid color.	_d'uni.	_dewnee.
_with stripes.	_à rayures.	_ah rayewr.
_with polka dots.	_à pois.	_ah pwah.
_in plaid.	_d'écossais.	_daykohseh.
_checked.	_à carreaux.	_ah kahroh.

Materials

I don't like this material. Do you have anything in . . .	Je n'aime pas ce tissu. Avez-vous quelque chose en . . .	Zhuh nehm pah suh teesew. Ahvay voo kehlkuh shohz ah(n) . . .
_corduroy?	_velours côtelé?	_vuhloor kohtlay?
_cotton?	_coton?	_kohtoh(n)?
_denim?	_toile?	_twahl?
_flannel?	_flanelle?	_flahnehl?
_lace?	_dentelle?	_dah(n)tehl?
_leather?	_cuir?	_kweer?
_linen?	_lin?	_la(n)?
_nylon?	_nylon?	_neeloh(n)?
_poplin?	_popeline?	_pohpleen?
_satin?	_satin?	_sahta(n)?

159

_silk?	_soie?	_swah?
_suede?	_daim?	_da(m)?
_velvet?	_velours?	_vuhloor?
_wool?	_laine?	_lehn?

Shoes

I'd like a pair of . . .	Je voudrais une paire de . . .	Zhuh voodreh ewn pehr duh . . .
_boots.	_bottes.	_boht.
_flats.	_chaussures à talons plats.	_shohsewr ah tahloh(n) plah.
_high heels.	_chaussures à talons hauts.	_shohsewr ah tahlon(n) oh.
_sandals.	_sandales.	_sah(n)dahl.
_shoes.	_chaussures.	_shohsewr.
_slippers.	_pantoufles.	_pah(n)toofl.
_sneakers.	_tennis.	_tehnees.
They fit me well.	Elles me vont bien.	Ehl muh voh(n) byeh(n).
They don't fit.	Elles ne me vont pas.	Ehl nuh muh voh(n) pah.
They're too . . .	Elles sont trop . . .	Ehl soh(n) troh . . .
_big.	_grandes.	_grah(n)d.
_small.	_petites.	_puhteet.
_wide.	_larges.	_lahrzh.
_narrow.	_étroites.	_aytrwaht.
I don't know my size.	Je ne connais pas ma pointure.	Zhuh nuh kuhneh pah mah pwa(n)tewr.
I wear size ____.	Je chausse du ____.	Zhuh shohs dew ____.
I'd like the same in brown.	Je voudrais les mêmes en marron.	Zhuh voodreh lay mehm ah(n) mahroh(n).

WOMEN'S CLOTHING SIZES

Coats, Dresses, Suits, Skirts, Slacks

U.S.	4	6	8	10	12	14	16
France	36	38	40	42	44	46	48

Blouses/Sweaters

U.S.	32/6	34/8	36/10	38/12	40/14	42/16
France	38/2	40/3	42/4	44/5	46/6	48/7

Shoes

U.S.	4	4½	5	5½	6	6½	7	7½	8	8½	9	9½	10
Europe	35	35	36	36	37	37	38	38	39	39	40	40	41

MEN'S CLOTHING SIZES

Suits/Coats

U.S.	34	36	38	40	42	44	46	48
France	44	46	48	50	52	54	56	58

Sweaters

U.S.	XS/36	S/38	M/40	L/42	XL/44
France	42/2	44/3	46–48/4	50/5	52–54/6

Shirts

U.S.	14	14½	15	15½	16	16½	17	17½	18
France	36	37	38	39	40	41	42	43	44

Slacks

U.S.	30	31	32	33	34	35	36	37	38	39
France	38	39–40	41	42	43	44–45	46	47	48–49	50

Socks

U.S.	9½	10	10½	11	11½	12	13
France	36–37	38–39	40–41	42–43	44–45	46–47	48–49

Shoes

U.S.	7	7½	8	8½	9	9½	10	10½	11
Europe	39	40	41	42	43	43	44	44	45

THE JEWELRY STORE (LA BIJOUTERIE)

Would you show me your . . .	Pourriez-vous me montrer vos . . .	Poo(r)eeay voo muh moh(n)tray-mwah voh
_alarm clocks?	_réveils?	_rayvehy?
_bracelets?	_bracelets?	_brahslay?
_brooches?	_broches?	_brohsh?
_chains?	_chaînes?	_shehn?
_cufflinks?	_boutons de manchettes?	_bootoh(n) duh mah(n)sheht?
_earrings?	**_boucles d'oreilles?**	**_bookl dohrehy?**
_gems?	_pierres précieuses?	_pyehr praysyuhz?
_jewelry boxes?	_coffres à bijoux?	_kohfray ah beezhoo?
_necklaces?	**_colliers?**	**_kohlyay?**
_pins?	_épingles?	_aypa(n)gl?
_rings?	_bagues?	_bahg?
_engagement rings?	_bagues de fiançailles?	_bahg duh fyah(n)sahy?
_wedding rings?	_alliances?	_ahlyah(n)s?
_watches?	_montres?	_moh(n)tr?
digital	digitales	deezheetahl
quartz	à quartz	a kwahrts
Do you have something . . .	Avez-vous quelque chose . . .	Ahvay-voo kehlkuh shohz . . .
_gold?	_en or?	_ah(n) nohr?
solid gold	en or massif	ah(n) nohr mahseef
gold-plated	en plaqué or	ah(n) plahkay ohr
_platinum?	_en platine?	_ah(n) plahteen?
_silver?	_en argent?	_ah(n) nahrzhah(n)?
Can you repair this?	Pouvez-vous réparer ceci?	Poovay-voo raypahray suhsee?
This is how many carats?	Combien y-a-t-il de carats?	Koh(m)bya(n) yahteel duh kahrah?
What is this made of?	**En quoi est-ce fait?**	**Ah(n) kwah ehs feh?**

It's . . .	C'est . . .	Seht . . .
_an amethyst.	_une améthyste.	_ewn ahmayteest.
_copper.	_en cuivre.	_ah(n) kweevr.
_coral.	_en corail.	_ah(n) kohrahy.
_crystal.	_en cristal.	_ah(n) kreestahl.
_a diamond.	_un diamant.	_uh(n) dyahmah(n).
_an emerald.	_une émeraude.	_ewn aymrohd.
_ivory.	_en ivoire.	_ah(n) neevwahr.
_jade.	_en jade.	_ah(n) zhahd.
_onyx.	_en onyx.	_ah(n) nohneeks.
_a pearl.	_une perle.	_ewn pehrl.
_a ruby.	_un rubis.	_uh(n) rewbee.
_a sapphire.	_un saphir.	_uh(n) sahfeer.
_a topaz.	_une topaze.	_ewn tohpahz.

MUSIC (LA MUSIQUE)

Do you have any ____	Avez-vous des ____	Ahvay-voo day ____
_CDs of Debussy?	_CDs de Debussy?	_sehdeh duh Duhbewsee?
_cassettes?	_cassettes?	_kahseht?
_compact discs?	_disques compacts?	_deesk koh(m)pahkt?
Is there a section for . . .	Y a-t-il un rayon où l'on trouve . . .	Yahteel uh(n) rahyoh(n) oo loh(n) troov . . .
_International music?	_des variétés internationales?	_day vahreeaytay zah(n)tehrnahsyohnahl?
_classical music?	_de la musique classique?	_duh lah mewzeek klahseek?
_folk music?	_de la musique folklorique?	_duh lah mewzeek fohklohreek?
_jazz?	_du jazz?	_dew "jazz"?
_musical comedy?	_des comédies musicales?	_day kohmaydee mewzeekahl?

163

_music of the region?	_de la musique de la région?	_duh lah mewzeek duh lah rayzhyoh(n)?
_opera?	_de l'opéra?	_duh lohpayrah?
_pop music?	_de la musique pop?	_duh lah mewzeek pohp?

THE PHOTO SHOP
(LE MAGASIN DE PHOTOS)

Do you sell . . .	Vendez-vous . . .	Vah(n)day-voo . . .
_cameras?	_des appareils photos?	_day zahpahrehy fohtoh?
_automatic cameras?	_des appareils automatiques?	_day zahpahray ohtohmahteek?
_movie cameras?	_des caméras?	_day kahmayrah?
_video cameras?	_des caméscopes?	_day kahmayskohp?
_filters?	_des filtres?	_day feeltr?
_batteries?	_des piles?	_day peel?
_light meters?	_des cellules photoélectriques?	_day sehlewl fohtoh-aylehktreek?
_lens caps?	_des capuchons d'objectif?	_day kahpewshoh(n) dohbzhehkteef?
_lenses?	_des objectifs?	_day zohbzhehkteef?
_telephoto lenses?	_des télé-objectifs?	_day taylay-ohbzhehkteef?
_wide-angle lenses?	_des grand angulaires?	_day grah(n)-tah(n)gewlehr?
_film?	_une pellicule?	_ewn pehleekewl?
I'd like a roll of . . .	Je voudrais une pellicule . . .	Zhuh voodreh ewn pehleekewl . . .
_color film.	_couleur.	_kooluhr.
_black-and-white film.	_noir et blanc.	_nwahr ay blah(n).
_film for a 35mm camera.	_pour un appareil 35mm.	_poor uh(n) nahpahray trah(n)t sa(n) meeleemehtr.
_24 exposures.	_de 24 poses.	_duh va(n)-kahtr pohz.

_36 exposures.	_de 36 poses.	_duh trah(n)t-see pohz.
_slide film.	_pour diapositives.	_poor deeahpohzeeteev.
_print film.	_pour épreuves.	_poor aypruhv.
_film this size.	_de ce format.	_duh suh fohrmah.
_film this ASA number.	_de ce chiffre ASA.	_duh suh sheefr ah ehs ah.
_film for artificial light.	_pour lumière artificielle.	_poor lewmyehr ahrteefeesyehl.
_film for natural light.	_pour lumière naturelle.	_poor lewmyehr nahtewrehl.
How much is it to develop a roll of film of this type?	Combien coûte le développement d'une pellicule de ce genre?	Koh(m)byeh(n) koot luh dayvehlohpmah(n) dewn pehleekewl duh suh zhah(n)r?
I'd like . . .	Je voudrais . . .	Zhuh voodreh . . .
_two prints of each one.	_deux épreuves de chacune.	_duh zaypruhv duh shahkewn.
_an enlargement.	_un agrandissement.	_uh(n) nagrah(n)deesmah(n).
_prints with a glossy finish.	_des épreuves en brillant.	_day zaypruhv ah(n) breeyah(n).
_prints with a matte finish.	_des épreuves en mat.	_day zaypruhv ah(n) maht.
When will they be ready?	Quand seront-elles prêtes?	Kah(n) suhroh(n)-tehl preht?
I'm having a problem with . . .	J'ai un petit problème avec . . .	Zheh uh(n) ptee prohblehm ahvehk . . .
_the flash.	_le flash.	_luh flahsh.
_the focus.	_la mise au point.	_lah meez oh pwa(n).
_the shutter.	_l'obturateur.	_lohbtewrahtuhr.
_the winding mechanism.	_le levier d'avancement.	_luh luhvyay dahvah(n)smah(n).
Do you do camera repairs?	Réparez-vous les appareils photos?	Raypahray-voo lay zahpahrehy fohtoh?

165

ELECTRICAL APPLIANCES

Make sure you check the voltage when buying or bringing in electrical appliances, since 220 volts AC is the rule all over Europe. You will thus need a transformer to use American equipment, as well as auxiliary adapter plugs.

What is the voltage?	Quel est le voltage?	Kehl eh luh vohltahzh?
I need batteries for this.	Il me faut des piles pour ceci.	Eel muh foh day peel poor suhsee.
It's broken; can you fix it?	C'est cassé; pouvez-vous le réparer?	Seh kahsay; poovay-voo luh raypahray?
I'd like . . .	Je voudrais . . .	Zhuh voodreh . . .
_a bulb.	_une ampoule.	_ewn ah(m)pool.
_a clock radio.	_un radio-réveil.	_uh(n) rahdyoh-rayvehy.
_a computer.	_un ordinateur.	_uh(n) ordeenahtuhr.
_a hair dryer.	_un sèche-cheveux.	_uh(n) sehsh-shuhvuh.
_a travel iron.	_un fer à repasser de voyage.	_uh(n) fehr ah ruhpahsay duh vwahyahzh.
_a lamp.	_une lampe.	_ewn lah(m)p.
_a plug.	_une prise.	_ewn preez.
_a radio (portable).	_un poste de radio (portatif).	_uh(n) pohst duh rah-dyoh (pohrtahteef).
_a CD player.	_un lecteur CD.	_uh(n) lehktewr sehdeh
_a shaver.	_un rasoir électrique.	_uh(n) rahzwahr aylehktreek.
_a tape recorder.	_un magnéto-phone.	_uh(n) mahnyay-tohfohn.
_a stereo.	_une chaîne.	_ewn shehn
_a black-and-white TV.	_un téléviseur noir et blanc.	_uh(n) taylayveezuhr nwahr ay blah(n).
_a color TV.	_un téléviseur couleur.	_uh(n) taylayveezuhr kooluhr.

_a transformer.	_un transformateur.	_uh(n) trah(n)sfohr-mahtuhr.
_a VCR.	_un magnétoscope.	_uh(n) manyay-tohskohp.
_a DVD player.	_un lecteur DVD.	_uh(n) lehkteur dehvehdeh.

BOOKS, MAGAZINES, AND PAPER GOODS

In France, bookstores (*les librairies* [lay leebrayree]) sell all kinds of books and writing supplies. Most bookstores have a small English-language section. Additional writing supplies are found at the stationery store (*la papeterie* [lah pahpehtree]). Your best bet for newspapers and magazines are the outdoor *kiosques* [keeohsk] or the numerous *bureaux de tabac* [bewroh duh tahbah]. For your convenience, we have included items from all of these categories in the section below.

When in Paris, you may enjoy a visit to Shakespeare & Co. (rue de la Bûcherie), an American bookstore run by an expatriate on the Paris scene since 1946. The store's name was appropriated from the famous bookshop owned and operated by Sylvia Beach, a friend of Hemingway and a patron of James Joyce, sixty-plus years ago. Other sources of English books are W.H. Smith (rue de Rivoli) and Brentano's (avenue de l'Opéra).

I'm looking for . . .	Je cherche . . .	Zhuh shehrsh . . .
_a bookstore.	_une librairie.	_ewn leebrehree.
_a stationer.	_une papeterie.	_ewn pahpehtree.
_a newsstand.	_un kiosque à journaux.	_uh(n) kyohsk ah zhoornoh.
Where are . . .	Où sont . . .	Oo soh(n) . . .
_books in English?	_les livres en anglais?	_lay leevr ah(n) nah(n)gleh?
_magazines in English?	_les magazines en anglais?	_lay mahgahzeen ah(n) nah(n)gleh?
_newspapers in English?	_les journaux en anglais?	_lay zhoornoh ah(n) nah(n)gleh?
Here is . . .	Voici . . .	Vwahsee . . .
_the title.	_le titre.	_luh teetr.

_the author.	_l'auteur.	_lohtuhr.
Do you have it in paperback?	L'avez-vous en livre de poche?	Lahvay-voo ah(n) leevr duh pohsh?
I'd like . . .	Je voudrais . . .	Zhuh voodreh . . .
_a ballpoint pen.	_un stylo à bille. or un bic	_uh(n) steeloh ah beey. uh(n) beek
_a book on ____.	_un livre sur ____.	_uh(n) leevr sewr ____.
_a calendar.	_un calendrier.	_uh(n) kahlah(n)-dreeay.
_crayons.	_des crayons de couleur.	_day krayoh(n) duh kooluhr.
_an English-French dictionary.	_un dictionnaire anglais-français.	_uh(n) deeksyohnehr ah(n)gleh-frah(n)seh.
_envelopes.	_des enveloppes.	_day zah(n)vuhlohp.
_an eraser.	_une gomme.	_ewn gohm.
_glue.	_de la colle.	_duh lah kohl.
_a travel guide.	_un guide de voyage.	_uh(n) gheed duh vwahyahzh.
_ink.	_de l'encre.	_duh lah(n)kr.
_labels.	_des étiquettes.	_day zayteekeht.
_a map.	_une carte.	_ewn kahrt.
city map	un plan de la ville	uh(n) plah(n) duh lah veel
road map	une carte routière	ewn kahrt rootyehr
_a felt-tip pen.	_un crayon feutre.	_uh(n) krayoh(n) fuhtr.
_a marker.	_un marqueur.	_uh(n) mahrkuhr.
_a notebook.	_un cahier.	_uh(n) kahyay.
_paper.	_du papier.	_dew pahpyay.
_paperclips.	_des trombones.	_day troh(m)bohn.
_a pen.	_un stylo.	_uh(n) steeloh.
_a pencil.	_un crayon.	_uh(n) krayoh(n).
_a pencil sharpener.	_un taille-crayon.	_uh(n) tahy-krayoh(n).
_a calculator.	_une calculatrice.	_ewn kahlkewlahtrees.
_a ruler.	_une règle.	_ewn rehgl.
_scotch tape.	_du scotch.	_dew skohtsh.

168

_a stapler.	_une agrafeuse.	_ewn ahgrahfuhz.
_staples.	_des agrafes.	_day zahgrahf.
_stationery.	_du papier à lettres.	_dew pahpyay ah lehtr.
_thumbtacks.	_des punaises.	_day pewnehz.
_printer paper.	_du papier pour imprimante.	_dew pahpyay poor eh(m)preemah(n)t.
_a writing pad.	_un bloc.	_uh(n) blohk.

THE TOBACCO SHOP (LE BUREAU DE TABAC)

In France, the sale of tobacco products is strictly controlled by—and is a monopoly of—the state, though there is no minimum age to buy. The red cone in cafés and bars indicates a state-approved tobacco outlet. (Incidentally, the final *c* in tabac is not pronounced, an exception to the *careful* rule on page 6.)

Give me a pack of cigarettes, please.	Donnez-moi un paquet de cigarettes, s'il vous plaît.	Dohnay mwah uh(n) pahkay duh seegahreht, seel voo play.
Do you have . . .	Avez-vous . . .	Ahvay-voo . . .
_American cigarettes?	_des cigarettes américaines?	_day seegahreht ah-mayreekehn?
_chewing gum?	_du chewing-gum?	_dew shooing-guhm?
_chocolate?	_du chocolat?	_dew shohkohlah?
_cigarette cases?	_des étuis à cigarettes?	_day zaytwee ah seegahreht?
_filtered cigarettes?	_des cigarettes avec filtre?	_day seegahreht ahvehk feeltr?
_French cigarettes?	_des cigarettes françaises?	_day seegahreht frah(n)sehz?
_king-size cigarettes?	_des cigarettes longues?	_day seegahreht loh(n)g?
_lighters?	_des briquets?	_day breekay?
_lighter fluid?	_de l'essence à briquet?	_duh lehsah(n)s ah breekay?
_matches?	_des allumettes?	_day zahlewmeht?

169

_mild cigarettes?	_des cigarettes douces?	_day seegahreht doos?
_pipe tobacco?	_du tabac à pipe?	_dew tahbah ah peep?
_strong cigarettes?	_des cigarettes fortes?	_day seegahreht fohrt?
_unfiltered cigarettes?	_des cigarettes sans filtre?	_day seegahreht sah(n) feeltr?

TOILETRIES

Perfume and cosmetics are available at many major department stores. You can also find them at a *parfumerie* [pahrfewmree]. Other toiletries may be found at a *pharmacie* [fahr mah see] or *supermarché* [soopehrmahrsheh], where prices are usually lower.

Do you have . . .	Avez-vous . . .	Ahvay-voo . . .
_aftershave lotion?	_de la lotion après-rasage?	_duh lah lohsyoh(n) ahpreh-rahzahzh?
_bobby pins?	_des épingles à cheveux?	_day zaypa(n)gl ah shuhvuh?
_a brush?	**_une brosse?**	**_ewn brohs?**
_bubble bath?	_du bain moussant?	_dew ba(n) moosah(n)?
_cleansing cream?	_une crème démaquillante?	_ewn krehm day-mahkeeyah(n)t?
_a comb?	**_un peigne?**	**_uh(n) pehnyuh?**
_some contraceptives?	_des contraceptifs?	_day koh(n)trahsehp-teef?
_curlers?	_des bigoudis?	_day beegoodee?
_a deodorant?	**_un déodorant?**	**_uh(n) day-ohdohrah(n)?**
_emery boards?	_des limes à ongles?	_day leem ah oh(n)gl?
_eyeliner?	_un eye liner?	_uh(n) nahy lahynehr?
_an eyebrow pencil?	_un crayon pour les yeux?	_uh(n) krayoh(n) poor lay zyuh?
_eye shadow?	_du fard à paupières?	_dew fahr ah poh-pyehr?

_face powder?	_de la poudre?	_duh lah poodr?
_hairspray?	_de la laque?	_duh lah lahk?
_hand cream?	_de la crème pour les mains?	_duh lah krehm poor lay ma(n)?
_lipstick?	_du rouge à lèvres?	_dew roozh ah lehvr?
_makeup?	_du maquillage?	_dew mahkeeyahzh?
_mascara?	_du mascara?	_dew mahskahrah?
_a mirror?	_un miroir?	_uh(n) meerwahr?
_moisturizing cream?	**_de la crème hydratante?**	**_duh lah krehm ee-drahtah(n)t?**
_nail clippers?	_un coupe-ongles?	_uh(n) koop-oh(n)gl?
_nail polish?	_du vernis à ongles?	_dew vehrnee ah oh(n)gl?
_nail polish remover?	_du dissolvant?	_dew deesohlvah(n)?
_perfume?	_du parfum?	_dew pahrfuh(m)?
_a razor?	**_un rasoir?**	**_uh(n) razwahr?**
_razor blades?	**_des lames de rasoir?**	**_day lahm duh rahzwahr?**
_rouge?	_du fard?	_dew fahr?
_safety pins?	_des épingles de nourrice?	_day zaypa(n)gl duh noorees?
_sanitary napkins?	_des serviettes hygiéniques?	_day sehrvyeht eezhyayneek?
_scissors?	_des ciseaux?	_day seezoh?
_setting lotion?	_du fixatif?	_dew feeksahteef?
_shaving cream?	_de la crème à raser?	_duh lah krehm ah rahzay?
_soap?	_du savon?	_dew sahvoh(n)?
_suntan lotion?	_de la crème solaire?	_duh lah krehm sohlehr?
_suntan oil?	_de l'huile solaire?	_duh lweel sohlehr?
_talcum powder?	_du talc?	_dew tahlk?
_tampons?	**_des tampons?**	**_day tah(m)poh(n)?**

171

_tissues?	_des mouchoirs en papier?	_day mooshwahr ah(n) pahpyay?
_toilet paper?	_du papier hygiénique?	_dew pahpyay eezhyayneek?
_toilet water?	_de l'eau de toilette?	_duh loh duh twahleht?
_a toothbrush?	_une brosse à dents?	_ewn brohs ah dah(n)?
_toothpaste?	_du dentifrice?	_dew dah(n)-teefrees?
_towels?	_des serviettes?	_day sehrvyeht?
_tweezers?	_des pinces à épiler?	_day pa(n)s ah aypeelay?

FOOD SHOPPING

The most famous food store of all is Fauchon (26 pl. de la Madeleine). E. Dehillerin (18–20 rue Coquillière), on the edge of Les Halles, is the world's number-one source for professional kitchenware, a veritable museum of utensils. Everything you always wanted for cooking and didn't know where to find is crammed into this traditional corner store.

Though supermarkets and *hypermarchés* [eepehrmahrshay] are increasingly popular, the French love to spend time selecting beautiful ingredients at their local markets. Paris has three kinds of markets: roving markets, which pop up around 8 AM and disappear at 1 PM; permanent covered markets; and street markets. Street and covered markets are open from 8 to 1 and 4 to 7 Tuesday through Saturday, and 8 to 1 Sunday. One of the best street markets is on rue Mouffetard in the 5th arrondissement; the enormous open-air Bastille market takes place Thursday and Sunday.

Measures and Containers

| I'd like . . . | Je voudrais . . . | Zhuh voodreh . . . |
| _a kilo of potatoes. | _un kilo de pommes de terre. | _uh(n) keeloh duh pohm duh tehr. |

_a can of peas.	_une boîte de petits pois.	_ewn bwaht duh puh-tee pwah.
_a can of coffee.	_une boîte de café.	_ewn bwaht duh kahfay.
_a dozen eggs.	_une douzaine d'oeufs.	_ewn doozehn duh.
_five slices of ham.	_cinq tranches de jambon.	_sa(n) trah(n)sh duh zha(m)boh(n).
_a piece of cheese.	_un morceau de fromage.	_uh(n) mohrsoh duh frohmahzh.
_a liter of mineral water.	_un litre d'eau minérale.	_uh(n) leetr doh meenayrahl.
_a box of chocolates.	_une boîte de chocolats.	_ewn bwaht duh shohkohlah.
_a bottle of milk.	_une bouteille de lait.	_ewn bootehy duh leh.
_of fruit juice.	_de jus de fruit.	_duh zhew duh frwee.
_200 grams of flour.	_deux cents grammes de farine.	_duh sah(n) grahm duh fahreen.

Additional Items

_a bottle of soda	_une bouteille de soda	_ewn bootehy duh sohdah
_some butter	_du beurre	_dew buhr
_some cookies	_des biscuits	_day beeskwee
_cold cuts	_de la charcuterie	_duh lah shahrkewtree
_ham	_du jambon	_dew zhah(m)boh(n)
_ice cream	_de la glace	_duh lah glahs
_a lemon	_un citron	_uh(n) seetroh(n)
_mustard	_de la moutarde	_duh lah mootahrd
_oranges	_des oranges	_day zohrah(n)zh
_pears	_des poires	_day pwahr
_pepper	_du poivre	_dew pwahvr
_potato chips	_des chips	_day sheep
_salt	_du sel	_dew sehl

_sausage	_des saucisses	_day sohsees
_sugar	_du sucre	_dew sewkr
_tea	_du thé	_dew tay
_yogurt	_des yaourts	_day yah-oort

Bread

Give me . . .	Donnez-moi . . .	Dohnay-mwah . . .
_a croissant.	_un croissant.	_uh(n) krwahsah(n).
_a brioche.	_une brioche.	_ewn breeyohsh.
_a chocolate roll.	_un pain au chocolat.	_uh(n) pa(n) oh shohkohlah.
_a roll.	_un petit pain.	_uh(n) puhtee pa(n).
(types of French bread)	_une ficelle. _une flûte. _une baguette. _un pain.	_ewn feesehl. _ewn flewt. _ewn bahgeht. _uh(n) pa(n).
_white bread.	_du pain de mie.	_dew pa(n) duh mee.
_a rye bread.	_un pain de seigle.	_uh(n) pa(n) duh sehgl.
_six rolls.	_six petits pains.	_see puhtee pa(n).
_a whole wheat bread.	_un pain complet.	_uh(n) pa(n) koh(m)-play.
_a multi-grain bread.	_un pain aux céréales.	_uh(n) pa(n) oh sehrayahl.
_a farmhouse bread.	_un pain de campagne.	_uh(n) pa(n) duh kah(m)pahnyuh.

WEIGHTS AND MEASURES

METRIC WEIGHT	U.S.
1 gram (g)	0.035 ounce
28.35 grams	1 ounce
100 grams	3.5 ounce
454 grams	1 pound
1 kilogram (kilo)	2.2 pounds

LIQUIDS	U.S.
1 liter (l)	4.226 cups
1 liter	2.113 pints
1 liter	1.056 quarts
3.785 liters	1 gallon

DRY MEASURE	U.S.
1 litre	0.908 quart
1 decalitre	1.135 pecks
1 hectolitre	2.837 bushels

One inch = 2.54 centimeters
One centimeter = .39 inch

inches	feet	yards	
1 mm.	0.039	0.003	0.001
1 cm.	0.39	0.03	0.01
1 dm.	3.94	0.32	0.10
1 m.	39.40	3.28	1.09

.39 (# of centimeters) = (# of inches)
2.54 (# of inches) = (# of centimeters)

inches	feet	yards	
1 mm.	0.039	0.003	0.001
1 cm.	0.39	0.03	0.01
1 dm.	3.94	0.32	0.10
1 m.	39.40	3.28	1.09

15
14
13
12
11
10
9
8
7
6
5
4
3
2
cm. 1

6
5
4
3
2
1
inches

ACTIVITIES AND
15 ENTERTAINMENT

SPORTS

Sports are a way of life in France, for both participants and spectators.

For an unforgettable spectator experience, you need only be on hand for the finish of the three-week Tour de France bicycle race as it reaches the Champs Élysées in late July. All Paris turns itself inside out for the occasion, a kind of Bastille Day without the parades and dancing in the streets. Parades and dancing do spontaneously break out when the French national soccer team wins a major tournament: the whole country rejoiced after France won the World Cup in 1998.

Just a few points lower on the enthusiasm scale for spectators are days at the Paris racetracks betting on the horses. When you are in Paris, try to get to Longchamps, considered the world's most beautiful racetrack, in a splendid Seine-side setting in the Bois de Boulogne. Also in the Bois is Auteuil, the city's steeplechase track.

Other spectator sports in the Paris area are polo at Pelouse de Bagatelle in the Bois de Boulogne, Sundays in summer, and tennis (national and international tournaments) at Stade Roland-Garros. Farther afield are auto races (*24 Hours of Le Mans* and *le Grand Prix*). Tickets are available from branches of Fnac.

Want to participate? Information on tennis courts around Paris is available from La Ligue de Tennis de Paris (109 bis ave. Mozart, 75016, tel. 01.44.14.67.89); and FFT (Fédération Française de Tennis), at Roland Garros (2 ave. Gordon Bennet, 75016; tel. 01.47.43.48.00). At the latter, queries in English are welcome.

For horseback riding call the Fédération Française d'Equitation (9 bd. Macdonald, 75019; tel. 01.53.26.15.50). There are also seasonal sports in different parts of France, such as fishing, hunting, and skiing. For all these, the French Government Tourist Office has detailed information.

DIALOGUE   Swimming (La Natation)

Jean-Pierre:	Qu'est-ce qu'il fait chaud!	Kehs keel fay shoh!
Mary Ann:	Oui! Si on allait se baigner?	Wee! See oh(n) nahlay suh behnyay?
Jean-Pierre:	Bonne idée! Qu'est-ce que tu préfères: la mer ou la piscine?	Bohn eeday! Kehskuh tew prayfehr: lah mehr oo lah peeseen?
Mary Ann:	J'adore la mer!	Zhahdohr lah mehr! Meh
	Mais . . . y a-t-il des courants dange- reux?	. . . yahteel day koo- rah(n) dah(n)zhuhruh?
Jean-Pierre:	Mais, non! La mer est plutôt calme par ici.	May noh(n)! Lah mehr ay plewtoh kahlm pahr eesee.
Mary Ann:	Tant mieux! D'ac- cord, rendez-vous sur la plage dans cinq minutes!	Tah(n) myuh. Dakohr, rah(n)day-voo sewr lah plahzh dah(n) sa(n) meenewt!
Jean-Pierre:	Entendu! Et n'ou- blie pas ton huile solaire!	Ah(n)tah(n)dew! Ay nooblee pah toh(n) nweel sohlehr!

Jean-Pierre:	It's so hot out!
Mary Ann:	Yes. What do you say we go swimming?
Jean-Pierre:	Good idea! Which do you prefer: the beach or the pool?
Mary Ann:	I love the sea! But . . . are there any danger- ous currents?
Jean-Pierre:	No! The sea is pretty calm around here.
Mary Ann:	So much the better! Okay, see you on the beach in five minutes.
Jean-Pierre:	Right! And don't forget your suntan lotion!

PARTICIPATORY SPORTS

Swimming

The Beach

Where are the best beaches?	**Où se trouvent les meilleures plages?**	Oo suh troov lay meh-yuhr plahzh?
How do we get there?	Comment y va-t-on?	Kohmah(n) ee vahtoh(n)?
Is it a private or public beach?	Est-ce une plage privée ou publique?	Ehs ewn plahzh pree-vay oo pewbleek?
Where is the life-guard?	**Où est le maître nageur?**	Oo eh luh mehtr nahzhuhr?
Ouch! The sand is hot. But the water is cool.	Aïe! Le sable est chaud. Mais l'eau est fraîche.	Ahy! Luh sahbl ay shoh. May loh ay frehsh.
Are there dangerous currents?	Y a-t-il des courants dangereux?	Yahteel day koorah(n) dah(n)zhuhruh?
No, there are only small waves.	Non, il n'y a que des petites vagues.	Nohn, eel neeyah kuh day puhteet vahg.
I'd like to rent . . .	**Je voudrais louer . . .**	Zhuh voodreh looway . . .
_a beach chair.	_une chaise longue.	_ewn shehz loh(n)g.
_a beach towel.	_une serviette de plage.	_ew sehrvyeht duh plahzh.
_a cabana.	_une cabine.	_ewn kahbeen.
_a pedal boat.	_un pédalo.	_uh(n) paydahloh.
_a rowboat.	_une barque.	_ewn bahrk.
_a sailboard.	_une planche à voile.	_ewn plah(n)sh ah vwahl.
_a sailboat.	_un voilier.	_uh(n) vwahlyay.
_skin-diving equipment.	_un équipement de plongée sous-marine.	_uh(n) naykeep-mah(n) duh ploh(n)zhay soo-mahreen.

_an umbrella.	_un parasol.	_uh(n) pahrahsohl.
_a surfboard.	_une planche de surf.	_ewn plah(n)sh duh sewrf.
_waterskis.	_des skis nautiques.	_day skee nohteek.
Don't forget to bring . . .	N'oubliez pas d'apporter . . .	Noobleeyay pah dahportay . . .
_sunglasses.	_des lunettes de soleil.	_day lewneht duh soh-lehy.
_suntan lotion.	_de la crème solaire.	_duh lah krehm sohlehr.

Poolside

Where is the pool?	Où se trouve la piscine?	Oo suh troov lah pee-seen?
Is the pool . . .	Est-ce une piscine . . .	Ehs ewn peeseen . . .
_outdoors?	_en plein air?	_ah(n) plehn ehr?
_indoors?	_couverte? (découverte?)	_koovehrt? (day-koo-vehrt?)
_heated?	_chauffée?	_shohfay?
When does the pool open/close?	A quelle heure ouvre/ferme la piscine?	Ah kehl uhr oovr/fehrm lah peeseen?

Other Active Sports

I like (to play) . . .	J'aime faire . . .	Zhem fehr . . .
_basketball.	_du basket.	_dew bahskeht.
_boxing.	_de la boxe.	_duh lah bohks.
_cycling.	_du cyclisme.	_dew seekleezm.
_deep-sea diving	_de la plongée sous-marine.	_duh lah ploh(n)zhay soo-mahreen.
_rugby.	_du rugby.	_dew rewgbee.
_running.	_du footing.	_dew footeeng.
_skiing (downhill).	_du ski alpin.	_dew skee ahlpa(n).
_skiing (cross-country).	_du ski de fond.	_dew skee duh foh(n).

179

_swimming.	_de la natation.	_duh nahtahsyoh(n).
_tennis.	_du tennis.	_dew tehnees.
_volleyball.	_du volley.	_dew vohlay.
Where can I find . . .	**Où y a-t-il . . .**	**Oo yahteel . . .**
_a tennis court?	**_un court de tennis?**	**_uh(n) koor duh tehnees?**
_a pool?	_une piscine?	_ewn peeseen?
_a racket?	_une raquette?	_ewn rahkeht?
_a golf course?	_un terrain de golf?	_uh(n) tehra(n) duh gohlf?
_a skating rink?	_une patinoire?	_ewn pahteenwahr?
How much is it . . .	Quel est le tarif . . .	Kehl eh luh tahreef . . .
_per hour?	_à l'heure?	_ah luhr?
_per day?	_à la journée?	_ah lah zhoornay?
Would you like to play . . .	**Voulez-vous jouer au . . .**	**Voolay-voo zhooay oh . . .**
_tennis?	_tennis?	_tehnees?
_golf?	**_golf?**	**_gohlf?**
We need to buy some balls.	Il faut qu'on achète des balles.	Eel foh koh(n) nahsheht day bahl.
You play very well.	Vous jouez très bien.	Voo zhooay treh byeh(n).
He plays fairly well.	Il joue assez bien.	Eel zhoo ahsay byeh(n).
I don't play well.	Je ne joue pas bien.	Zhuh nuh zhoo pah byeh(n).
What's the score?	Quel est le score?	Kehl eh luh skohr?
Who's winning?	Qui gagne?	Kee gahnyuh?

Note: Two popular American sports that are not played much in France, Belgium, or Switzerland are baseball and football. The French word *le football* [luh footbohl] always refers to soccer. Say *le football américain* [ah-mehreeka(n)] when referring to U.S.-style football. Baseball is, not surprisingly, *le baseball* (lah baysbohl).

180

Skiing

Would you like to go skiing?	Voulez-vous faire du ski?	Voolay-voo fehr dew skee?
What is the best ski area?	Quelle est la meilleure station de ski?	Kehl eh lah mehyuhr stahsyoh(n) duh skee?
I like Val d'Isère.	J'aime bien Val d'Isère.	Zhehm byeh(n) Vahl Deezehr.
Are there slopes for . . .	Y a-t-il des pistes pour . . .	Yahteel day peest poor . . .
_beginners?	_débutants?	_daybewtah(n)?
_intermediates?	_skieurs moyens?	_skeeuhr mwohya(n)?
_experts?	_très bons skieurs?	_treh boh(n) skeeuhr?
I'm going to take a lesson.	Je vais prendre une leçon.	Zhuh vay prah(n)dr ewn luhsoh(n).
What are the conditions like now?	Quelles sont les conditions en ce moment?	Kehl soh(n) lay koh(n)-deesyoh(n) ah(n) suh mohmah(n)?
There's lots of snow.	Il y a beaucoup de neige.	Eel yah bohkoo duh nehzh.
Where are the lifts?	Où sont les télésièges?	Oo soh(n) lay taylaysyehzh?
How much is a ski-pass?	Combien coûte un forfait?	Koh(m)byeh(n) koot uh(n) fohrfeh?
_for half a day?	_demi-journée?	_duhmee-zhoornay?
_for a day?	_journée?	_zhoornay?
I'd like to rent . . .	Je voudrais louer . . .	Zhuh voodreh looay . . .
_ski equipment	_un équipement de ski.	_uh(n) naykeep-mah(n) duh skee.
_skis.	_des skis.	_day skee.
_ski boots.	_des chaussures de ski.	_day shohsewr duh skee.
_poles.	_des bâtons.	_day bahtoh(n).

181

CAMPING

Camping is a highly popular pastime in France and cuts across the divisions of class and geography. The well-organized system reflects the French passion for classification and evaluation. Campsites receive from one to four stars according to the quality and number of the facilities. Reservations in summer are a must. *Le camping sauvage* [luh kah(m)peeng sohvahzh], i.e., unofficial camping "in the wild," is common, but you must ask the landowner for permission.

I'm looking for a campsite with . . .	Je cherche un camping avec . . .	Zhuh shehrsh uh(n) kah(m)peeng ahvehk . . .
_electricity.	_l'électricité.	_duh laylehktreeseetay.
_a grocery.	_une épicerie.	_ewn aypeesree.
_a pool.	_une piscine.	_ewn peeseen.
_butane gas.	_du butane.	_dew bewtahn.
What does it cost for one night?	Quel est le tarif pour une nuit?	Kehl eh luh tahreef poor ewn nwee?
Can we camp here?	Pouvons-nous camper ici?	Poovoh(n)-noo kah(m)-pay eesee?
Is there room for a trailer?	Y a-t-il de la place pour une caravane?	Yahteel duh lah plahs poor ewn kahrahvahn?
I'd like to rent a mobile home.	J'aimerais louer un mobile-home.	Zhehmreh looay uh(n) mohbeel-hohm.

SPECTATOR SPORTS

Let's go to the stadium!	Allons au stade!	Ahloh(n) zoh stahd!
I'd like to see . . .	J'aimerais voir . . .	Zhehmreh vwahr . . .
_a tennis match.	_un match de tennis.	_uh(n) mahtsh duh tehnees.
_horse racing.	_une course de chevaux.	_ewn koors duh shuhvoh.
_a soccer game.	_un match de football.	_uh(n) mahtsh duh footbohl.

_a boxing match.	_un match de boxe.	_uh(n) mahtsh duh bohks.
How much do tickets cost?	Combien coûtent les billets?	Koh(m)byeh(n) koot lay beeyay?
When does the match begin?	A quelle heure commence le match?	Ah kehl uhr kohmah(n)s luh mahtsh?
Who's playing?	**Qui joue?**	**Kee zhoo?**
Who won?	**Qui a gagné?**	**Kee ah gah(n)yay?**
What are the teams?	Quelles sont les équipes?	Kehl soh(n) lay zay-keep?

MOVIES

Parisians adore movies, and not just great art films but real junk flicks as well. Foreign films play in different versions in different theaters, either dubbed or in the original language with French subtitles. The latter is indicated by the letters *v.o.* (*version originale* [vehrsyoh(n) ohreezheenahl]). Prices are typically reduced for matinée shows and sometimes all day Monday or Wednesday.

The easiest way to find out what's playing at Paris theaters is to pick up one of the weekly entertainment guides such as *Pariscope*. Here you will find complete listings and times for all movie and legitimate theaters in Paris, along with brief synopses of prominent recent films. A new publication, *Zurban*, is also useful, though it doesn't have an English section.

Let's go to the movies!	**Allons au cinéma!**	**Ahloh(n) zoh seenaymah!**
What's playing?	**Qu'est-ce qu'on joue?**	**Kehs koh(n) zhoo?**
What kind of film is it?	**Quel genre de film est-ce?**	**Kehl zhah(n)r duh feelm ehs?**
Is it in French or English?	Est-ce en français ou en anglais?	Ehs ah(n) frah(n)seh oo ah(n) nah(n)gleh?
Is it dubbed?	**Est-ce doublé?**	**Ehs dooblay?**
I prefer to see . . .	Je préfère voir . . .	Zhuh prehfehr vwahr . . .
_the original version with subtitles.	_la version originale avec des soustitres.	_lah vehrsyoh(n) ohreezheenahl ahvehk day sooteetr.

183

_a comedy.	_une comédie.	_ewn kohmaydee.
_science fiction.	_un film de science-fiction.	_uh(n) feelm duh seeah(n)s feek-syoh(n).
_a musical comedy.	_une comédie musicale.	_ewn kohmaydee mu-zeekahl.
_a drama.	_un drame.	_uh(n) drahm.
_a political film.	_un film politique.	_uh(n) feelm poh-leeteek.
_a war film.	_un film de guerre.	_uh(n) feelm duh ghehr.
_a love story.	_une histoire d'amour.	_ewn eestwahr dah-moor.
_a western.	_un western.	_uh(n) wehstehrn.
When does the show start?	A quelle heure commence le film?	Ah kehl uhr kohmah(n)s luh feelm?
How much are the tickets?	Combien coûtent les places?	Koh(m)bya(n) koot lay plahs?
What theater is showing the new film by ____ with ____?	Dans quel cinéma passe le nouveau film de ____ avec ____?	Dah(n) kehl seenaymah pahs luh noovoh feelm duh ____ ahvehk ____?

THEATER, CONCERTS, OPERA, AND BALLET

For those who speak or understand French, there is an incredible variety of theater available in Paris, with important efforts in major cities such as Lyon, Strasbourg, Bordeaux, and Marseille. For summer theater at its best, check out the July Festival de théâtre d'Avignon, in the south of France. For variety, innovation, and quality of performance, it is one of the best theater festivals in the world. In addition to the established theatrical groups, such as *La Comédie-Française,* look for appearances by Third World troupes based in France and by the wildly innovative experimental groups. The daily press in Paris lists schedules and programs.

You should be aware that theaters, like so many establishments in France, are closed in August. During the rest of the year, you will find a nonstop parade of the world's greatest orchestras, soloists, dancers, and opera companies. Reservations are recommended.

What's playing at the theater?	**Qu'est-ce qu'on joue au théâtre?**	Kehs koh(n) zhoo oh tayahtr?
What kind of play is it?	**Quel genre de pièce est-ce?**	Kehl zhah(n)r duh pyehs ehs?
It's an avant-garde play.	C'est une pièce avant-gardiste.	Seh tewn pyehs ahvah(n)-gahrdeest.
Who wrote it?	Qui l'a écrite?	Kee lah aykreet?
Are there tickets for tonight?	Y a-t-il des places pour ce soir?	Yahteel day plahs poor suh swahr?
How much are the least expensive seats?	Combien coûtent les places les moins chères?	Koh(m)bya(n) koot lay plahs lay mwa(n) shehr?
I'd like . . .	**Je voudrais . . .**	Zhuh voodreh . . .
_an orchestra seat.	_une place à l'orchestre.	_ewn plahs ah lohrkehstr.
_a balcony seat.	_une place au balcon.	_ewn plahs oh bahlkoh(n).
_two tickets for the Saturday matinee.	_deux billets pour samedi en matinée.	_duh beeyay poor sahmdee ah(n) mahteenay.
_two seats in the balcony not too far back.	_deux places au balcon pas trop loin.	_duh plahs oh bahlkoh(n) pah troh lwa(n).
A program, please.	Un programme, s'il vous plaît.	Uh(n) prohgrahm, seel voo pleh.
I'd like to see . . .	**J'aimerais voir . . .**	Zhehmreh vwahr . . .
_a concert.	_un concert.	_uh(n) koh(n)sehr.
_a classical music concert.	_un concert de musique classique.	_uh(n) koh(n)sehr duh muzeek klahseek.
_a jazz concert.	_un concert de jazz.	_uh(n) koh(n)sehr duh dzhahz.
_an opera.	_un opéra.	_uh(n) nohpayrah.
_a ballet.	_un ballet.	_uh(n) bahlay.

What's playing tonight at the opera?	Qu'est-ce qu'on joue ce soir à l'opéra?	Kehs koh(n) zhoo suh swahr ah lohpayrah?
Who's . . .	Qui . . .	Kee . . .
_playing?	_joue?	_zhoo?
_singing?	_chante?	_shah(n)t?
_dancing?	_danse?	_dah(n)s?
_the conductor?	_est le chef d'orchestre?	_eh luh shehf dohrkehstr?
Do we need a reservation?	Faut-il réserver?	Fohteel rayzehrvay?

CLUBS, DISCOS, AND CABARETS

Renowned for its exciting night life, Paris offers everything from sophisticated political satire to bawdy extravaganzas. Jazz is especially popular, with both traditional and contemporary fare widely appreciated. Paris is a late town; many shows do not begin until 10 PM. If you go clubbing, remember that jeans and sneakers are frowned upon. One of the best new clubs is the Batofar, a boat moored on the Seine.

Montreal also has an active jazz and nightlife scene.

I'd like to go to . . .	Je voudrais aller dans . . .	Zhuh voodreh ahlay dah(n) . . .
_a disco.	_une discothèque.	_zewn deeskohtehk.
_a nightclub.	_une boîte de nuit.	_zewn bwaht duh nwee.
_a jazz club.	_un club de jazz.	_zuh(n) kluhb duh dzhahz.
I'd like to go dancing.	Je voudrais aller danser.	Zhuh voodray zahlay dah(n)say.
There's a small cover charge.	Il y a un petit prix d'entrée.	Eel yah uh(n) puhtee pree dah(n)tray.
Would you like to dance?	Voulez-vous danser?	Voolay-voo dah(n)say?
Is there a floor show?	Y a-t-il un spectacle?	Yahteel uhn spehktahkl?

TRAVELING WITH CHILDREN IN PARIS

Children can have a ball in Paris, where they will find amusement parks, aquariums, marionette shows, museums, playgrounds, and zoos.

Baby-sitting services are available from the following organizations, which will send a student at an hourly rate. If sitting goes beyond midnight (last Métro service), there's an extra charge for taxi fare home.

- Ababa, 8 ave. du Maine, 75015; Tel. 01.45.49.46.46.
- Allô Service Maman Poule, 7 villa Murat, 75016. Tel. 01.42.20.96.96.
- Baby Sitting Service, 18 rue Tronchet, 75008. Tel. 01.46. 37.51.24.

Jardin du Luxembourg has a pond to sail boats, a playground, and marionette and puppet shows. Playgrounds and ponds are also in the Tuileries Gardens and at the foot of the Eiffel Tower. Other puppet shows are in the Champ de Mars and in the rotary of the Champs-Élysées, avenue Gabriel.

There's a wax museum, the Musée Grevin (10 bd. Montmartre), open from 1 to 7 PM; an aquarium in the Bois de Vincennes at the eastern edge of the city; and a zoo in the Jardin des Plantes (3 Quai St-Bernard) on the Left Bank of the Seine, not far from Notre Dame.

A far more famous and extensive zoo (Parc Zoologique de Paris) is in the Bois de Vincennes. There are playgrounds, another zoo, and an amusement park in the Bois de Boulogne, on the western rim of Paris. In fact, the Jardin d'Acclimatation de Paris in the Bois de Boulogne could be considered a total world of amusements, rides, distractions, and sports for the young.

COOKING SCHOOLS

Learn how to make the perfect soufflé or a tasty coq-au-vin at the following world-renowned schools:

La Varenne, Château du Fey, 89300 Villecien. Tel. 03.86.63. 18.34. In the United States: Tel. 800/537-6486, www.lavarenne. com. Bilingual courses in different aspects of French cooking are given in a 17th-century château. One week courses are

$2,800–$3,600 and include transportation to and from Paris, accommodations, meals, and excursions.

Le Cordon Bleu, 8 rue Léon Delhomme, 75015 Paris; tel. 01.53.68.22.50. In the United States: Tel. 845/426-7400. Four-day specialized courses start at $760. Demonstration tickets are about $45 each.

Ritz-Escoffier Ecole de Gastronomie Française, 38 rue Cambon, 75001 Paris; tel. 01.43.16.30.50. Bilingual courses in different aspects of French cooking are given. A demonstration costs about $50 while a hands-on workshop costs $100 and up. The full program is on the Internet at www.ritzparis.com.

With *Traveltalk*, you can find and use phrases you need without formal grammar study. However, by learning some of the basic grammatical patterns of the language, you will be able to construct an unlimited number of your own sentences and greatly increase your range of expression.

NOUNS AND ARTICLES

Definite Article—*the*

All nouns are either masculine or feminine. As there is not one systematic way to tell the gender of most nouns from their spelling or meaning, it is best to learn the definite article with the noun.

Masculine Singular—*le*

the pen	le stylo	luh steeloh
the menu	le menu	luh muhnew
the man	l'homme	lohm

Remember, the vowel in the definite article is dropped when the next word begins with a vowel and with some words beginning with *h*—this is referred to as elision (see page 8).

Feminine Singular—*la*

the lady	la dame	lah dahm
the page	la page	lah pazh
the orange	l'orange	lohrahnzh

Plural—*les*

Les is the definite article for all plural nouns, whether masculine or feminine.

Masculine Plural:

the pens	les stylos	lay steeloh

Feminine Plural:

the pages	les pages	lay pahzh
the oranges	les oranges	lay zohrah(n)zh

You will note from the examples above that to make a noun plural, we simply add an *s* to the spelling. The *s*, however, is silent (but note the liaison with the plural article when the following noun begins with a vowel). In speaking, therefore, we can tell if a noun is plural only from the preceding article.

the boy	le garçon	luh gahrsoh(n)
the boys	les garçons	lay gahrsoh(n)

Indefinite Articles—*a, some*

Masculine Singular—*un*

a pen	un stylo	uh(n) steeloh
a menu	un menu	uh(n) muhnew
a friend	un ami	uh(n) nahmee

Feminine Singular—*une*

a lady	une dame	ewn dahm
a page	une page	ewn pahzh
an orange	une orange	ewn ohrah(n)zh

Plural—*des*

Des is the indefinite article for all nouns, whether masculine or feminine.

some pens	des stylos	day steeloh
some pages	des pages	day pahzh
some oranges	des oranges	day zohrah(n)zh (note the liaison here)

Article System

	Singular	Plural
Definite	m. le	les
	f. la	
Indefinite	m. un	des
	f. une	

Note: The *n* of *un* is not pronounced before a consonant but *is* pronounced in *liaison* when the next word begins with a vowel.

PRONOUNS

Pronouns stand for or replace nouns and perform several distinct functions.

Subject Pronouns are the subjects of sentences or clauses and are usually found in sentence-initial position

I am going to the restaurant.	*Je* vais au restaurant.
You speak English.	*Vous* parlez anglais.

Direct Object Pronouns represent the persons or objects acted upon by the verb. They agree in number and gender with the nouns they replace. Note: They are identical with the forms of the definite article *the*—le, la, les.

Do you understand French?	Est-ce que vous comprenez le français?
Yes, I understand *it*.	Oui, je *le* comprends.
Do you like the desserts here?	Vous aimez les desserts ici?
Yes, I like *them*.	Oui, je *les* aime.

As seen from the above examples, direct object pronouns generally come between the subject and the verb. However, they *follow* an imperative:

Take *it*!	Prenez-*la*!

Indirect Object Pronouns receive the action of the verb indirectly and are usually represented in English as "to him, to her, to me," etc.

I am speaking *to him* (or her).	Je *lui* parle.
He's giving his map *to me*.	Il *me* donne sa carte.

Indirect object pronoun placement is the same as for direct object pronouns: between subject and verb, except for commands.

Write *to him*!	Ecrivez-*lui*!

Pronouns as Objects of Prepositions always follow the preposition.

I'm going *with him*.	Je vais *avec lui*.

The following chart shows the forms of all the sets of pronouns discussed above.

Subject	Direct Object	Indirect Object	After a Preposition
I je	me me	to me me	me moi
you tu*	you te	to you te	you toi
he il	him le	to him lui	him lui
she elle	her la	to her lui	her elle
we nous†	us nous	to us nous	us nous
you vous*	you vous	to you vous	you vous
they ils (masculine/mixed)	them les	to them leur	them eux
they elles (feminine)	them les	to them leur	them elles

We speak French here (idiomatic). On parle français ici.

One speaks French here (literal).

Note: Before a verb beginning with a vowel, a pronoun that ends in *e* or *a* drops that letter. This is an example of elision.

I like/love . . .	Je aime . . . → J'aime . . .
He's listening to me.	Il me écoute. → Il m'écoute.
We have it.	Nous la avons. → Nous l'avons.

ADJECTIVES

Placement

Most adjectives are placed *after* the noun.

| an amusing book | un livre amusant |
| a French friend | un ami français |

Tu, Vous—French, like many other languages, has preserved a distinction between familiar and formal *you* (the *thou* and *you* distinction that has disappeared from English). *Tu* is used for children, close friends, and relatives. *Vous* is used when addressing anyone else and is also used exclusively in the plural. As a traveler, you most probably will give and receive only *vous*. Children under sixteen or seventeen should be prepared to hear *tu* but would address only other children as *tu*, addressing adults as *vous*. Note the verbs tutoyer (to say *tu* to someone) and vouvoyer (to say *vous* to someone).

†*On* (one) is often used in place of *nous* (we) in the spoken language.

A few common, short adjectives occur *before* the noun. Most of these can be grouped in pairs for easy learning.

small	petit
big, great	grand
young	jeune
old	vieux
good	bon
bad	mauvais
pretty	joli
good weather	le beau temps
bad weather	le mauvais temps
a young man	un jeune homme

Gender

Adjectives agree in gender with the nouns they modify. Adjectives which end in a silent final consonant in the masculine, add an *e* and sound the preceding consonant in the feminine.

an amusing book	un livre amusant	uh(n) leevr ahmew-zah(n)
an amusing play	une pièce amusante	ewn pyehs ahmew-zah(n)t

Adjectives that end in a vowel in the masculine, add *e* to form the feminine but don't change their pronunciation. Adjectives ending in *e* with no accent mark remain the same.

pretty (*m*)	joli	zhohlee
(*f*)	jolie	zhohlee
sincere (*m*)	sincère	sa(n)sehr
(*f*)	sincère	sa(n)sehr
pleased (*m*)	enchanté	ah(n)shah(n)tay
(*f*)	enchantée	ah(n)shah(n)tay

Adjectives ending in *-ier* add *e* to form the feminine and add an accent grave as in the following. Note the pronunciation change.

entire (*m*)	entier	ah(n)tyay
(*f*)	entière	ah(n)tyehr

Adjectives that end in a vowel + *n* in the masculine double the *n* and add *e* in the feminine.

good (m)	bon	boh(n)
(f)	bonne	bohn
Italian (m)	italien	eetahlya(n)
(f)	italienne	eetahlyehn

Number

Like the nouns they describe, adjectives add *s* to the singular form to indicate the plural, masculine, or feminine as required. The *s* is not pronounced.

| some amusing friends | des amis amusants | day zahmee zahmew-zah(n) |
| some amusing women | des femmes amusantes | day fahm zahmew-zah(n)t |

If the singular adjective ends in *s*, there is no change for the plural.

| a French book | un livre français |
| some French books | des livres français |

Possessive Adjectives

Possessive adjectives denote ownership: *my* hat, *your* coat, *his* tickets, etc. In French, possessive adjectives agree in number and gender with the *thing possessed*.

	Singular masculine feminine	Plural (same for m/f)
my	mon ma	mes
your	ton* ta*	tes*
his/her	son sa	ses
our	notre notre	nos
your	votre votre	vos
their	leur leur	leurs

---

*The distinction between *tu* and *vous*, described under *Pronouns*, is also found in the possessive adjectives.

Here are some examples of the use of possessive adjectives.

my wife	ma femme	his aunt	sa tante
my book	mon livre	his ideas	ses idées
my friends	mes amis	our house	notre maison
your suitcase	ta valise	your child	votre enfant
your friend	ton ami	their book	leur livre
his pencil	son crayon		

Note: We have seen how liaison and elision help preserve the pleasing alternation of vowel and consonant. For the same reason, we do not use *ma, ta,* or *sa* before a feminine noun beginning with a vowel. Instead, we use the masculine variants *mon, ton,* and *son.*

my friend (f.)	mon amie	moh(n) nahmee
his (or her) omelette (f.)	son omelette	soh(n) nohmleht

Demonstrative Adjectives

	Singular This/That	Plural These/Those
Masculine	ce	ces
Masculine before vowel or "h"	cet	ces
Feminine	cette	ces

Here are some examples of demonstrative adjectives.

this/that boy	ce garçon
this/that man	cet homme
this/that woman	cette femme
these/those boys	ces garçons
these/those men	ces hommes
these/those women	ces femmes

Comparative and Superlative Adjectives

Positive	Comparative	Superlative
big	bigger	biggest
grand(e)	plus grand(e)	le/la/les plus grand(e)(s)

| interesting | more interesting | most interesting |
| intéressant(e) | plus intéressant(e) | le/la/les plus intéressant(e)(s) |

Here are some examples of comparative and superlative adjectives.

This hat is big.

Ce chapeau est grand.

This hat is bigger than the other.

Ce chapeau est plus grand que l'autre.

This hat is the biggest in the store.

Ce chapeau est le plus grand du magasin.

These hats are the biggest.

Ces chapeaux sont les plus grands.

Comparatives of the Lesser Degree To say that something is less ____ or the least ____, we use the same pattern as above, simply substituting the word *moins* for *plus*.

This hat is less interesting than the other.

Ce chapeau est moins intéressant que l'autre.

This hat is the least interesting.

Ce chapeau est le moins intéressant.

Note the following irregular comparisons and superlatives.

Positive	Comparative	Superlative
good	better	best
bon(ne)	meilleur(e)	le/la/les meilleur(e)(s)
bad	worse	worst
mauvais(e)	pire	le/la/les pire(s)

Here are some examples using these irregular comparisons/superlatives.

It's the best ice cream in the world!

C'est la meilleure glace du monde!

This hotel is worse than the other.

Cet hôtel est pire que l'autre.

ADVERBS

In general, adverbs are formed by adding *-ment* to the feminine form of the corresponding adjective.

rapid	rapidly
rapide	rapidement
serious	seriously
sérieux(euse)	sérieusement

Note the following common adverbs that are irregular.

fast	vite	veet
well	bien	byeh(n)
badly	mal	mahl
better	mieux	myuh
worse	pire	peer

PREPOSITIONS

_about	_de	_duh
_according to	_selon	_suhloh(n)
_across	_à travers	_ah trahvehr
_after	_après	_ahpreh
_among	_parmi	_pahrmee
_around	_autour de	_ohtoor duh
_at	_à	_ah
_at (+ name of person or profession)	_chez	_shay
_before	_avant	_ahvah(n)
_behind	_derrière	_dehryehr
_between	_entre	_ah(n)tr
_by	_par	_pahr
_during	_pendant	_pah(n)dah(n)
_except	_sauf	_sohf
_for	_pour	_poor
_from	_de	_duh

197

_in	_dans, en	_dah(n), ah(n)
_in front of	_devant	_duhvah(n)
_on	_sur	_sewr
_opposite	_en face de	_ah(n) fahs duh
_through	_à travers	_ah trahvehr
_to	_à	_ah
_toward	_vers	_vehr
_under	_sous	_soo
_until	_jusqu'à	_zhewskah
_with	_avec	_ahvehk
_without	_sans	_sah(n)

CONTRACTIONS

The common prepositions *à* (to, at) and *de* (of, from) have special contracted forms when combined with certain forms of the definite article:

à + le = au   de + le = du

à + les = aux   de + les = des

(There are no contractions with *à la*, *à l'*, *de la*, or *de l'*.)

I'm going to the movies.	Je vais *au* cinéma.
I'm coming from the movies.	Je viens *du* cinéma.
Peter is going to go to the museums.	Pierre va aller *aux* musées.

NEGATIVE SENTENCES

Negative sentences require two negative elements, one preceding and one following the verb.

not (simple negation)	ne (verb) pas
never	ne (verb) jamais
nothing	ne (verb) rien
no longer	ne (verb) plus
no one	ne (verb) personne

Here are some examples of negative forms.

I know.	Je sais*.
I don't know his name.	Je ne sais pas son nom.
I know nothing.	Je ne sais rien.
I no longer know.	Je ne sais plus.
I know nobody.	Je ne connais* personne.

QUESTIONS

The easiest way to ask a question that can be answered by *yes* or *no* is simply to say a declarative sentence using rising intonation, i.e., raise your voice at the end as you would with a question in English.

We're going to the restaurant.	On va au restaurant.
Shall we go to the restaurant?	On va au restaurant?
You're French.	Vous êtes français.
Are you French?	Vous êtes français?

Another common way to ask a yes/no question is to place the phrase *Est-ce que* [ehskuh] before a declarative sentence:

Are you French?	Est-ce que vous êtes français?

WH-questions are another major category. These are the questions which in English begin with *wh*.

who	qui	kee
what	que, quoi	kuh, kwah
where	où	oo
when	quand	kah(n)
why	pourquoi	poorkwah
how	comment	kohmah(n)

In French, WH questions are formed as follows.

WH-word + est-ce que + declarative

*Note: Both *savoir* and *connaître* mean *to know*. *Savoir* is used when referring to facts. *Connaître* is used when referring to people and places.

| When does the train leave? | Quand est-ce que le train part? |
| Where can I change my money? | Où est-ce que je peux changer mon argent? |

You may also hear *pronoun-verb inversion questions:*

| Do you speak French? | Parlez-vous français? |
| Do you like ice cream? | Aimez-vous la glace? |

Note: Pronoun inversion may be used to form a question with any pronoun except, in most cases, *je* (I). Here you generally use the *est-ce que* structure.

| Are we on time? | Sommes-nous à l'heure? |
| Am I on time? | Est-ce que je suis à l'heure? |

To change the expression *Il y a* (There is) to a question, a *t* is added for easier pronunciation—*y a-t-il* (Is there?), pronounced *yahteel.*

VERBS

There are three principal types of verb conjugations in French, each signaled by a distinctive verb ending or infinitive.

-er Verbs

Verbs ending in *-er,* such as *parler* (to speak), are by far the most common verb category.

I speak	je parle	zhuh parl
you speak	tu parles	tew parl
he/she/one speaks	il/elle/on parle	eel/ehl/oh(n) parl
we speak	nous parlons	noo parloh(n)
you speak	vous parlez	voo parlay
they speak	ils/elles parlent	eel/ehl parl
Speak!	Parlez!	Parlay!

The following is a list of some of the more common *-er* verbs that are conjugated according to the regular pattern above.

to like, love	aimer	to close	fermer
to change	changer	to eat	manger
to look for	chercher	to speak	parler
to cost	coûter	to look at	regarder

to eat dinner	dîner	to work	travailler
to give	donner	to find	trouver
to listen to	écouter	to travel	voyager

-ir Verbs

The second type of verb ends in -ir, such as *finir* (to finish).

I finish	je finis	zhuh feenee
you finish	tu finis	tew feenee
he/she/one finishes	il/elle/on finit	eel/ehl/oh(n) feenee
we finish	nous finissons	noo feeneesoh(n)
you finish	vous finissez	voo feeneesay
they finish	ils/elles finissent	eel/ehl feenees
Finish!	Finissez!	Feeneesay!

-re Verbs

The third category of verb ends in -re, such as *rendre* (to give back).

I give back	je rends	zhuh rah(n)
you give back	tu rends	tew rah(n)
he/she/one gives back	il/elle/on rend	eel/ehl/oh(n) rah(n)
we give back	nous rendons	noo rah(n)doh(n)
you give back	vous rendez	voo rah(n)day
they give back	ils/elles rendent	eel/ehl rah(n)d
Give it back!	Rendez-le/la!	Rah(n)day-luh/lah!

The following is a list of several common -re verbs that are conjugated according to the regular pattern above.

to wait	attendre
to descend, get off	descendre
to hear	entendre
to give back	rendre
to answer	répondre (à)

201

Most Common Irregular Verbs

As in most languages, the French verbs used most frequently are those that show the greatest irregularities. Here are conjugations of a few of the most common irregular verbs.

Infinitive:	Être (Be)	Avoir (Have)	Aller (Go)	Faire (Make/Do)
je	suis	ai	vais	fais
tu	es	as	vas	fais
il/elle/on	est	a	va	fait
nous	sommes	avons	allons	faisons
vous	êtes	avez	allez	faites
ils/elles	sont	ont	vont	font
imperative	soyez	ayez	allez	faites

Infinitive:	Venir (Come)	Pouvoir (Be able)	Vouloir (Want)
je	viens	peux	veux
tu	viens	peux	veux
il/elle/on	vient	peut	veut
nous	venons	pouvons	voulons
vous	venez	pouvez	voulez
ils/elles	viennent	peuvent	veulent
imperative	venez	—	—

Future Action

As in English, you may express upcoming action in French by using the conjugated form of the helping verb *to go—aller—* plus the infinitive of the main verb.

I'm going to leave tomorrow.	Je vais partir demain.
We're going to visit Paris tomorrow.	Nous allons visiter Paris demain.

Past Tense

To express an action in the past, French uses the following structure: Subject + proper form of helping verb *avoir* + past participle.

Pierre sang.	Pierre a chanté.
We ate.	Nous avons mangé.

The past participle of regular verbs is predictable from the type of infinitive ending.

_Type of Infinitive	-er	-ir	-re
_Past Participle	-é	-i	-u

Verb		Infinitive	Past Participle
-er	to speak	parler	parlé
	to sing	chanter	chanté
	to love	aimer	aimé
-ir	to finish	finir	fini
	to choose	choisir	choisi
	to lose weight	maigrir	maigri
-re	to give back	rendre	rendu
	to sell	vendre	vendu
	to wait	attendre	attendu

I sold my ticket.	J'ai vendu mon billet.
They chose a hotel.	Ils ont choisi un hôtel.
We sang a French song.	Nous avons chanté une chanson française.

Note: a number of common verbs are conjugated with *être* as the helping verb instead of *avoir* to form the past tense. In this case, the past participle must agree with the subject (masculine or feminine) of the sentence. These verbs, with their corresponding past participles, are shown on the following page.

Verb	Infinitive	Past Participle
to arrive	arriver	arrivé(e)
to return	retourner	retourné(e)
to go up	monter	monté(e)
to go down	descendre	descendu(e)
to enter	entrer	entré(e)
to return	rentrer	rentré(e)
to leave	sortir	sorti(e)
to leave	partir	parti(e)
to go	aller	allé(e)

to die	mourir	mort(e)
to be born	naître	né(e)

Pierre left at two o'clock.	Pierre est parti à deux heures.
Marie left at three o'clock.	Marie est partie à trois heures.
Nicole was born in 1952.	Nicole est née en 1952.
We went to the concert yesterday.	Nous sommes allés au concert hier.

Irregular Past Participles: Some of the most commonly used French verbs have irregular past participles. A number of these are listed below.

Verb	Infinitive	Past Participle
to have	avoir	eu
to be	être	été
to be able	pouvoir	pu
to make/do	faire	fait
to see	voir	vu
to want	vouloir	voulu
to drink	boire	bu
to open	ouvrir	ouvert
to write	écrire	écrit
to take	prendre	pris

I had (literally: took) my breakfast at 7 AM.	J'ai pris mon petit déjeuner à 7 heures.
They saw the Eiffel Tower yesterday.	Ils ont vu la Tour Eiffel hier.

Reflexive Verbs

Reflexive verbs are those for which the subject and the object of the action are one and the same, i.e., the subject performs the action on himself or herself. The following sentence pattern is used with reflexive verb forms: Subject + reflexive pronoun + verb.

I am washing myself.	Je me lave.	zhuh muh lahv.
Pierre is shaving himself.	Pierre se rase.	Pyehr suh rahz.
We are hurrying.	Nous nous dépêchons.	Noo noo daypeh-shoh(n).

The *reflexive pronoun* must agree with the subject of the sentence.

Subject	Reflexive Pronoun
je	me
tu	te
il, elle, on	se
nous	nous
vous	vous
ils, elles	se

A number of verbs which are not reflexive in English are reflexive in French. The most common ones include:

to be called	s'appeler
to sit down	s'asseoir
to change clothes	se changer
to go to bed	se coucher
to hurry	se dépêcher
to get undressed	se déshabiller
to get dressed	s'habiller
to get up	se lever
to take a walk	se promener
to wake up	se réveiller
to make a mistake	se tromper

ENGLISH/FRENCH DICTIONARY

The gender of nouns is indicated by *m.* (masculine) or *f.* (feminine). Nouns commonly used in the plural are shown in the plural form and are followed by the notation *pl.*

Adjectives are listed in the masculine singular form. The formation of feminine and plural adjectives is described in the chapter on grammar. Irregular feminine and plural adjective forms are listed in the dictionary.

A

a, an un, m. *[uh(n)]* une, f. *[ewn]*

to be able to pouvoir *[poovwahr]*

above dessus *[duhsew]*

abroad à l'étranger *[ah laytrah(n)zhay]*

to accept accepter *[ahksehptay]*

to accompany accompagner *[ahkoh(m)pahnyay]*

accompanying vegetables garniture, f. *[gahrneetewr]*

according to selon *[suhloh(n)]*

acquaintance connaissance, f. *[koynehsah(n)s]*

address adresse, f. *[ahdrehs]*

to adore adorer *[ahdohray]*

adult adulte, m. *[ahdewlt]*

to be afraid of avoir peur de *[ahvwahr puhr duh]*

after après *[ahpreh]*

afternoon après-midi, m. or f. *[ahpreh-meedee]*

afterward ensuite *[ah(n)sweet]*

again encore *[ah(n)kohr]*

against contre *[koh(n)tr]*

age âge, m. *[ahzh]*

agency agence, f. *[ahzhah(n)s]*

ago il y a *[eel yah]*

agreed entendu *[ah(n)tah(n)dew]*, d'accord *[dahkohr]*

air-conditioned climatisé *[kleemahteezay]*

airplane avion, m. *[ahvyoh(n)]*

airport aéroport, m. *[ahayrohpohr]*

alarm clock réveil, m. *[rayvehy]*

all tout *[too]*

all directions toutes directions *[toot deerehksyoh(n)]*

almonds amandes, f.pl. *[ahmah(n)d]*

almost presque *[prehsk]*

alone seul *[suhl]*

also aussi *[ohsee]*

America Amérique, f. *[Ahmayreek]*

American américain *[ahmayreeka(n)]*

among parmi *[pahrmee]*

to amuse (s')amuser *[(s)ahmewzay]*

anchovies anchois, m.pl. *[ah(n)shwah]*

and et *[ay]*

answer réponse, f. *[raypoh(n)s]*

to answer répondre *[raypoh(n)dr]*

antique dealer antiquaire, m., f. *[ah(n)teekehr]*

antiques antiquités, f.pl.
[ah(n)teekeetay]

aperitif apéritif, m. [ahpay-
reeteef]

apology excuses, f.pl.
[ehkskews]

to apologize s'excuser
[sehkskewzay]

appetite appétit, m. [ahpay-
tee]

appetizers hors d'oeuvre,
m. [ohr duhvr]

apple pomme, f. [pohm]

appointment rendez-vous,
m. [rah(n)day-voo]

apricot abricot, m. [ah-
breekoh]

April avril [ahvreel]

are there . . .? y a-t-il . . .?
[yahteel . . .?]

area code indicatif, m.
[a(n)deekahteef]

arm bras, m. [brah]

armchair fauteuil, m. [fo-
htuhy]

to arrive arriver [ahreevay]

art art, m. [ahr]

art gallery galerie d'art, f.
[gahlree dahr]

artichoke artichaut, m.
[ahrteeshoh]

artichoke heart fond d'artichaut, m. [foh(n)
dahrteeshoh] coeur d'ar-
tichaut, m. [kuhr dahrteeshoh]

article article, m. [ahrteekl]

ashtray cendrier, m.
[sah(n)dreeay]

to ask demander [duhman(n)-
day]

asparagus asperge, f. [ah-
spehrzh]

at à [ah]

at the house of chez [shay]

to attach attacher [ahtah-
shay]

attention attention, f.
[ahtah(n)syoh(n)]

attic grenier, m. [gruhnyay]

attraction curiosité, f.
[kewryohzeetay]

August août [oot]

aunt tante, f. [tah(n)t]

automatic automatique
[ohtohmahteek]

autumn automne, m.
[ohtohn]

avocado avocat, m.
[ahvohkah]

B

baby-sitter garde d'enfants,
f. [gahrd dah(n)fah(n)]

back dos, m. [doh]

in back of derrière [dehryehr]

bacon lard, m. [lahr]

bad mauvais [mohvay]

badly mal [mahl]

bag sac, m. [sahk]

baggage locker consigne
automatique, f. [koh(n)seen
yohtohmahteek]

bakery boulangerie, f.
[boolah(n)zhree]

balcony balcon, m.
[bahlkoh(n)]

banana banane, f. [bahnahn]

bank banque, f. [bah(n)k]

bar bar, m. [bahr]

barber coiffeur, m. [kwah-
fuhr]

basement sous-sol, m. [soo-
sohl]

basket panier, m. [pahnyay]

basketball basket, m.
[bahskeht]

bath bain, m. [ba(n)]

to bathe (se) baigner [(suh)
behnyay]

bathing suit maillot de bain,
m. [mahyoh duh ba(n)]

bathrobe robe de chambre,
f. [rohb duh shah(m)br]

bathroom salle de bain, f. *[sahl duh ba(n)]*

battery pile, f. *[peel]*

to be être *[ehtr]*

to be out of gas être en panne d'essence *[ehtr pahn dehsah(n)s]*

beach plage, f. *[plahzh]*

bean haricot, m. *[ahreekoh]*

beard barbe, f. *[bahrb]*

beautiful beau, m. *[boh]* belle, f. *[behl]*

beauty parlor salon de beauté, m. *[sahlon(n)duh bo-htay]*

because parce que *[pahrs kuh]*

to become devenir *[duhvuh-neer]*

bed lit, m. *[lee]*

bed-and-breakfast chambre d'hôte, f. *[shah(m)br doht]*

bedroom chambre, f. *[shah(m)br]*

beef boeuf, m. *[buhf]*

beer bière, f. *[byehr]*

beet betterave, f. *[behtrahv]*

before avant *[ahvah(n)]*

to begin commencer *[kohmah(n)say]*

beginner débutant, m. *[day-bewtah(n)]*

behind derrière *[dehryehr]*

Belgian belge *[behlzh]*

Belgium Belgique, f. *[Behlzheek]*

to believe croire *[krwahr]*

bellboy chasseur, m. (in big hotels only) *[shahsuhr]*

below en bas *[ah(n) bah]*

belt ceinture, f. *[sa(n)tewr]*

beneath dessous *[duhsoo]*

beside à côté de *[ah kohtay duh]*

better (adj.) meilleur *[mehyuhr]*

better (adv.) mieux *[myuh]*

between entre *[ah(n)tr]*

beyond au delà de *[oh duh-lah duh]*

big grand *[grah(n)]*

bill addition, f. *[ahdeesyah(n)]* note, f. *[noht]*

birthday anniversaire, m. *[ahneevehrsehr]*

bitter amer *[ahmehr]*

black noir *[nwahr]*

blanket couverture, f. *[koovehrtewr]*

blinker clignotant, m. *[kleenyohtah(n)]*

blond blond *[bloh(n)]*

blood sang, m. *[sah(n)]*

blouse chemisier, m. *[shuh-meeseeyay]*

blue bleu *[bluh]*

boarding pass carte d'embarquement, f. *[kahrt da(m)bahrkmah(n)]*

boat barque, f. *[bahrk]* bâteau, m. *[bahtoh]*

body corps, m. *[kohr]*

boiled bouilli *[booyee]*

bone os, m. *[ohs]*

book livre, m. *[leevr]*

book (of tickets) carnet, m. *[kahrnay]*

bookstore librairie, f. *[lee-brehree]*

boot botte, f. *[boht]*

booth cabine, f. *[kahbeen]*

border frontière, f. *[froh(n)-tyehr]*

born né *[nay]*

to borrow emprunter *[ah(m)pruh(n)tay]*

boss chef, m. *[shehf]*

to bother gêner *[zhehnay]*

bottle bouteille, f. *[bootehy]*

box boîte, f. *[bwaht]*

boy garçon, m. *[gahrsoh(n)]*

bracelet bracelet, m. *[brah-slay]*

brain cervelle, f. *[sehrvehl]* or cerveau, m. *[sehrvoh]*

brakes freins, m.pl. *[fra(n)]*

bread pain, m. *[pa(n)]*

to break briser *[breezay]*

breakdown (car) panne, f. *[pahn]*

breakfast petit déjeuner, m. *[puhtee dayzhuhnay]*

bridge pont, m. *[poh(n)]*

briefcase serviette, f. *[sehr-vyeht]*

to bring amener *[ahmnay]* apporter *[ahpohrtay]*

broken cassé *[kahsay]*

brother frère, m. *[frehr]*

brother-in-law beau-frère, m. *[boh-frehr]*

brown brun *[bruh(n)]*; marron *[mahroh(n)]*

brush brosse, f. *[brohs]*

Brussels Bruxelles *[Brewsehl]*

brussels sprout chou de Bruxelles, m. *[shoo duh Brewsehl]*

to buckle attacher *[ahtah-shay]*

bulb ampoule, f. *[ah(m)pool]*

to burn brûler *[brewlay]*

bus autobus, m. *[ohtohbews]* bus, m. *[bews]* car, m. *[kahr]*

bus stop arrêt de bus, m. *[ahreh duh bews]*

business affaires, f.pl. *[ah-fehr]*

busy occupé *[ohkewpay]*

but mais *[meh]*

butcher shop boucherie, f. *[booshree]*

butter beurre, m. *[buhr]*

button bouton, m. *[bootoh(n)]*

buy acheter *[ahshtay]*

by par *[pahr]*

C

cabaret cabaret, m. *[kah-bahray]*

cabbage chou, m. *[shoo]*

café café, m. *[kahfay]*

to call (by name) (s')appeler *[(s)ahplay]*

to call back rappeler *[rah-play]*

calm tranquille *[trah(n)keel]*

camera appareil-photo, m. *[ahpahrehy fohtoh]*

camomile camomille, f. *[kahmohmeel]*

to camp camper *[kah(m)pay]*

can I . . . ? puis-je . . . ? *[pweezh]*

Canada Canada, m. *[Kah-nahdah]*

Canadian canadien *[kah-nahdya(n)]*

to cancel annuler *[ahnewlay]*

candle bougie, f. *[boozhee]*

car voiture, f. *[vwahtewr]*

car rental agency agence de location de voitures f. *[ahzhah(n)s duh lohkahsyoh(n) duh vewahtewr]*

carafe carafe, f. *[kahrahf]*

carbonated gazeux *[gahzuh]*

carburetor carburateur, m. *[kahrbewrahtuhr]*

card fiche, f. *[feesh]*

carefully avec soin *[ahvehk swa(n)]*

caretaker concierge m. or f. *[koh(n)syehrzh]*

carrot carotte, f. *[kahroht]*

to carry porter *[pohrtay]*

cart chariot, m. *[shahryoh]*

cash register caisse, f. *[kehs]*

cashier caissier, m. *[kehsyay]*

castle château, m. *[shahtoh]*

cat chat, m. *[shah]*

to catch attraper *[ahtrahpay]*

cathedral cathédrale, f. *[kahtaydrahl]*

cauliflower chou-fleur, m. *[shoo-fluhr]*

cave grotte, f. *[groht]*

CD player lecteur CD, m. *[lehktuhr sehdeh]*

ceiling plafond, m. *[plahfoh(n)]*

celery céleri, m. *[saylree]*

cell cellule, f. *[sehlewl]*

cellar cave, f. *[kahv]*

cell phone téléphone portable, m. *[taylayfohn pohrtabl]*

cemetery cimetière, m. *[seemtyehr]*

cent. (1/100 euro) cent, m. *[sah(n)]*

center centre, m. *[sah(n)tr]*

certainly certainement *[sehrtehnmah(n)]*

chain chaîne, f. *[shehn]*

chair chaise, f. *[shehz]*

change monnaie, f. *[mohneh]*

to change changer *[shah(n)zhay]*

change of train/bus changement, m. *[shah(n)zhmah(n)]*

chapel chapelle, f. *[shahpehl]*

cheap bon marché *[boh(n) mahrshay]*

check chèque, m. *[shehk]*

to check enregistrer (les bagages) *[ah(n)rehzheestray]*

cheese fromage, m. *[frohmahzh]*

cherry cerise, f. *[suhreez]*

chest poitrine, f. *[pwahtreen]*

chicken poulet, m. *[poolay]*

child enfant, m. or f. *[ah(n)fah(n)]*

chin menton, m. *[mah(n)toh(n)]*

choice choix, m. *[shwah]*

to choose choisir *[shwahzeer]*

church église, f. *[aygleez]*

cider cidre, m. *[seedr]*

cigar cigare, m. *[seegahr]*

cigarette cigarette, f. *[seegahreht]*

cigarette case étui à cigarettes, m. *[aytwee ah seegahreht]*

cinnamon cannelle, f. *[kahnehl]*

city ville, f. *[veel]*

classic classique *[klahseek]*

clean propre *[prohpr]*

to clean nettoyer *[nehtwahyay]*

clear clair *[klehr]*

cliff falaise, f. *[fahlehz]*

clock pendule, f. *[pah(n)dewl]*

to close fermer *[fehrmay]*

closet armoire, f. *[ahrmwahr]*

clothes vêtements, m.pl. *[vehtmah(n)]*

cloudy couvert *[koovehr]*

coast côte, f. *[koht]*

coat manteau, m. *[mah(n)toh]*

cod morue, f. *[mohrew]*

coffee café, m. *[kahfay]*

coffee with milk café au lait, m. *[kahfay oh leh]*

cognac cognac, m. *[kohnyahk]*

cold froid *[frwah]*

cold (virus) rhûme, m. *[rewm]*

cold (weather) froid, m. *[frwah]*

cold cuts charcuterie, f. *[shahrkewtree]*

collar col, m. *[kohl]*

colleague collègue, m. or f. *[kohlehg]*

collect (call) en P.C.V. *[ah(n) pay say vay]*

color couleur, f. *[kooluhr]*

comb peigne, m. *[pehnyuh]*

to come venir *[vuhneer]*

to come back revenir *[ruhvuhneer]*

company compagnie, f. *[koh(m)pahnyee]*

compartment compartiment, m. *[koh(m)pahrteemah(n)]*

complaint plainte, f. *[pla(n)t]*

concert concert, m. *[koh(n)sehr]*

to confirm confirmer *[koh(n)feermay]*

congratulations! félicitations! *[fayleeseetahsyoh(n)!]*

contact lens verre de contact, m. *[vehr duh koh(n)tahkt]* lentille, f. *[lah(n)teel]*

contents contenu, m. *[koh(n)tuhnew]*

continental breakfast petit déjeuner complet, m. *[puh-tee dayzhuhnay koh(m)play]*

to continue continuer *[koh(n)teenway]*

cook cuisinier, m. *[kweezeenyay]*

to cook faire cuire *[fehr kweer]*; faire la cuisine *[fehr lah kweezeen]*

cooked cuit *[kwee]*

cookies biscuits *[beeskwee]*

cooking cuisine, f. *[kweezeen]*

cool frais *[freh]*

corduroy velour côtelé, m. *[vuhloor kohtuhlay]*

corkscrew tire-bouchon, m. *[teer-booshoh(n)]*

corn maïs, m. *[mah-ees]*

corner coin, m. *[kwa(n)]*

correspondence correspondance, f. *[kohrehspoh(n)dah(n)s]*

to cost coûter *[kootay]*

cotton coton, m. *[kohtoh(n)]*

cough toux, f. *[too]*

to cough tousser *[toosay]*

to count compter *[koh(m)tay]*

country (landscape) campagne, f. *[kah(m)pahnyuh]*

country (nation) pays, m. *[payee]*

course cours, m. *[koor]*

courthouse palais de justice, m. *[pahleh duh zhew-stees]*

cousin cousin, m. *[kooza(n)]* cousine, f. *[koozeen]*

to cover couvrir *[koovreer]*

cover charge couvert, m. *[koovehr]*

covered couvert *[koovehr]*

crab crabe, m. *[krahb]*

cream crème, f. *[krehm]*

credit card carte de crédit, f. *[kahrt duh kraydee]* carte bleue, f. *[kahrt bluh]*

creole créole *[krayahl]*

creperie crêperie, f. *[kreh-pree]*

to cross (go across) traverser *[trahvehrsay]*

crosswalk passage clouté, m. *[pahsahzh klootay]* passage piétons, m. *[pahsahzh peeaytoh(n)]*

crust croûte, f. *[kroot]*

to cry pleurer *[pluhray]*

cucumber concombre, m. *[koh(n)koh(m)br]*

cup tasse, f. *[tahs]*

curl boucle, f. *[bookl]*

curlers bigoudis, m.pl. *[bee-goodee]*

currency monnaie, f. *[mohnay]* devise, f. *[duhveez]*

currency exchange office bureau de change, m. *[be-wroh duh shah(n)zh]*

custard flan, m. *[flah(n)]*

customer client, m. *[kleeah(n)]*

customs douane, f. *[dwahn]*

cut coupe, f. *[koop]*

to cut, cut off couper *[koo-pay]*

cutlet côtelette, f. *[kohtleht]*

cycling cyclisme, m. *[seek-leezm]*

D

daily quotidien *[kohteedya(n)]*

dance danse, f. *[dah(n)s]*

to dance danser *[dah(n)say]*

211

dangerous dangereux
[dah(n)zhuhruh]
dark foncé *[foh(n)say]*
date (fruit) datte, f. *[daht]*
daughter fille, f. *[feey]*
day jour, m. *[zhoor]*
by the day à la journée *[ah
lah zhoornay]*
the day after tomorrow
après-demain *[ahpreh-
duhma(n)]*
dead end voie sans issue, f.
[vwah sah(n) zeesew]
dear cher *[shehr]*
decaffeinated décaféiné
[daykahfayeenay]
December décembre *[day-
sah(m)br]*
to decide décider *[daysee-
day]*
to declare déclarer *[day-
klahray]*
deep-sea diving plongée
sous-marine, f. *[ploh(n)zhay
soo-mahreen]*
delay retard, m. *[ruhtahr]*
delicatessen charcuterie, f.
[shahrkewtree]
delighted enchanté *[ah(n)-
shah(n)tay]*
department store grand magasin, m. *[grah(n) mah-
gahza(n)]*
desire envie, f. *[ah(n)vee]*
desk bureau, m. *[bewroh]*
detour déviation, f.
[dayvyah-syoh(n)]
diabetic diabétique *[dyah-
bayteek]*
to dial composer *[koh(m)po-
hzay]*
diamond diamant, m.
[dyahmah(n)]
diaper couche, f. *[koosh]*
dictionary dictionnaire, m.
[deeksyohnehr]
diesel fuel gas-oil, m.
[gahzwahl]

diet régime, m. *[rayzheem]*
different différent
[deefayrah(n)]
difficult difficile *[deefeeseel]*
to diminish diminuer
[deemeeneway]
to dine dîner *[deenay]*
dining room salle à manger,
f. *[sahl ah mah(n)zhay]*
dinner dîner, m. *[deenay]*
direct flight vol direct, m.
[vohl deerehkt]
direction direction, f.
[deerehksyoh(n)]
sens, m. *[sah(n)s]*
directory (telephone) annuaire, m. *[ahnwehr]*
dirty sale *[sahl]*
disappointed déçu *[daysew]*
dish plat, m. *[plah]*
distance distance, f.
[deestah(n)s]
to disturb déranger
[dayrah(n)zhay]
divorced divorcé *[deevohrsay]*
do . . . ? est-ce que . . . ?
[ehskuh . . . ?]
to do faire *[fehr]*
doctor médecin, m.
[maydsa(n)]
dog chien, m. *[shyeh(n)]*
door porte, f. *[pohrt]*
doughnut beignet, m.
[behnyay]
downstairs en bas *[ah(n)bah]*
downtown centre ville, m.
[sah(n)truh veel]
dozen douzaine, f.
[doozehn]
drama drame, m. *[drahm]*
théâtre, m. *[tayahtr]*
dress robe, f. *[rohb]*
to dress s'habiller *[sah-
beeyay]*
dried fruit fruits secs m.pl.
[frwee sehk]
drink boisson, f.
[bwahsoh(n)]

to drink boire *[bwahr]*

to drive (a car) conduire *[koh(n)dweer]*

to drop off déposer *[daypohzay]*

drunk ivre *[eevr]*

dry sec *[sehk]*

to dry clean nettoyer à sec *[nehtwahyay ah sehk]*

dry cleaner pressing, m. *[prehseeng]*

dubbed doublé *[dooblay]*

duck canard, m. *[kahnahr]*

duckling caneton, m. *[kahntoh(n)]*

during pendant *[pah(n)dah(n)]*

duty-free shop magasin, m. *[mahgahza(n)]* duty-free *[dewtee free]*

E

each chaque *[shahk]*

each one chacun *[shahkuh(n)]*

ear oreille, f. *[ohrehy]*

early tôt *[toh]*

to earn gagner *[gahnyay]*

earring boucle d'oreille, f. *[bookl dohrehy]*

east est, m. *[ehst]*

easy facile *[fahseel]*

to eat manger *[mah(n)zhay]*

éclair (type of pastry) éclair, m. *[ayklehr]*

eel anguille, f. *[ah(n)geey]*

egg oeuf, m. *[uhf]*

eggplant aubergine, f. *[ohbehrzheen]*

eight huit *[weet]*

eighteen dix-huit *[dee-zweet]*

eighty quatre-vingts *[kahtr-va(n)]*

eldest aîné *[ehnay]*

electricity électricité, f. *[aylehktreeseetay]*

elevator ascenseur, m. *[ahsah(n)suhr]*

eleven onze *[oh(n)z]*

elsewhere ailleurs *[ahyuhr]*

emergency urgence, f. *[ewrzhah(n)s]*

emergency road service dépannage, m. *[daypahnahzh]*

empty vide *[veed]*

end fin, f. *[fa(n)]*

to end terminer *[tehrmeenay]*

England Angleterre, f. *[Ah(n)gluhtehr]*

English anglais *[ah(n)gleh]*

enlargement agrandissement, m. *[ahgrah(n)deesmah(n)]*

enough assez *[ahsay]*

entire entier *[ah(n)tyay]*

entrance entrée, f. *[ah(n)tray]*

entry prohibited défense d'entrer *[dayfah(n)s dah(n)tray]*

environment milieu, m. *[meelyuh]*

error erreur, f. *[ehruhr]*

euro euro, m. *[uhroh]*

evening soir, m. *[swahr]*

evening party soirée, f. *[swahray]*

every chaque *[shahk]*

everybody tout le monde *[too luh moh(n)d]*

everything tout *[too]*

everywhere partout *[pahrtoo]*

example exemple, m. *[ehgzah(m)pl]*

excellent excellent *[eksehlah(n)]*

exchange change, m. *[shah(n)zh]*

to exchange échanger *[ayshah(n)zhay]*

exchange office bureau de change, m. *[bewroh duh shah(n)zh]*

excursion excursion, f. *[ehkskewrsyoh(n)]*

excuse me pardon! *[pahrdoh(n)]*

to excuse excuser
  [ehkskewsay]
exhausted épuisé *[ayp-
  weezay]*
exit sortie, f. *[sohrtee]*
expensive cher *[shehr]*
extra supplément, m. *[sew-
  playmah(n)]*
eye oeil, m. *[uhy]*
eyeglasses lunettes, f.pl.
  [lewneht]
eyelash cil, m. *[seel]*

F

face visage, m. *[veezahzh]*
factory usine, f. *[ewzeen]*
fall (season) automne, m.
  [ohtohn]
to fall tomber *[toh(m)bay]*
false faux *[foh]*
to be familiar with connaître
  [kohnehtr]
family famille, f. *[fahmeey]*
far loin *[lwa(n)]*
farm ferme, f. *[fehrm]*
fast rapide *[rahpeed]*
fat gros *[groh]*
father père, m. *[pehr]*
father-in-law beau-père, m.
  [boh-pehr]
faucet robinet, m. *[ro-
  hbeenay]*
fear peur, f. *[puhr]*
to fear avoir peur de
  [ahvwahr puhr duh]
February février *[fayvreeyay]*
to feel se sentir *[suh sah(n)-
  teer]*
fever fièvre, f. *[fyehvr]*
few peu de *[puh duh]*
field champ, m. *[shah(m)]*
fifteen quinze *[ka(n)z]*
fifty cinquante *[se(n)kah(n)t]*
fig figue, f. *[feeg]*
fillet filet, m. *[feelay]*

fill it up faites le plein *[feht
  luh pla(n)]*
film cinéma, m. *[seenaymah]*
film cartridge pellicule, f.
  [pehleekewl]
to find trouver *[troovay]*
fine arts beaux arts, m.pl.
  [boh zahr]
finger doigt, m. *[dwah]*
to finish finir *[feeneer]*
fire feu, m. *[fuh]*
first premier *[pruhmyay]*
fish poisson, m. *[pwahsoh(n)]*
five cinq *[sa(n)]*
fixed fixe *[feeks]*
fixed-price menu menu à
  prix fixe, m. *[muhnew ah
  pree feeks]*
flashlight lampe de poche,
  f. *[lah(m)p duh pohsh]*
flat plat *[plah]*
flavor parfum, m.
  [pahrfuh(m)]
flea market marché aux
  puces, m. *[mahrshay oh pews]*
flight vol, m. *[vohl]*
flight attendant hôtesse de
  l'air, f. *[ohtehs duh lehr]*
floor plancher, m.
  [plah(n)shay]
flour farine, f. *[fahreen]*
flower fleur, f. *[fluhr]*
flute flûte, f. *[flewt]*
to fly voler *[vohlay]*
fog brouillard, m. *[brooyahr]*
folkloric folklorique *[fohlk-
  lohreek]*
to follow suivre *[sweevr]*
food nourriture, f.
  [nooreetewr]
foot pied, m. *[pyay]*
on foot à pied *[ah pyay]*
for pour *[poor]*
forbidden interdit
  [a(n)tehrdee]
foreign étranger
  [aytrah(n)zhay]

foreigner étranger, m. *[ay-trah(n)zhay]*

forest forêt, f. *[fohreh]*

to forget oublier *[oobleeyay]*

to forgive pardonner *[pahrdohnay]*

fork fourchette, f. *[foorsheht]*

form formulaire, m. *[fohrmewlehr]*

format format, m. *[fohrmah]*

fortress forteresse, f. *[fohrtuhrehs]*

forty quarante *[kahrah(n)t]*

forward en avant *[ah(n)nahvah(n)]*

fountain fountaine, f. *[foh(n)tehn]*

four quatre *[kahtr]*

fourteen quatorze *[kahtohrz]*

fowl volaille, f. *[vohlahy]*

franc franc, m. *[frah(n)]*

France France, f. *[Frah(n)s]*

free libre *[leebr]*

French français *[frah(n)say]*

French bread baguette, f. *[bahgeht]*

fresh frais *[freh]*

Friday vendredi *[vah(n)druhdee]*

fried frit *[free]*

friend ami, m. *[ahmee]* amie, f. *[ahmee]*

friendship amitié, f. *[ahmeetyay]*

frog grenouille, f. *[gruhnooy]*

from de *[duh]*

in front of devant *[duhvah(n)]*

frost verglas, m. *[vehrglah]*

frozen glacé *[glahsay]*

fruit fruit, m. *[frwee]*

to have fun s'amuser *[sahmewzay]*

furnished meublé *[muhblay]*

furniture meubles, m.pl. *[muhbl]*

G

to gain weight grossir *[grohseer]*

game (child's play) jeu, m. *[zhuh]*

game (wild) gibier, m. *[zheebyay]*

garage garage, m. *[gahrahzh]*

garden jardin, m. *[zhahrda(n)]*

garlic ail, m. *[ahy]*

gasoline essence, f. *[ehsah(n)s]*

gastronomical gastronomique *[gahstrohnohmeek]*

general delivery poste restante, f. *[pohst rehstah(n)t]*

German allemand *[ahlmah(n)]*

Germany Allemagne, f. *[Ahlmahnyuh]*

to get off descendre *[dehsah(n)dr]*

to get up se lever *[suh luhvay]*

gift cadeau, m. *[kahdoh]*

ginger gingembre, m. *[zha(n)zhah(m)br]*

girl fille, f. *[feey]*

to give donner *[dohnay]*

glass verre, m. *[vehr]*

glove gant, m. *[gah(n)]*

to go aller *[ahlay]*

to go down descendre *[dehsah(n)dr]*

to go up monter *[moh(n)tay]*

gold or, m. *[ohr]*

golf course terrain de golf, m. *[tehra(n) duh gohlf]*

good bon *[boh(n)]*

good-bye au revoir *[oh rvwahr]*

goodness! mon dieu! *[Moh(n) dyuh]*

goose oie, f. *[wah]*

215

gourmet cooking grande cuisine, f. *[grah(n)d kweezeen]*

gourmet menu menu gastronomique, m. *[muhnew gahstrohnohmeek]*

granddaughter petite fille, f. *[puhteet feey]*

grandfather grand-père, m. *[grah(n)-pehr]*

grandmother grand-mère, f. *[grah(n)-mehr]*

grandson petit fils, m. *[puhtee fees]*

grape raisin, m. *[rayza(n)]*

grapefruit pamplemousse, m. *[pah(m)pluhmoos]*

grass herbe, f. *[ehrb]*

grave tombe, f. *[toh(m)b]*

gray gris *[gree]*

great super *[sewpehr]*

green vert *[vehr]*

green beans haricots verts, m.pl. *[ahreekoh vehr]*

grilled grillé *[greeyay]*

grocery épicerie, f. *[aypeesree]*

ground sol, m. *[sohl]*

ground floor rez-de-chaussée, m. *[ray-duh-shohsay]*

guide guide, m. or f. *[geed]*

guided guidé *[geeday]*

H

hair cheveux, m.pl. *[shuhvuh]*

hair dryer sèche-cheveux, m. *[sehsh-shuhvuh]*

haircut coupe de cheveux, f. *[koop duh shuhvuh]*

hairdresser coiffeur, m. *[kwahfuhr]*

hairdresser's shop salon de beauté, m. *[sahloh(n) duh bohtay]*; salon de coiffure, m. *[sahloh(n) duh kwahfuhr]*

hairpin épingle à cheveux, f. *[aypa(n)gl ah shuhvuh]*

half demi *[duhmee]*

half bottle demi-bouteille, f. *[duhmee-bootehy]*

hall porter portier, m. *[pohrteeyay]*

ham jambon, m. *[zhah(m)boh(n)]*

hand main, f. *[ma(n)]*

handbag sac à main, m. *[sahk ahma(n)]*

handicapped handicapé *[a(n)deekahpay]*

handkerchief mouchoir, m. *[mooshwahr]*

handmade fait main *[feh ma(n)]*

handsome beau *[boh]*

hanger cintre, m. *[sa(n)tr]*

happy heureux *[uhruh]*

harbor port, m. *[pohr]*

hardware store quincaillerie, f. *[ka(n)kahyree]*

to have avoir *[ahvwahr]*

to have fun s'amuser *[sah-mewzay]*

he il *[eel]*

head tête, f. *[teht]*

headlights phares, m.pl. *[fahr]*

health santé, f. *[sah(n)tay]*

to hear entendre *[ah(n)tah(n)dr]*

heart coeur, m. *[kuhr]*

hearty appetite bon appétit *[boh(n) nahpaytee]*

heat chauffage, m. *[shohfahzh]*

heavy lourd *[loor]*

heel talon, m. *[tahloh(n)]*

height hauteur, f. *[ohtuhr]*

hello bonjour *[boh(n)zhoor]*

help secours, m. *[suhkoor]*

to help aider *[ehday]*

hen poule, f. *[pool]*

her (possessive) sa/son/ses *[sah/soh(n)/say]*

her (herself) se/lui/la
 [suh/lwee/lah]
herb herbe, f. *[ehrb]*
here ici *[eesee]*
here is . . . voici . . . *[vwah-
 see . . .]*
high haut *[oh]*
high school lycée, m. *[leesay]*
high tide marée haute, f.
 [mahray oht]
higher supérieur *[sew-
 payryuhr]*
highway autoroute, f.
 [ohtohroot]
highway ends fin d'autoroute *[fa(n) dohtohroot]*
hill colline, f. *[kohleen]* côte,
 f. *[koht]*
him se/lui/le *[suh/lwee/luh]*
to hire louer *[looay]*
his sa/son/ses
 [sah/soh(n)/say]
history histoire, f. *[eestwahr]*
to hit frapper *[frahpay]*
hole trou, m. *[troo]*
holiday jour férié, m. *[zhoor
 fehryay]*
to hope espérer *[ehspayray]*
horse cheval, m. *[shuhvahl]*
hospital hôpital, m. *[oh-
 peetahl]*
host (restaurant) maître
 d'hôtel, m. *[mehtr dohtehl]*
hot chaud *[shoh]*
hotel hôtel, m. *[ohtehl]*
hour heure, f. *[uhr]*
house maison, f. *[mehzoh(n)]*
at the house of chez *[shay]*
household appliances ap-
 pareils ménagers, m.pl.
 [ahpahrehy maynahzhay]
how comment *[kohmah(n)]*
how do you say . . . ? comment dit-on . . . ?
 [kohmah(n) deetoh(n) . . .]
how many, how much combien *[koh(m)byeh(n)]*
hundred cent *[sah(n)]*

hunger faim, f. *[fa(m)]*
to hurry se dépêcher *[suh
 daypehshay]*
husband mari, m. *[mahree]*

I

I je *[zhuh]*
ice glace, f. *[glahs]*
ice cream glace, f. *[glahs]*
ice-cream cone cornet de
 glace, m. *[kohrnay duh glahs]*
ice cube glaçon, m. *[glah-
 soh(n)]*
iced glacé *[glahsay]*
if si *[see]*
ill malade *[mahlahd]*
illness maladie, f.
 [mahlahdee]
important important
 [a(m)pohrtah(n)]
impossible impossible
 [a(m)pohseebl]
in dans *[dah(n)]* en *[ah(n)]*
in back of derrière *[dehryehr]*
in front of devant *[duhvah(n)]*
in spite of malgré *[mahlgray]*
included compris *[koh(m)pree]*
to indicate indiquer
 [a(n)deekay]
to inform renseigner
 [rah(n)sehnyay]
information renseignements, m.pl.
 [rah(n)sehnyuhmah(n)]
infusion infusion, f.
 [a(n)fewzyoh(n)]
in-laws beaux-parents,
 m.pl. *[boh-pahrah(n)]*
inn auberge, f. *[ohbehrzh]*
inside dedans *[duhdah(n)]*
instant coffee café soluble,
 m. *[kahfay sohlewbl]*
instead of au lieu de *[oh lyuh
 duh]*
intelligent intelligent
 [a(n)tehleezhah(n)]

217

to be interested in s'intéresser à [sa(n)tayrehsay ah]
interesting intéressant
[a(n)tayrehsah(n)]
intersection carrefour, m.
[kahrfoor]
to introduce présenter
[prayzah(n)tay]
to invite inviter [a(n)veetay]
iron fer, m. [fehr]
to iron repasser [ruhpahsay]
is . . . ? est-ce que . . . ?
[ehskuh . . . ?]
it is, this is c'est [seh]
island île, f. [eel]
ivory ivoire, f. [eevwahr]

J

jack cric, m. [kreek]
jacket veste, f. [vehst]
jam confiture, f.
[koh(n)feetewr]
January janvier [zhah(n)vyay]
jar bocal, m. [bohkahl]
jewelry box coffret à bijoux, m. [kohfray ah beezhoo]
jewelry shop bijouterie, f.
[beezhootree]
jewels bijoux, m.pl.
[beezhoo]
job travail, m. [trahvahy]
jogging footing, m.
[footeeng] jogging, m. [zho-
hgeeng]
joke plaisanterie, f.
[playzah(n)tree]
to judge juger [zhewzhay]
juice jus, m. [zhew]
July juillet [zhweeay]
June juin [zhwa(n)]

K

to keep garder [gahrday]
keep right serrez à droite
[sehray ah drwaht]

key clé, f. [klay]
kilometer kilomètre, m.
[keelohmehtr]
kiosk kiosque, m. [keeohsk]
to kiss embrasser [ah(m)brah-
say]
kitchen cuisine, f. [kweezeen]
knee genou, m. [zhuhnoo]
knife couteau, m. [kootoh]
to knock frapper [frahpay]
to know (be familiar with)
connaître [kohnehtr]
to know (facts) savoir
[sahvwahr]
kosher kasher [kahshehr]

L

lace dentelle, f. [dah(n)tehl]
lack manque, m. [mah(n)k]
to lack manquer [mah(n)kay]
ladder échelle, f. [ayshehl]
lake lac, m. [lahk]
lamb mouton, m. [mootoh(n)]
land terre, f. [tehr]
landscape paysage, m.
[payeezahzh]
language langue, f. [lah(n)g]
last dernier [dehrnyay]
to last durer [dewray]
late tard [tahr]
to laugh rire [reer]
laundromat laverie automatique, f. [lahvree ohtohmah-
teek]
laundry blanchisserie, f.
[blah(n)sheesree]
lawyer avocat, m.
[ahvohkah]
layover escale, f. [ehskahl]
to learn apprendre
[ahprah(n)dr]
at least au moins [oh mwa(n)]
leather cuir, m. [kweer]
to leave (depart) partir
[pahrteer]

to leave (behind) laisser *[lehsay]*

leek poireau, m. *[pwahroh]*

left gauche, f. *[gohsh]*

leg jambe, f. *[zhah(m)b]*

lemon citron, m. *[seetroh(n)]*

lemonade (fizzy) limonade, f. *[leemohnahd]* **(still)** citron-nade, f. *[seetrohnahd]*

to lend prêter *[prehtay]*

lens objectif, m. *[ohbzhehk-teef]* lentille, f. *[lah(n)teey]*

less moins *[mwa(n)]*

lesson leçon, f. *[luhsoh(n)]*

to let laisser *[lehsay]*

letter lettre, f. *[lehtr]*

lettuce laitue, f. *[lehtew]*

level niveau, m. *[neevoh]*

lever levier, m. *[layvyay]*

library bibliothèque, f. *[bee-bleeohtehk]*

license permis, m. *[pehrmee]*

life vie, f. *[vee]*

lifeguard maître nageur, m. *[mehtrnahzhur]*

light (adj.) léger *[layzhay]*

light lumière, f. *[lewmyehr]*

to light allumer *[ahlewmay]*

light meal repas léger, m. *[ruhpah layzhay]*

light wine vin léger, m. *[va(n) layzhay]*

lighter briquet, m. *[breekay]*

like, as comme *[kohm]*

to like aimer *[ehmay]*

I'd like je voudrais *[zhuh voodreh]*

lime citron vert, m. *[seetroh(n) vehr]*

line ligne, f. *[leenyuh]*

line (of people) queue, f. *[kuh]*

linen lin, m. *[la(n)]*

lipstick rouge à lévre, m. *[roozh ah lehvr]*

liquor liqueur, f. *[leekuhr]*

list liste, f. *[leest]*

to listen écouter *[aykootay]*

liter litre, m. *[leetr]*

little, few peu *[puh]*

to live habiter *[ahbeetay]*

liver foie, m. *[fwah]*

living room salon, m. *[sahloh(n)]*

lobster homard, m. *[ahmahr]* langouste, f. *[lah(n)goost]*

local local *[lohkahl]*

local wine vin du pays, m. *[va(n) dew payee]*

long long *[loh(n)]*

for a long time longtemps *[loh(n)tah(m)]*

to look at regarder *[ruhgahr-day]*

to look for chercher *[shehr-shay]*

to lose perdre *[pehrdr]*

to lose weight maigrir *[mehgreer]*

lost perdu *[pehrdew]*

lost and found bureau des objets trouvés, m. *[bewroh dohbzhay troovay]*

a lot beaucoup *[bohkoo]*

lotion lotion, f. *[lohsyoh(n)]*

love amour, m. *[ahmoor]*

to love adorer *[ahdohray]* aimer *[ehmay]*

low bas *[bah]*

low tide marée basse, f. *[mahray bahs]*

luck chance, f. *[shah(n)s]*

good luck! bonne chance! *[bohn shah(n)s!]*

luggage bagages, m.pl. *[bahgahzh]*

lunch déjeuner, m. *[dayzhuh-nay]*

luxury luxe, m. *[lewks]*

M

machine appareil, m. *[ah-pahrehy]*

madam madame *[mahdahm]*

magazine magazine, m.
[mahgahzeen]

mail courrier, m. *[kooryay]*

to mail poster *[pohstay]*

mailbox boîte aux lettres, f.
[bwaht oh lehtr]

maître d' maître d'hôtel, m.
[mehtr dohtehl]

to make faire *[fehr]*

makeup maquillage, m.
[mahkeeyahzh]

man homme, m. *[ohm]*

manager gérant, m.
[zhayrah(n)] directeur, m.
[deerehktewr]

manicurist manucure,
f. or m. *[mahnewkewr]*

many beaucoup *[bohkoo]*

map carte, f. *[kahrt]* plan,
m. *[plah(n)]*

March mars *[mahrs]*

marjoram marjolaine, f.
[mahrzhohlehn]

market marché, m. *[mahr-shay]*

married marié *[mahryay]*

marvelous merveilleux
[mehrvehyuh]

mass messe, f. *[mehs]*

match allumette, f.
[ahlewmeht]

What's the matter? Qu'est-
ce qu'il y a? *[Kehs keel yah?]*

May mai *[meh]*

maybe peut-être *[puh-tehtr]*

mayonnaise mayonnaise, f.
[mahyohnehz]

me me/moi *[muh/mwah]*

meal repas, m. *[ruhpah]*

to mean vouloir dire *[vool-wahr deer]*

meaning sens, m. *[sah(n)s]*
signification, f. *[see-nyeefeekahsyoh(n)]*

means moyens, m.pl.
[mwahya(n)]

meat viande, f. *[vyah(n)d]*

mechanic mécanicien, m.
[maykahneesya(n)]

medicine médecine, f.
[maydseen]

medieval médiéval *[maydyay-vahl]*

to meet rencontrer
[rah(n)koh(n)tray]

meeting réunion, f.
[rayewnyoh(n)]

melon melon, m. *[muhloh(n)]*

menu carte, f. *[kahrt]* menu,
m. *[muhnew]*

merchant marchand, m.
[mahrshah(n)]

middle milieu, m. *[meelyuh]*

in the middle of au milieu
de *[oh meelyuh duh]*

midnight minuit *[meenwee]*

mileage kilométrage, m.
[keelohmehtrahzh]

milk lait, m. *[leh]*

with milk au lait *[oh leh]*

mineral minéral *[meenayrahl]*

mineral water eau
minérale, f. *[oh meenayrahl]*

mint menthe, f. *[mah(n)t]*

minute minute, f. *[meenewt]*

mirror miroir, m, *[meerwahr]*

miss (woman) mademoiselle
[mahdmwahzehl]

to miss manquer *[mah(n)kay]*

mistake faute, f. *[foht]*

mister, sir monsieur *[muh-syuh]*

moment moment, m.
[mohmah(n)]

monastery monastère, m.
[mohnahstehr]

Monday lundi *[luh(n)dee]*

money, change monnaie, f.
[mohneh]

money, silver argent, m.
[ahrzhah(n)]

month mois, m. *[mwah]*

moon lune, f. *[lewn]*

more plus *[plew]*

morning matin, m. *[mahta(n)]*

mosque mosquée, f. *[mohskay]*

mother mère, f. *[mehr]*

mother-in-law belle-mère, f. *[behl-mehr]*

mountain montagne, f. *[moh(n)tahnyuh]*

mountain pass col, m. *[kohl]*

mousse mousse, f. *[moos]*

mouth bouche, f. *[boosh]*

movies, movie theater cinéma, m. *[seenaymah]*

Mr. monsieur *[muhsyuh]*

Mrs. madame *[mahdahm]*

much beaucoup *[bohkoo]*

museum musée, m. *[mewzay]*

mushroom champignon, m. *[shah(m)peenyoh(n)]*

music musique, f. *[mewzeek]*

mussels moules, f.pl. *[mool]*

mustache moustache, f. *[moostahsh]*

mustard moutarde, f. *[mootahrd]*

my ma/mon/mes *[mah/moh(n)/may]*

N

nail ongle, m. *[oh(n)gl]*

nail cutter coupe-ongles, m. *[koop-oh(n)gl]*

nail file lime à ongles, f. *[leem ah oh(n)gl]*

nail polish vernis à ongles, m. *[vehrnee ah oh(n)gl]*

name nom, m. *[noh(m)]*

to be named s'appeler *[sah-play]*

napkin serviette, f. *[sehrvyeht]*

napoleon (type of pastry) mille-feuille, m. *[meel-fuhy]*

narrow étroit *[aytrwah]*

nationality nationalité, f. *[nahsyohnahleetay]*

nature nature, f. *[nahtewr]*

near près (de) *[preh (duh)]*

nearby proche *[prohsh]*

necessary nécessaire *[naysehsehr]*

it is necessary il faut *[eel foh]*

neck cou, m. *[koo]*

necklace collier, m. *[kohlyay]*

necktie cravate, f. *[krahvaht]*

nectarine brugnon, m. *[brewnyoh(n)]*

to need avoir besoin de *[ahvwahr buhzwa(n) duh]*

neighbor voisin, m. *[vwahza(n)]*

neighborhood quartier, m. *[kahrtyay]*

net filet, m. *[feelay]*

never jamais *[zhahmay]*

new nouveau, m. *[noovoh]* nouvelle, f. *[noovehl]*

new cuisine nouvelle cuisine, f. *[noovehl kweezeen]*

newspaper/s journal/journaux, m. *[zhoornal/zhoornoh]*

newsstand kiosque à journaux, m. *[keeohsk ah zhoornoh]*

next (adj.) prochain *[prohsha(n)]*

next ensuite *[ah(n)sweet]*

nice gentil *[zhah(n)teey]*

night nuit, f. *[nwee]*

nightclub boîte de nuit, f. *[bwaht duh nwee]*

nine neuf *[nuhf]*

nineteen dix-neuf *[deez-nuhf]*

ninety quatre-vingt-dix *[kahtruh-va(n)-dees]*

no non *[noh(n)]*

nonsmoking section salle non-fumeurs, f. *[sahl noh(n)-fumuhr]*

noodles nouilles, f. *[nooy]*

noon midi *[meedee]*

north nord, m. *[nohr]*

nose nez, m. *[nay]*

not at all pas du tout *[pah dew too]*

notebook cahier, m. *[kahyay]*
nothing rien *[reeya(n)]*
to notice remarquer *[ruhmahrkay]*
novel roman, m. *[rohmah(n)]*
November novembre *[no-hvah(m)br]*
now maintenant *[ma(n)tuh-nah(n)]*
number chiffre, m. *[sheefr]* numéro, m. *[newmayroh]* nombre, m. *[noh(m)br]*
numbered numéroté *[new-mayrohtay]*
nurse infirmière, f. *[a(n)feer-myehr]*
nut noix, f. *[nwah]*

O

object objet, m. *[ohbzhay]*
to be obliged to devoir *[duhvwahr]*
to obtain obtenir *[ohbtuhneer]*
ocean océan, m. *[ohsayah(n)]*
October octobre *[ohktohbr]*
odd impair *[a(m)pehr]*
of, from de *[duh]*
of course bien sûr *[byeh(n)-sewr]*
to offer offrir *[ohfreer]*
office bureau, m. *[bewroh]*
often souvent *[soovah(n)]*
oil huile, f. *[weel]*
okay d'accord *[dahkohr]*
old vieux, m. *[vyuh]* vieille, f. *[vyehy]*
omelette omelette, f. *[ohm-leht]*
on sur *[sewr]*
on foot à pied *[ah pyay]*
on time à l'heure *[ah luhr]*
one un, m. *[uh(n)]* une, f. *[ewn]*
one (we) on *[oh(n)]*
one-way sens unique *[sah(n)s ewneek]*

one-way ticket aller simple, m. *[ahlay sa(m)pl]*
onion oignon, m. *[ohnyoh(n)]*
only seulement *[suhlmah(n)]*
open ouvert *[oovehr]*
to open ouvrir *[oovreer]*
operator opérateur, m. *[oh-payrahtewr]*
opportunity occasion, f. *[ohkahzyoh(n)]*
opposite contraire, m. *[koh(n)trehr]*
opposite (across from) en face de *[ah(n)fahs duh]*
or ou *[oo]*
orange orange, f. *[ohrah(n)zh]*
orangeade orangeade, f. *[ohrah(n)zhahd]*
orchestra orchestre, m. *[ohrkehstr]*
orchestra leader chef d'orchestre, m. *[shehf dohrkehstr]*
to order commander *[kohmah(n)day]*
ordinary ordinaire *[ohrdeenehr]*
oregano origan, m. *[ohree-gah(n)]*
other autre *[ohtr]*
our notre/nos *[nohtr/noh]*
outdoors plein air *[pleh nehr]*
outfit tenue, f. *[tuhnew]*
outside en plein air *[ah(n)-pleh nehr]* dehors *[dehohr]*
oven four, m. *[foor]*
over dessus *[duhsew]*
overcoat manteau, m. *[mah(n)toh]*
overseas à l'étranger *[ah laytrah(n)zhay]*
to owe devoir *[duhvwahr]*
own propre *[prohpr]*
owner propriétaire, m. *[prohpreeaytehr]*
oyster huître, f. *[weetr]*

P

pack paquet, m. *[pahkay]*

package colis, m. *[kohlee]*

packet paquet, m. *[pahkay]*

pain douleur, f. *[dooluhr]*

painter peintre, m. *[pa(n)tr]*

painting peinture, f.
[pa(n)tewr] tableau, m. *[tah-bloh]*

pair paire, f. *[pehr]*

pajamas pyjama, m.
[peezhahmah]

pancake crêpe, f. *[krehp]*

panorama panorama, m.
[pahnohrahmah]

pants pantalon, m.
[pah(n)tahloh(n)]

paper papier, m. *[pahpyay]*

park parc, m. *[pahrk]*

to park (se) garer
[(suh)gahray]

parking stationnement, m.
[stahsyohnmah(n)]

parking lot parking, m.
[pahrkeeng]

parking meter parcmètre,
m. *[pahrkmehtr]*

parking prohibited stationnement interdit *[stahsyohn-
mah(n) a(n)tehrdee]*

parking side côté du sta-
tionnement, m. *[kohtay dew
stahsyohnmah(n)]*

parsley persil, m. *[persee]*

part partie, f. *[pahrtee]*

party fête f. *[feht]*; soirée, f.
[swahreh]

to pass passer *[pahsay]*

passage passage, m. *[pah-
sahzh]*

passport passeport, m.
[pahspohr]

pasta pâtes, f.pl. *[paht]*

pastry shop pâtisserie, f.
[pahteesree]

to pay payer *[payay]*

peach pêche, f. *[pehsh]*

peak sommet, m. *[sohmay]*

pear poire, f. *[pwahr]*

peas petits pois, m.pl. *[puh-
tee pwah]*

pedestrian piéton, m. *[pyay-
toh(n)]*

pedestrian crosswalk pas-
sage piétons, m. *[pahsahzh
peeaytoh(n)]*

pedestrians prohibited interdit aux piétons *[a(n)tehrdee
oh pyaytoh(n)]*

pen stylo, m. *[steeloh]*

pencil crayon, m. *[krayoh(n)]*

people gens, f.pl. *[zhah(n)]*

pepper poivre, m. *[pwahvr]*

perfect parfait *[pahrfeh]*

performance représenta-
tion, f. *[ruhprayzah(n)tah-
syoh(n)]*

perfume parfum, m.
[pahrfuh(m)]

perhaps peut-être *[puh-tehtr]*

period période, f. *[payryohd]*

permanent wave mise en
plis, f. *[meez ah(n) plee]*

to permit permettre *[pehrme-
htr]*

person personne, f.
[pehrsohn]

personal personnel
[pehrsohnehl]

to persuade persuader *[pehr-
swahday]*

pharmacy pharmacie, f.
[fahrmahsee]

phone téléphone, m. *[taylay-
fohn]*

phone directory annuaire,
m. *[ahnewehr]*

photograph photo, f. *[fohtoh]*

to photograph photogra-
phier *[fohtohgrahfyay]*

pickle cornichon, m.
[kohrneeshoh(n)]

pie tarte, f. *[tahrt]*

pig cochon, m. *[kohshoh(n)]*

pill pillule, f. *[peelewl]*
pillow oreiller, m. *[ohrehyay]*
pin épingle, f. *[aypa(n)gl]*
pineapple ananas, m. *[ah-nahnahs]*
pink rose *[rohz]*
place endroit, m. *[ah(n)drwah]*
plan plan, m. *[plah(n)]*
planetarium planétarium, m. *[plahnaytahryuhm]*
plate assiette, f. *[ahsyeht]*
platform quai, m. *[keh]*
play (literary) pièce de théâtre, f. *[pyehs duh tayahtr]*
to play jouer *[zhooay]*
player joueur, m. *[zhoouhr]*
playground terrain de jeu, m. *[tehra(n) duh zhuh]*
please s'il vous plaît *[seel voo pleh]*
pleasure plaisir, m. *[ple-hzeer]*
plum prune, f. *[prewn]*
pocket poche, f. *[pohsh]*
pocketbook sac, m. *[sahk]*
police station commissariat, m. *[kohmeesahryah]* poste de police, m. *[pohst duh pohlees]*
policeman agent de police, m. *[ahzhah(n) duh pohlees]*
pond étang, m. *[aytah(n)]*
pool piscine, f. *[peeseen]*
poor pauvre *[pohvr]*
pork porc, m. *[pohr]*
porter porteur, m. *[pohrtuhr]*
portion portion, f. *[pohrsyoh(n)]*
to possess posséder *[pohsay-day]*
post office bureau de poste, m. *[bewroh duh pohst]* poste; f. *[pohst]*
postcard carte postale, f. *[kahrt pohstahl]*
potato pomme de terre, f. *[pohm duh tehr]*
pottery poterie, f. *[pohtree]*

practical pratique *[prahteek]*
precious stone pierre précieuse, f. *[pyehr praysyuhz]*
to prefer préférer *[pray-fayray]*
pregnant enceinte *[ah(n)sa(n)t]*
to prepare préparer *[pray-pahray]*
prescription ordonnance, f. *[ohrdohnah(n)s]*
present cadeau, m. *[kahdoh]*
to present présenter *[prayzah(n)tay]*
pressure pression, f. *[prehsyoh(n)]*
pretty joli *[zhohlee]*
price (cost) prix, m. *[pree]*
price (rate) tarif, m. *[tahreef]*
priest prêtre, m. *[prehtr]*
print épreuve, f. *[aypruhv]*
priority priorité, f. *[preeohreetay]*
private privé *[preevay]*
private property propriété privée, f. *[prohpreeaytay preevay]*
profession profession, f. *[prohfehsyoh(n)]*
to prohibit interdire *[a(n)tehrdeer]*
to promise promettre *[prohmehtr]*
to pronounce prononcer *[prohnoh(n)say]*
to protect protéger *[pro-htayzhay]*
prune pruneau, m. *[prewnoh]*
public public *[peubleek]*
purchase achat, m. *[ahshah]*
purple violet *[vyohlay]*
to push pousser *[poosay]*
to put, put on mettre *[mehtr]*

Q

quality qualité, f. *[kahleetay]*

quarter quart, m. *[kahr]*
question question, f. *[kehstyoh(n)]*
quiche quiche, f. *[keesh]*
quickly vite *[veet]*

R

rabbi rabbin, m. *[rahba(n)]*
rabbit lapin, m. *[lahpa(n)]*
radiator radiateur, m. *[rahdyahtuhr]*
radio poste de radio, m. *[pohst duh rahdyoh]* radio, f. *[radyoh]*
railroad chemin de fer, m. *[shuhma(n) duh fehr]*
railroad crossing passage à niveau, m. *[pahsahzh ah neevah]*
railroad station gare, f. *[gahr]*
rain pluie, f. *[plwee]*
it's raining il pleut *[eel pluh]*
raisins raisins secs, m.pl. *[rayza(n) sehk]*
rapid rapide *[rahpeed]*
rare (meat) saignant *[sehnyah(n)]*
raspberry framboise, f. *[frah(m)bwahz]*
rather plutôt *[plewtoh]*
raw vegetables crudités, f.pl. *[krewdeetay]*
razor rasoir, m. *[rahzwahr]*
to read lire *[leer]*
ready prêt *[preh]*
really vraiment *[vrehhmah(n)]*
reason raison, f. *[rehzoh(n)]*
reasonable raisonnable *[rehzohnahbl]*
receipt reçu, m. *[ruhsoo]*
to receive recevoir *[ruhsuhvwahr]*
recent récent *[raysah(n)]*
to recommend recommander *[ruhkohmah(n)day]*

recording enregistrement, m. *[ah(n)rehzheestruhmah(n)]*
red rouge *[roozh]*
red wine vin rouge, m. *[va(n) roozh]*
reduction réduction, f. *[raydewksyoh(n)]*
refreshing rafraîchissant *[rahfrehsheesah(n)]*
to refuse refuser *[ruhfewzay]*
to register, check enregistrer *[ah(n)rehzheestray]*
to regret regretter *[ruhgrehtay]*
to reimburse rembourser *[rah(m)boorsay]*
to remain rester *[rehstay]*
to remember se rappeler *[suh rahplay]*
rent loyer, m. *[lwahyay]*
to rent louer *[looay]*
to repair réparer *[raypahray]*
to repeat répéter *[raypaytay]*
to represent représenter *[ruhprayzah(n)tay]*
to resemble ressembler *[ruhsah(m)blay]*
reservation réservation, f. *[rayzehrvahsyoh(n)]*
to reserve réserver *[rayzehrvay]*
reserved for buses réservé aux (auto)bus *[rayzehrvay oh zohtohbews]*
responsible responsable *[rehspoh(n)sahbl]*
rest repos, m. *[ruhpoh]*
to rest se reposer *[suh ruhpohzay]*
restaurant restaurant, m. *[rehstohrah(n)]*
result résultat, m. *[rayzewltah]*
retirement retraite, f. *[ruhtreht]*
to return (something) rendre *[rah(n)dr]*

225

to return (to) rentrer
[rah(n)tray]
returned de retour *[duh ruh-toor]*
rice riz, m. *[ree]*
right (direction) droite, f. *[dr-waht]*
right (legal/moral) droit, m. *[drwah]*
right away tout de suite *[tood sweet]*
ring bague, f. *[bahg]*
risk risque, m. *[reesk]*
river fleuve, m. *[fluhv]* riv-ière f. *[reevyehr]*
road (highway) route, f. *[root]*
road (way) chemin, m. *[shuhma(n)]*
road map carte routière, f. *[kahrt rootyehr]*
roast rôti, m. *[rohtee]*
roast beef rosbif, m. *[rohs-beef]*
roll (bread) petit pain, m. *[puhtee pa(n)]*
roll of film pellicule, f. *[pehleekewl]*
to roll, drive rouler *[roolay]*
roof toit, m. *[twah]*
room salle, f. *[sahl]* pièce, f. *[pyehs]*
room (bedroom) chambre, f. *[shah(m)br]*
room service service d'é-tage, m. *[sehrvees daytahzh]*
room with all meals pension complète, f. *[pah(n)syoh(n) koh(m)pleht]*
rooster coq, m. *[kohk]*
rosé wine vin rosé, m. *[va(n) rohzay]*
rosemary romarin, m. *[rohmahra(n)]*
round-trip ticket aller-retour, m. *[ahlay-ruhtoor]*
rowboat barque, f. *[bahrk ah rahm]*

rug tapis, m. *[tahpee]*
ruins ruines, f.pl. *[rween]*
rule règle, f. *[rehgl]*
to run courir *[kooreer]*
running footing, m. *[footeeng]*, jogging, m. *[zho-hgeeng]*
rye seigle, m. *[sehgl]*

S

sad triste *[treest]*
safe coffre-fort, m. *[kohfruh-fohr]*
safety pin épingle de sûreté, f. *[aypa(n)gl duh sewr-tay]* épingle de nourrice, f. *[aypa(n)gl duh noorees]*
sale vente, f. *[vah(n)t]*
salesman vendeur, m. *[vah(n)duhr]*
saleswoman vendeuse, f. *[vah(n)duhz]*
salt sel, m. *[sehl]*
salted salé *[sahlay]*
same même *[mehm]*
sand sable, m. *[sahbl]*
sandals sandales, f.pl. *[sah(n)dahl]*
sanitary napkins serviettes hygiéniques, f.pl. *[sehrvyeht eezhyayneek]*
Saturday samedi *[sahmdee]*
saucer soucoupe, f. *[sookoop]*
sausage saucisse, f. *[sohsees]* saucisson, m. *[sohseesoh(n)]*
to say dire *[deer]*
scenic route circuit touris-tique, m. *[seerkwee tooreesteek]*
schedule horaire, m. *[ohrehr]*
school école, f. *[aykohl]*
scissors ciseaux, m.pl. *[see-zoh]*

226

screwdriver tournevis, m. *[toornuhvees]*

sculpture sculpture, f. *[skewltewr]*

sea mer, f. *[mehr]*

seafood fruits de mer, m.pl. *[frwee duh mehr]*

season saison, f. *[sehzoh(n)]*

seat place, f. *[plahs]*

second deuxième *[duhzyehm]*

section, shelf rayon, m. *[rayoh(n)]*

to see voir *[vwahr]*

to seem sembler *[sah(m)blay]*

to sell vendre *[vah(n)dr]*

to send envoyer *[ah(n)vwahyay]*

senior citizens personnes agées, f.pl. *[pehrsohn zahzhay]*

sentence (grammatical) phrase, f. *[frahz]*

September septembre *[sehptah(m)br]*

serious sérieux *[sayryuh]*

to serve servir *[sehrveer]*

service station station-service, f. *[stahsyoh(n)-sehrvees]*

seven sept *[seht]*

seventeen dix-sept *[dee-seht]*

seventy soixante-dix *[swahsah(n)t-dees]*

several plusieurs *[plewzyuhr]*

shampoo shampooing, m. *[shah(m)pwa(n)]*

to share partager *[pahrtahzhay]*

to shave raser *[rahzay]*

shaving cream crème à raser, f. *[krehm ah rahzay]*

she elle *[ehl]*

sheep, lamb agneau, m. *[ahnyoh]*

sheet (bed) drap, m. *[drah]*

shelf, section rayon, m. *[rayoh(n)]*

shell coquillage, m. *[kohkeeyahzh]*

shirt chemise, f. *[shuhmeez]*

shoe chaussure, f. *[shohsewr]*

shoe size pointure, f. *[pwa(n)tewr]*

shop boutique, f. *[booteek]* magasin, m. *[mahgahza(n)]*

to shop faire des achats *[fehr day zahshah]*

shopping center centre commercial, m. *[sah(n)tr kohmehrsyahl]*

short court *[koor]*

shoulder épaule, f. *[aypohl]*

show spectacle, m. *[spehktahkl]*

to show montrer *[moh(n)tray]*

shower douche, f. *[doosh]*

shrimp crevette, f. *[kruhveht]*

shrunk rétréci *[raytraysee]*

shutter obturateur, m. *[ohbtewrahtuhr]*

sick malade *[mahlahd]*

sickness maladie, f. *[mahlahdee]*

side côté, m. *[kohtay]*

sidewalk trottoir, m. *[trohtwahr]*

sign enseigne, f. *[ah(n)sehnyuh]* panneau, m. *[pahnoh]*

to sign signer *[seenyay]*

silk soie, f. *[swah]*

silver argent, m. *[ahrzhah(n)]*

since depuis *[duhpwee]*

since when? depuis quand? *[duhpwee kah(n)]*

to sing chanter *[shah(n)tay]*

single (unmarried) célibataire *[sayleebahtehr]*

sister soeur, f. *[suhr]*

sister-in-law belle-soeur, f. *[behl-suhr]*

to sit down s'asseoir *[sahswahr]*

site site, m. *[seet]*

six six *[sees]*

sixteen seize *[sehz]*

sixty soixante *[swahsah(n)t]*

size taille, f. *[tahy]*

skating rink patinoire, f. *[pahteenwahr]*

ski equipment équipement de ski, m. *[aykeepmah(n) duh skee]*

ski lift télésiege, m. *[taylaysyehzh]*

skiing ski, m. *[skee]*

skiing, cross-country ski de fond, m. *[skee duh foh(n)]*

skin peau, f. *[poh]*

skirt jupe, f. *[zhewp]*

sky ciel, m. *[syehl]*

to sleep dormir *[dohrmeer]*

sleeping berth couchette, f. *[koosheht]*

sleeping car wagon-lit, m. *[vahgoh(n)-lee]*

slice tranche, f. *[trah(n)sh]*

slide (photographic) diapositive, f. *[dyahpohzeeteev]*

slippers pantoufles, f.pl. *[pah(n)toofl]*

slippery glissant *[gleesah(n)]*

slow lent *[lah(n)]*

to slow down ralentir *[rahlah(n)teer]*

slowly lentement *[lah(n)tuhmah(n)]*

small petit *[puhtee]*

smile sourire, m. *[sooreer]*

smoked fumé *[fumay]*

smokers fumeurs, m.pl. *[foomuhr]*

snack bar buffet-express, m. *[bewfay-ehksprehs]* snack-bar, m. *[snahk-bahr]*

snail escargot, m. *[ehskahrgoh]*

snow neige, f. *[nehzh]*

to snow neiger *[nehzhay]*

so many, so much tant *[tah(n)]*

so much the better tant mieux *[tah(n) myuh]*

so much the worse tant pis *[tah(n) pee]*

soap savon, m. *[sahvoh(n)]*

sock chaussette, f. *[shohseht]*

soft doux, m. *[doo]* douce, f. *[doos]*

solid uni *[ewnee]*

some quelque(s) *[kehlkuh]*

someone quelqu'un *[kehlkuh(n)]*

something quelque chose *[kehlkuh shohz]*

sometimes parfois *[pahrfwah]*

somewhere quelque part *[kehlkuh pahr]*

son fils, m. *[fees]*

song chanson, f. *[shah(n)soh(n)]*

soon bientôt *[bya(n)toh]*

sorry désolé *[dayzohlay]*

sort genre, m. *[zhah(n)r]*

soufflé soufflé, m. *[sooflay]*

soup, chowder bisque, f. *[beesk]*

south sud, m. *[sewd]*

spaghetti spaghetti, m.pl. *[spahghetee]*

Spain Espagne, f. *[ehspah-nyuh]*

Spanish espagnol *[ehspahny-ohl]*

sparkling wine vin mousseux, m. *[va(n) moosuh]*

to speak parler *[pahrlay]*

specialty spécialité, f. *[spaysyahleetay]*

speed vitesse, f. *[veetehs]*

to spell épeler *[ayplay]*

to spend dépenser *[daypah(n)say]*

to spend (time) passer *[pahsay]*

spice piment, m. *[peemah(n)]*

spinach épinards, m.pl. *[aypeenahr]*

spoon cuillère, f. *[kweeyehr]*

spouse époux, m. *[aypoo]* épouse, f. *[aypooz]*

spring (season) printemps, m. *[pra(n)tah(m)]*

square (town) place, f. *[plahs]*

squash courge, f. *[koorzh]*

stadium stade, m. *[stahd]*

staircase escalier, m. *[ehskahlyay]*

stamp (postage) timbre, m. *[ta(m)br]*

to start (a car) démarrer *[daymahray]*

starter (on a car) démarreur, m. *[daymahruhr]*

state état, m. *[aytah]*

station station, f. *[stahsyoh(n)]*

stationery papier à lettres, m. *[pahpyay ah lehtr]*

stationery store papeterie, f. *[pahpehtree]*

statue statue, f. *[stahtew]*

stay séjour, m. *[sayzhoor]*

to stay (lodge) loger *[lohzhay]*

to stay (remain) rester *[rehstay]*

steak biftek, m. *[beeftehk]* steak, m. *[stehk]*

to steal voler *[vohlay]*

stew ragoût, m. *[rahgoo]*

stick, pole bâton, m. *[bah-toh(n)]*

still, again encore *[ah(n)kohr]*

stock exchange bourse, f. *[boors]*

stockings bas, m.pl. *[bah]*

stomach estomac, m. *[ehstohmah]*

stone pierre, f. *[pyehr]*

stop (along the way) escale, f. *[ehskahl]*

to stop arrêter *[ahrehtay]*

store magasin, m. *[mah-gahza(n)]*

store window vitrine, f. *[vee-treen]*

storm tempête, f. *[tah(m)peht]*

story (of a building) étage, m. *[aytahzh]*

story (tale) histoire, f. *[eestwahr]*

strange bizarre *[beezahr]*

strawberry fraise, f. *[frehz]*

street rue, f. *[rew]*

string ficelle, f. *[feesehl]*

string beans haricots, m.pl. *[ahreekoh]*

stripe rayure, f. *[rayewr]*

strong fort *[fohr]*

suburb banlieue, f. *[bah(n)lyuh]*

subway métro, m. *[maytroh]*

subway station station de métro, f. *[stahsyoh(n) duh maytroh]*

suede daim, m. *[da(m)]*

sugar sucre, m. *[sewkr]*

suit costume, m. *[kohstewm]*

suitcase valise, f. *[vahleez]*

sum somme, f. *[sohm]*

summer été, m. *[aytay]*

sun soleil, m. *[sohlehy]*

Sunday dimanche *[dee-mah(n)sh]*

sunglasses lunettes de soleil, f.pl. *[lewneht duh sohlehy]*

suntan lotion huile solaire, f. *[weel sohlehr]*

superior, higher supérieur *[sewpayryuhr]*

supermarket supermarché, m. *[sewpehrmahrshay]*

supplement supplément, m. *[sewplaymah(n)]*

sure sûr *[sewr]*

surfboard planche de surf, f. *[plah(n)sh duh sewrf]*

sweater pull, m. *[pool]*

sweet doux, m. *[doo]* douce, f. *[doos]* sucré *[sewkray]*

sweet wine vin doux, m. *[va(n) doo]*

to swim nager *[nahzhay]* se baigner *[suh behnyay]*

swimmer nageur, m. *[nahzhuhr]*

swimming natation, f. *[nah-tahsyoh(n)]*

swimming pool piscine, f. *[peeseen]*

Swiss suisse *[swees]*

Switzerland Suisse, f. *[Swees]*

synagogue synagogue, f. *[seenahgohg]*

T

table table, f. *[tahbl]*

tailor tailleur, m. *[tahyuhr]*

to take prendre *[prah(n)dr]*

tampon tampon, m. *[tah(m)poh(n)]*

tangerine mandarine, f. *[mah(n)dahreen]*

tap (water faucet) robinet, m. *[rohbeenay]*

to taste goûter *[gootay]*

tavern, restaurant bar, m. *[bahr]* restaurant, m. *[rehstohrah(n)]*

tax taxe, f. *[tahks]*

taxi taxi, m. *[tahksee]*

tea thé, m. *[tay]*

tearoom salon de thé, m. *[sahloh(n) duh tay]*

to teach, learn apprendre *[ahprah(n)dr]*

team équipe, f. *[aykeep]*

telephone téléphone, m. *[taylayfohn]*

to telephone téléphoner *[taylayfohnay]*

telephone directory annuaire, m. *[ahnwehr]*

television télévision, f. *[taylayveezyoh(n)]*

to tell raconter *[rahkon(n)tay]*

ten dix *[dees]*

tennis tennis, m. *[tehnees]*

tent tente, f. *[tah(n)t]*

terrace terrasse, f. *[tehrahs]*

to thank remercier *[ruh-mehrsyay]*

thank you merci *[mehrsee]*

that (thing) ça *[sah]* cela *[suh-lah]*

that (which) que *[kuh]*

the le/la/les *[luh/lah/lay]*

theater théâtre, m. *[tayahtr]*

their leur/leurs *[luhr/luhr]*

them les/leur/se *[lay/luhr/suh]*

then donc *[doh(n)k]*

there là *[lah]*

there, there is voilà *[vwahlah]*

there is il y a *[eel yah]*

therefore donc *[doh(n)k]*

these ces *[say]*

they ils, m.pl. *[eel]* elles, f.pl. *[ehl]*

thief voleur, m. *[vohluhr]*

thigh cuisse, f. *[kwees]*

thin mince *[man(n)s]*

thing chose, f. *[shohz]*

to think penser *[pah(n)say]*

third troisième *[trwahzyehm]*

thirst soif, f. *[swahf]*

to be thirsty avoir soif *[ahvwahr swahf]*

thirteen treize *[trehz]*

thirty trente *[trah(n)t]*

this ce/cet, m. *[suh/seht]* cette, f. *[seht]*

this one ceci *[suhsee]* celui *[suhlwee]*

those ces *[say]*

thousand mille *[meel]*

three trois *[trwah]*

throat gorge, f. *[gohrzh]*

through à travers *[ah trahvehr]*

Thursday jeudi *[zhuhdee]*

thyme thym, m. *[ta(m)]*

ticket billet, m. *[beeyay]*

ticket window guichet, m. *[gheeshay]*

tie cravate, f. *[krahvaht]*

time heure, f. *[uhr]* temps, m. *[tah(m)]*

on time à l'heure *[ah luhr]*

What time is it? Quelle heure est-il? *[Kehl uhr ehteel?]*

tip pourboire, m. *[poorbwahr]*

tire pneu, m. *[pnuh]*

tired fatigué *[fahteegay]*

tissue mouchoir en papier, m. *[mooshwahr ah(n) pahpyay]*

to à *[ah]*

to the à la, f. *[ah lah]* au, m. *[oh]* aux, m.pl. and f.pl. *[oh]*

toast pain grillé, m. *[pa(n) greeyay]*

tobacco tabac, m. *[tahbah]*

tobacco shop bureau de tabac, m. *[bewroh duh tah-bah]*

today aujourd'hui *[ohzhoord-wee]*

together ensemble *[ah(n)sah(m)bl]*

toilet, bathroom toilettes, f.pl. *[twahleht]* W.C., m.pl. *[vay say]*

toilet paper papier hygiénique, m. *[pahpyay eezhyayneek]*

toilet water eau de toilette, f. *[oh duh twahleht]*

token jeton, m. *[zhuhtoh(n)]*

toll péage, m. *[payahzh]*

tomato tomate, f. *[tohmaht]*

tomorrow demain *[duhma(n)]*

tongue langue, f. *[lah(n)g]*

too many, too much trop *[troh]*

tooth dent, f. *[dah(n)]*

toothpaste dentifrice, m. *[dah(n)teefrees]*

toothpick cure-dent, m. *[kewr-dah(n)]*

to touch toucher *[tooshay]*

to touch up retoucher *[ruh-tooshay]*

tour tour, m. *[toor]*; visite, f. *[veeseet]*

tourism tourisme, m. *[tooreezm]*

tourist touriste, m. or f. *[tooreest]*

touristic touristique *[tooreesteek]*

toward vers *[vehr]*

towel serviette, f. *[sehrvyeht]*

tower tour, f. *[toor]*

town ville. f. *[veel]*

town hall hôtel de ville, m. *[ohtehl duh veel]*

traffic circulation, f. *[seerkewlahsyoh(n)]*

traffic lights feux de circulation, m.pl. *[fuh duh seerkewlahsyoh(n)]*

trailer caravane, f. *[kahrah-vahn]*

train train, m. *[tra(n)]*

bullet train TGV, m. *[tay zhay vay]*

train station gare, f. *[gahr]*

to translate traduire *[trahd-weer]*

travel agency agence de voyage, f. *[ahzhah(n)s duh vwahyahzh]*

traveler's check chèque de voyage, m. *[shehk duh vwahyahzh]*

tree arbre, m. *[ahrbr]*

trip trajet, m. *[trahzhay]* voyage, m. *[vwahyahzh]*

trouble difficulté, f. *[deefeekewltay]*

trout truite, f. *[trweet]*

truck camion, m. *[kahmyoh(n)]*

true vrai *[vreh]*

trunk malle, f. *[mahl]* coffre, m. *[kohfr]*

truth vérité, f. *[vayreetay]*

to try essayer *[ehsayay]*

Tuesday mardi *[mahrdee]*
tune-up mise au point, f.
    [meez oh pwa(n)]
turkey dinde, f. *[da(n)d]*
turn virage, m. *[veerahzh]*
    tour, m. *[toor]*
to turn tourner *[toornay]*
turnip navet, m. *[nahvay]*
TV set téléviseur, m. *[tay-layveezuhr]*
twelve douze *[dooz]*
twenty vingt *[va(n)]*
two deux *[duh]*
type, sort genre, m.
    [zhah(n)r]
typical typique *[teepeek]*

U

ugly laid *[leh]*
umbrella parapluie, m.
    [pahrahplwee]
unbelievable incroyable
    [a(n)krwahyahbl]
uncle oncle, m. *[oh(n)kl]*
under sous *[soo]*
underpants slip, m. *[sleep]*
to understand comprendre
    [koh(m)prah(n)dr]
understood, included com-
    pris *[koh(m)pree]*
underwear sous-vêtements,
    m.pl. *[soo-vehtmah(n)]*
unhappy malheureux
    [mahluhruh]
unique unique *[ewneek]*
united, solid uni *[ewnee]*
United States Etats-Unis,
    m.pl. *[aytah-zewnee]*
university université, f.
    [ewneevehrseetay]
unlimited illimité *[eeleemee-tay]*
unmarried célibataire
    [sayleebahtehr]
until jusqu'à *[zhewskah]*

up, upstairs en haut *[ah(n) oh]*
urgent urgent *[ewrzhah(n)]*
us nous *[noo]*
to use employer *[ah(m)-plwahyay]*
useful utile *[ewteel]*
useless inutile *[eenewteel]*
usher ouvreuse, f. *[oovruhz]*
U-turn demi-tour, m. *[duh-mee-toor]*

V

vacation vacances, f.pl.
    [vahkah(n)s]
valley vallée, f. *[vahlay]*
value valeur, f. *[vahluhr]*
varied varié *[vahryay]*
veal veau, m. *[voh]*
vegetable légume, m.
    [laygewm]
velvet velours, m. *[vuhloor]*
to verify vérifier *[vayreefyay]*
vervain (infusion) verveine,
    f. *[vehrvehn]*
very très *[treh]*
video recorder magnéto-
    scope, m. *[mahnyaytohskohp]*
view vue, f. *[vew]*
villa villa, f. *[veelah]*
village village, m. *[veelahzh]*
vineyard vignoble, m.
    [veenyohbl]
visit visite, f. *[veezeet]*

W

waist, size taille, f. *[tahy]*
wait attente, f. *[ahtah(n)t]*
to wait for attendre
    [ahtah(n)dr]
waiter garçon, m.
    [gahrsoh(n)] serveur, m.
    [sehrvuhr]
waiting room salle d'at-
    tente, f. *[sahl dahtah(n)t]*

waitress serveuse, f.
  [sehrvuhz]
walk promenade, f.
  [prohmuhnahd]
to walk marcher [mahrshay]
to take a walk faire une
  promenade [fehr ewn
  prohmuhnahd]
wall mur, m. [mewr]
wallet porte-feuille, m.
  [pohrtuh-fuhy]
to want vouloir [voolwahr]
war guerre, f. [ghehr]
warm chaud [shoh]
to wash laver [lahvay]
watch montre, f. [moh(n)tr]
to watch regarder [ruhgahr-
  day]
water eau, f. [oh]
waterskiing ski nautique,
  m. [skee nohteek]
waterfall cascade, f. [kah-
  skahd]
watermelon pastèque, f.
  [pahstehk]
way moyen, m. [mwahya(n)]
way out issue, f. [eesew]
  sortie, f. [sohrtee]
we nous [noo]
weak faible [fehbl]
to wear porter [pohrtay]
weather temps, m. [tah(m)]
weather forecast météo, f.
  [maytayoh]
wedding ring alliance, f.
  [ahlyah(n)s]
Wednesday mercredi
  [mehrkruhdee]
week semaine, f. [suhmehn]
to weigh peser [puhzay]
weight poids, m. [pwah]
welcome bienvenue [bya(n)-
  vuhnew]
you're welcome de rien [duh
  reeya(n)]
well bien [byeh(n)]
well, then alors [ahlohr]

well-done (meat) bien cuit
  [bya(n) kwee]
west ouest, m. [wehst]
wet mouillé [mooyay]
wharf, platform quai, m.
  [keh]
what quel/quelle [kehl] quoi
  [kwah] qu'est-ce que
  [kehskuh]
when quand [kah(n)]
where où [oo]
which quel/quelle [kehl]
white blanc [blah(n)]
white bread pain de mie,
  m. [pa(n) duh mee]
white wine vin blanc, m.
  [va(n) blah(n)]
who qui [kee]
whole entier [ah(n)tyay]
whole wheat bread pain
  complet, m. [pa(n)
  koh(m)play]
why pourquoi [poorkwah]
wide large [lahrzh]
widow veuve, f. [vuhv]
widower veuf, m. [vuhf]
wife femme, f. [fahm]
wild sauvage [sohvahzh]
win gagner [gahnyay]
wind vent, m. [vah(n)]
window fenêtre, f. [fuhnehtr]
windsurfing planche à
  voile, f. [plah(n)sh ah vwahl]
wine vin, m. [va(n)]
wine cellar cave, f. [kahv]
winter hiver, m. [eevehr]
wish envie, f. [ah(n)vee]
  souhait, m. [sooweh]
to wish souhaiter [soowehtay]
with avec [ahvehk]
without sans [sah(n)]
wolf loup, m. [loo]
woman, wife femme, f.
  [fahm]
wonderful merveilleux
  [mehrvehyuh]
wool laine, f. [lehn]
word mot, m. [moh]

work travail, m. *[trahvahy]*
to work travailler *[trah-vahyay]*
work site chantier, m. *[shah(n)tyay]*
workshop atelier, m. *[ah-tuhlyay]*
world monde, m. *[moh(n)d]*
it is worth il vaut *[eel voh]*
to wrap up emballer *[ah(m)bahlay]*
wrist poignet, m. *[pwahnyay]*
to write écrire *[aykreer]*
written écrit *[aykree]*
to be wrong avoir tort *[ahvwahr tohr]*

X

X ray radio, f. *[rahdyoh]*

Y

year an, m. *[ah(n)]* année, f. *[ahnay]*
yellow jaune *[zhohn]*
yes oui *[wee]*

yesterday hier *[yehr]*
yet encore *[ah(n)kohr]*
yield cédez le passage *[say-day luh pahsahzh]*
yogurt yaourt, m. *[yahoort]*
you (singular, familiar) tu/te/toi *[tew/tuh/twah]*
you (plural or formal) vous *[voo]*
young jeune *[zhuhn]*
younger cadet *[kahday]* plus jeune *[ploo zhuhn]*
your (s. or familiar) ta/ton/tes *[tah/toh(n)/tay]*
your (pl. or formal) votre/vos *[votr/voh]*

Z

zero zéro *[zayroh]*
zipper fermeture éclair, f. *[fehrmuhtewr ayklehr]*
zoo jardin zoologique, m. *[zhahrda(n) zoh-ohlohzheek]* zoo, m. *[zoh]*
zucchini courgette, f. *[koorzheht]*

FRENCH/ENGLISH DICTIONARY

See usage note under English/French Dictionary.

A

à [ah] at, to

abricot, m. [ahbreekoh] apricot

accepter [ahksehptay] to accept

accompagner [ahkoh(m)pahnyay] to accompany

acheter [ahshtay] to buy

addition, f. [ahdeesyoh(n)] bill

adorer [ahdohray] to adore, love

adresse, f. [ahdrehs] address

adulte, m.,f. [ahdewlt] adult

aéroport, m. [ah-ehrohpohr] airport

affaires, f.pl. [ahfehr] business

âge, m. [ahzh] age

agence, f. [ahzhah(n)s] agency

agence de location de voitures, f. [ahzhah(n)s duh lohkahsyoh(n) duh vwahtewr] car rental agency

agence de voyage, f. [ahzhah(n)s duh vwahyahzh] travel agency

agent de police, m. [ahzhah(n) duh pohlees] policeman, policewoman

agrandissement, m. [ahgrah(n)deesmah(n)] enlargement

aider [ehday] to help

ailleurs [ahyuhr] elsewhere

aimer [ehmay] to like, love

aîné [ehnay] eldest

Allemagne, f. [ahluhmahnyuh] Germany

allemand [ahluhmah(n)] German

aller [ahlay] to go

aller-retour, m. [ahlay-ruhtoor] round-trip ticket

aller simple, m. [ahlay sa(m)pl] one-way ticket

alliance, f. [ahlyah(n)s] wedding ring

allumer [ahlewmay] to light

allumette, f. [ahlewmeht] match

alors [ahlohr] well, then

amandes, f.pl. [ahmah(n)d] almonds

amener [ahmnay] to bring

amer [ahmehr] bitter

Amérique, f. [Ahmayreek] America

américain [ahmayreeka(n)] American

ami, m. [ahmee] friend

amie, f. [ahmee] friend

amitié, f. [ahmeetyay] friendship

amour, m. [ahmoor] love

ampoule, f. [ah(m)pool] bulb

(s')amuser [sahmewzay] to amuse, have fun

an, m. [ah(n)] year

ananas, m. [ahnahnahs] pineapple

anchois, m. [ah(n)shwah] anchovy

andouille, f. [ah(n)dooy] type of sausage

anglais [ah(n)glay] English

Angleterre, f. [Ah(n)gluhtehr] England

anguille, f. [ah(n)gheey] eel

année, f. [ahnay] year

anniversaire, m. [ahneevehrsehr] birthday

annuaire, m. *[ahnwehr]* phone directory

annuler *[ahnewlay]* to cancel

antiquaire, m.,f. *[ah(n)teekehr]* antique dealer

antiquités, f.pl. *[ah(n)teekeetay]* antiques

août *[oot]* August

apéritif, m. *[ahpayreeteef]* aperitif

appareil, m. *[ahpahrehy]* machine

appareil photo, m. *[ahpahrehy fohtoh]* camera

(s')appeler *[sahplay]* to call, be named

appétit, m. *[ahpaytee]* appetite

apporter *[ahpohrtay]* to bring

apprendre *[ahprah(n)dr]* to teach, learn

après *[ahpreh]* after

après-demain *[ahpreh-duhma(n)]* day after tomorrow

après-midi, m. or f. *[ahprehmeedee]* afternoon

arbre, m. *[ahrbr]* tree

argent, m. *[ahrzhah(n)]* money, silver

armoire, f. *[ahrmwahr]* closet

arrêt de bus, m. *[ahray duh bews]* bus stop

arrêter *[ahrehtay]* to stop

arriver *[ahreevay]* to arrive

art, m. *[ahr]* art

artichaut, m. *[ahrteeshoh]* artichoke

article, m. *[ahrteekl]* article

ascenseur, m. *[ahsah(n)suhr]* elevator

asperge, f. *[ahspehrzh]* asparagus

assez *[ahsay]* enough

(s')asseoir *[sahswahr]* to sit down

assiette, f. *[ahsyeht]* plate

atelier, m. *[ahtuhlyay]* workshop

attacher *[ahtahshay]* to attach, buckle

attendre *[ahtah(n)dr]* to wait for

attente, f. *[ahtah(n)t]* wait

attention, f. *[ahtah(n)syoh(n)]* attention

attraper *[ahtrahpay]* to catch

au *[oh]* to the, at

au delà de *[oh duhlah duh]* beyond

au lait *[oh leh]* with milk

au revoir *[oh rvwahr]* good-bye

auberge, f. *[ohbehrzh]* inn

aubergine, f. *[ohbehrzheen]* eggplant

aujourd'hui *[ohzhoordwee]* today

aussi *[ohsee]* also

auto, f. *[ohtoh]* car

autobus, m. *[ohtohbews]* bus

automatique *[ohtohmahteek]* automatic

automne, m. *[ohtohn]* autumn

autoroute, f. *[ohtohroot]* highway

autre *[ohtr]* other

aux, pl. *[oh]* to the, at

avant *[ahvah(n)]* before

en avant *[ah(n) nahvah(n)]* forward

avec *[ahvehk]* with

avion, m. *[ahvyoh(n)]* airplane

avocat, m. *[ahvohkah]* avocado, lawyer

avoir *[ahvwahr]* to have

avoir besoin de *[ahvwahr buhzwa(n) duh]* to need

avril *[ahvreel]* April

B

bagages, m.pl. *[bahgahzh]* luggage

bague, f. *[bahg]* ring

baguette, f. *[bahgeht]* French bread

(se) baigner *[(suh) behnyay]* to bathe, swim

bain, m. *[ba(n)]* bath

balcon, m. *[bahlkoh(n)]* balcony

banane, f. *[bahnahn]* banana

banlieue, f. *[bah(n)lyuh]* suburb

banque, f. *[bah(n)k]* bank

bar, m. *[bahr]* bar

barbe, f. *[bahrb]* beard

barque, f. *[bahrk]* boat, rowboat

bas *[bah]* low

bas, m.pl. *[bah]* stockings

basket, m. *[bahskeht]* basketball

bateau, m. *[bahtoh]* boat

bâton, m. *[bahtoh(n)]* stick, pole

beau, m. *[boh]* beautiful, handsome

beau-frère, m. *[boh-frehr]* brother-in-law

beau-père, m. *[boh-pehr]* father-in-law

beaucoup *[bohkoo]* much, many, a lot

beaux arts, m.pl. *[boh zahr]* fine arts

beaux-parents, m.pl. *[boh-pahrah(n)]* in-laws

beignet, m. *[behnyay]* doughnut

belge *[behlzh]* Belgian

Belgique, f. *[Behlzheek]* Belgium

belle, f. *[behl]* beautiful

belle-mère, f. *[behl-mehr]* mother-in-law

belle-soeur, f. *[behl-suhr]* sister-in-law

betterave, f. *[behtrahv]* beet

beurre, m. *[buhr]* butter

bibliothèque, f. *[beebleeohtehk]* library

bien *[byeh(n)]* well

bien cuit *[byeh(n) kwee]* well-done (meat)

bien sûr *[byeh(n) sewr]* of course

bientôt *[byeh(n)toh]* soon

bienvenue *[byeh(n)vuhnew]* welcome

bière, f. *[byehr]* beer

biftek, m. *[beeftehk]* steak

bigoudis, m.pl. *[beegoodee]* curlers

bijouterie, f. *[beezhootree]* jewelry shop

bijoux, m.pl. *[beezhoo]* jewels

billet, m. *[beeyay]* ticket

biscuits, m.pl. *[beeskwee]* cookies

bisque, f. *[beesk]* soup, chowder

bistrot, m. *[beestroh]* bar, café

bizarre *[beezahr]* strange

blanc *[blah(n)]* white

blanchisserie, f. *[blah(n)sheesree]* laundry

bleu *[bluh]* blue

blond *[bloh(n)]* blond

bocal, m. *[bohkahl]* jar

boeuf, m. *[buhf]* beef

boire *[bwahr]* to drink

boisson, f. *[bwahsoh(n)]* drink

boîte, f. *[bwaht]* box

boîte aux lettres, f. *[bwaht oh lehtr]* mailbox

boîte de nuit, f. *[bwaht duh nwee]* nightclub

bon, m. *[boh(n)]* good

bon appétit *[boh(n) nahpaytee]* hearty appetite

bon marché *[boh(n) mahrshay]* cheap

bonjour *[boh(n)zhoor]* hello

bonne, f. *[bohn]* good

bonne chance! *[bohn shah(n)s!]* good luck!

botte, f. *[boht]* boot

bouche, f. *[boosh]* mouth

boucherie, f. *[booshree]* butcher shop

boucle, f. *[bookl]* curl

boucle d'oreille, f. *[bookl dohrehy]* earring

bougie, f. *[boozhee]* candle

bouillabaisse, f. *[booyahbehs]* fish soup

bouilli *[booyee]* boiled

boulangerie, f. *[boolah(n)zhree]* bakery

bourse, f. *[boors]* stock exchange

bouteille, f. *[bootehy]* bottle

boutique, f. *[booteek]* shop

bouton, m. *[bootoh(n)]* button

bracelet, m. *[brahslay]* bracelet

bras, m. *[brah]* arm

briquet, m. *[breekay]* lighter

briser *[breezay]* to break

brosse, f. *[brohs]* brush

brouillard, m. *[brooyahr]* fog

brugnon, m. *[brewnyoh(n)]* nectarine

brûler *[brewlay]* to burn

brun *[bruh(n)]* brown

Bruxelles *[Brewsehl]* Brussels

buffet-express, m. *[bewfay-ehksprehs]* snack bar

bureau, m. *[bewroh]* office, desk

bureau de change, m. *[bewroh duh shah(n)zh]* currency exchange office

bureau des objets trouvés, m. *[bewroh dayz ohbzhay troovay]* lost and found

bureau de poste, m. *[bewroh duh pohst]* post office

bureau de tabac, m. *[bewroh duh tahbah]* tobacco shop

bus, m. *[bews]* bus

C

ça *[sah]* that

cabaret, m. *[kahbahray]* cabaret

cabine, f. *[kahbeen]* booth

cadeau, m. *[kahdoh]* gift

cadet *[kahday]* younger

café, m. *[kahfay]* café, coffee

café au lait, m. *[kahfay oh leh]* coffee with milk

café soluble, m. *[kahfay sohlewbl]* instant coffee

cahier, m. *[kahyay]* notebook

caisse, f. *[kehs]* cash register

caissier, m. *[kehsyay]* cashier

camion, m. *[kahmyoh(n)]* truck

camomille, f. *[kahmohmeel]* camomile

campagne, f. *[kah(m)pahnyuh]* country (landscape)

camper *[kah(m)pay]* to camp

Canada, m. *[Kahnahdah]* Canada

canadien *[kahnadya(n)]* Canadian

canard, m. *[kahnahr]* duck

caneton, m. *[kahntoh(n)]* duckling

cannelle, f. *[kahnehl]* cinnamon

car, m. *[kahr]* bus

carafe, f. *[kahrahf]* carafe

caravane, f. *[kahrahvahn]* trailer

carburateur, m. *[kahrbewrahtuhr]* carburetor

carnet, m. *[kahrnay]* book of tickets

carotte, f. *[kahroht]* carrot

carrefour, m. *[kahrfoor]* intersection

carte, f. *[kahrt]* map, menu

carte bleue, f. *[kahrt bluh]* credit card

carte d'embarquement, f. *[kahrt da(m)bahrkmah(n)]* boarding pass

carte de crédit, f. *[kahrt duh kraydee]* credit card

carte postale, f. *[kahrt pohstahl]* postcard

carte routière, f. *[kahrt rootyehr]* road map

cascade, f. *[kahskahd]* waterfall

cassé *[kahsay]* broken

cathédrale, f. *[kahtaydrahl]* cathedral

cave, f. *[kahv]* (wine) cellar

ce, m. *[suh]* this

ceci *[suhsee]* this

cédez le passage *[sayday luh pahsahzh]* yield

ceinture, f. *[sa(n)tewr]* belt

cela *[suhlah]* that

céleri, m. *[saylree]* celery

célibataire *[sayleebahtehr]* single (unmarried)

cellule, f. *[sehlewl]* cell

celui *[suhlwee]* this one

cendrier, m. *[sah(n)dreeay]* ashtray

cent *[sah(n)]* hundred

cent, m. *[sah(n)]* 1/100 euro

centime, m. *[sah(n)teem]* centime (1/100 franc)

centre, m. *[sah(n)tr]* center

centre commercial, m. *[sah(n)tr kohmehrsyahl]* shopping center

centre ville, m. *[sah(n)truh veel]* downtown

cerise, f. *[suhreez]* cherry

certainement *[sehrtehnmah(n)]* certainly

cerveau, m. *[sehrvoh]* or **cervelle**, f. *[sehrvehl]* brain

ces, pl. *[say]* these, those

c'est *[seh]* it is, this is

cet, m. *[seht]* this

cette, f. *[seht]* this

chacun *[shahkuh(n)]* each one

chaîne, f. *[shehn]* chain

chaise, f. *[shehz]* chair

chambre, f. *[shah(m)br]* room, bedroom

chambre d'hôte, f. *[shah(m)br doht]* bed-and-breakfast

champ, m. *[shah(m)]* field

champignon, m. *[shah(m)peenyoh(n)]* mushroom

chance, f. *[shah(n)s]* luck

change, m. *[shah(n)zh]* currency, exchange

changer *[shah(n)zhay]* to change

chanson, f. *[shah(n)soh(n)]* song

chanter *[shah(n)tay]* to sing

chantier, m. *[shah(n)tyay]* work site

chapelle, f. *[shahpehl]* chapel

chaque *[shahk]* every, each

charcuterie, f. *[shahrkewtree]* delicatessen, cold cuts

chariot, m. *[shahryoh]* cart

chasseur, m. *[shahsuhr]* bellboy, hunter

chat, m. *[shah]* cat

château, m. *[shahtoh]* castle

chaud *[shoh]* warm, hot

chauffage, m. *[shohfahzh]* heat

chaussette, f. *[shohseht]* sock

chaussure, f. *[shohsewr]* shoe

chef, m. *[shehf]* boss

chef d'orchestre, m. *[shehf dohrkehstr]* orchestra leader

chemin, m. *[shuhma(n)]* way, path

chemin de fer, m. *[shuhma(n) duh fehr]* railroad

chemise, f. *[shuhmeez]* shirt

chemisier, m. *[shuhmeezyay]* blouse

chèque, m. *[shehk]* check

chèque de voyage, m. *[shehk duh vwahyahzh]* traveler's check

cher *[shehr]* dear, expensive

chercher *[shehrshay]* to look for

cheval, m. *[shuhvahl]* horse

cheveux, m.pl. *[shuhvuh]* hair

chez *[shay]* at the house of

chien, m. *[shya(n)]* dog

chiffre, m. *[sheefr]* number

choisir *[shwahzeer]* to choose

choix, m. *[shwah]* choice

chose, f. *[shohz]* thing

chou, m. *[shoo]* cabbage

chou de Bruxelles, m. *[shoo duh Brewsehl]* brussels sprout

chou-fleur, m. *[shoo-fluhr]* cauliflower

chute d'eau, f. *[shewt doh]* waterfall

cidre, m. *[seedr]* cider

ciel, m. *[syehl]* sky

cigare, m. *[seegahr]* cigar

cigarette, f. *[seegahreht]* cigarette

cil, m. *[seel]* eyelash

cimetière, m. *[seemtyehr]* cemetery

cinéma, m. *[seenaymah]* film, movies, movie theater

cinq *[sa(n)k]* five

cinquante *[sa(n)kah(n)t]* fifty

cintre, m. *[sa(n)tr]* hanger

circuit touristique, m. *[seerkwee tooreesteek]* scenic route

circulation, f. *[seerkewlahsyoh(n)]* traffic

ciseaux, m.pl. *[seezoh]* scissors

citron, m. *[seetroh(n)]* lemon

citronnade, f. *[seetrohnahd]* lemonade (still)

citron vert, m. *[seetroh(n) vehr]* lime

clair *[klehr]* clear

classique *[klahseek]* classic

clé, f. *[klay]* key

client, m. *[kleeah(n)]* customer

clignotant, m. *[kleenyohtah(n)]* blinker

climatisé, m. *[kleemahteezay]* air-conditioned

cochon, m. *[kohshoh(n)]* pig

coeur, m. *[kuhr]* heart

coeur d'artichaut, m. *[kuhr dahrteeshoh]* (artichoke heart)

coffre (car), m. *[kohfr]* trunk

coffre-fort, m. *[kohfruh-fohr]* safe

coffret à bijoux, m. *[kohfray ah beezhoo]* jewelry box

cognac, m. *[kohnyahk]* cognac

coiffeur, m. *[kwahfuhr]* hairdresser, barber

coin, m. *[kwa(n)]* corner

col, m. *[kohl]* mountain pass, collar

colis, m. *[kohlee]* package

collègue, m. or f. *[kohlehg]* colleague

collier, m. *[kohlyay]* necklace

colline, f. *[kohleen]* hill

combien *[koh(m)bya(n)]* how many, how much

commander *[kohmah(n)day]* to order

comme *[kohm]* like, as

commencer *[kohmah(n)say]* to begin

comment *[kohmah(n)]* how

comment dit-on . . . ? *[kohmah(n) dee toh(n) . . .]* how do you say . . . ?

commissariat, m. *[kohmeesahryah]* police station

compagnie, f. *[koh(m)pahnyee]* company

compartiment, m. *[koh(m)pahrteemah(n)]* compartment

composer *[koh(m)pohzay]* to dial, to compose

comprendre *[koh(m)prah(n)dr]* to understand

compris *[koh(m)pree]* understood, included

compter *[koh(m)tay]* to count

concert, m. *[koh(n)sehr]* concert

concierge, m. or f. *[koh(n)syehrzh]* caretaker (building) porter (big hotels only)

concombre, m. *[koh(n)koh(m)br]* cucumber

conduire *[koh(n)dweer]* to drive

confirmer *[koh(n)feermay]* to confirm

confiture, f. *[koh(n)feetewr]* jam

connaissance, f. *[kohnehsah(n)s]* acquaintance

connaître *[kohnehtr]* to know (be familiar with)

consigne automatique, f. *[koh(n)seen yohtohmahteek]* baggage locker

contenu, m. *[koh(n)tuhnew]* contents

continuer *[koh(n)teeneeway]* to continue

contraire, m. *[koh(n)trehr]* opposite

contre *[koh(n)tr]* against

coq, m. *[kohk]* rooster, cock

coquillage, m. *[kohkeeyahzh]* shell

cornet de glace, m. *[kohrnay duh glahs]* ice-cream cone

cornichon, m. *[kohrneeshoh(n)]* pickle

corps, m. *[kohr]* body

correspondance, f. *[kohrehspoh(n)dah(n)s]* correspondence, train or bus to . . .

costume, m. *[kohstewm]* costume, suit

côte, f. *[koht]* hill, rib, coast

côté, m. *[kohtay]* side

côté du stationnement, m. *[kohtay dew stahsyohnmah(n)]* parking side

côtelette, f. *[kohtleht]* cutlet

coton, m. *[kohtoh(n)]* cotton

cou, m. *[koo]* neck

couche, f. *[koosh]* diaper

couchette, f. *[koosheht]* sleeping berth

couleur, f. *[kooluhr]* color

coupe, f. *[koop]* cut, haircut

coupe de cheveux, f. *[koop duh shuhvuh]* haircut

coupe-ongles, m. *[koop-oh(n)gl]* nail cutter

couper *[koopay]* to cut, cut off

courge, f. *[koorzh]* squash

courgette, f. *[koorzheht]* zucchini

courir *[kooreer]* to run

courrier, m. *[kooryay]* mail

cours, m. *[koor]* course

court *[koor]* short

cousin, m. *[kooza(n)]* cousin

cousine, f. *[koozeen]* cousin

couteau, m. *[kootoh]* knife

coûter *[kootay]* to cost

couvert *[koovehr]* cloudy, covered

couvert, m. *[koovehr]* cover charge

couverture, f. *[koovehrtewr]* blanket

couvrir *[koovreer]* to cover

crabe, m. *[krahb]* crab

cravate, f. *[krahvaht]* necktie, tie

crayon, m. *[krayoh(n)]* pencil

crème, f. *[krehm]* cream

crème à raser, f. *[krehm ah rahzay]* shaving cream

créole *[krayohl]* creole

crêpe, f. *[krehp]* pancake

crêperie, f. *[krehpree]* creperie

crevette, f. *[kruhveht]* shrimp

cric, m. *[kreek]* jack (car)

croire *[krwahr]* to believe

croûte, f. *[kroot]* crust

crudités, f.pl. *[krewdeetay]* raw vegetables

cuillère, f. *[kweeyehr]* spoon

cuir, m. *[kweer]* leather

cuisine, f. *[kweezeen]* kitchen, cooking

cuisinier, m. *[kweezeenyay]* cook (chef)

cuisse, f. *[kwees]* thigh

cuit *[kwee]* cooked

curiosité, f. *[kewryohzeetay]* attraction

cyclisme, m. *[seekleezm]* cycling

D

d'accord *[dahkohr]* okay, agreed

daim, m. *[da(m)]* suede

dangereux *[dah(n)zhuhruh]* dangerous

241

dans *[dah(n)]* in
danse, f. *[dah(n)s]* dance
danser *[dah(n)say]* to dance
datte, f. *[daht]* date (fruit)
de *[duh]* of, from
débutant, m. *[daybewtah(n)]* beginner
décaféiné *[daykahfayeenay]* decaffeinated
décembre *[daysah(m)br]* December
décider *[dayseeday]* to decide
déclarer *[dayklahray]* to declare
déçu *[daysew]* disappointed
dedans *[duhdah(n)]* inside
défense d'entrer *[dayfah(n)s dah(n)tray]* no entry, entry prohibited
dehors *[dehohr]* outside
déjeuner, m. *[dayzhuhnay]* lunch
demain *[duhma(n)]* tomorrow
demander *[duhmah(n)day]* to ask
démarrer *[daymahray]* to start (a car)
démarreur, m. *[daymahruhr]* starter
demi *[duhmee]* half
demi-bouteille, f. *[duhmee-bootehy]* half bottle
demi-tour, m. *[duhmee-toor]* U-turn
dent, f. *[dah(n)]* tooth
dentelle, f. *[dah(n)tehl]* lace
dentifrice, m. *[dah(n)teefrees]* toothpaste
dépannage, m. *[daypahnahzh]* emergency road service
se dépêcher *[suh daypehshay]* to hurry
dépenser *[daypah(n)say]* to spend
déposer *[daypohzay]* to drop off
depuis *[duhpwee]* since
Depuis quand? *[Duhpwee kah(n)?]* Since when?

déranger *[dayrah(n)zhay]* to disturb
dernier *[dehrnyay]* last (adj.)
derrière *[dehryehr]* in back of, behind
des (pl.) *[day]* of the, from the
descendre *[dehsah(n)dr]* to go down, get off
désolé *[dayzohlay]* sorry
dessous *[duhsoo]* beneath
dessus *[duhsew]* above, over
deux *[duh]* two
deuxième *[duhzyehm]* second
devant *[duhvah(n)]* in front of
devenir *[duhvuhneer]* to become
déviation, f. *[dayvyahsyoh(n)]* detour
devoir *[duhvwahr]* to be obliged to
diabétique *[dyahbayteek]* diabetic
diamant, m. *[dyahmah(n)]* diamond
diapositive, f. *[dyahpohzeeteev]* slide (photographic)
dictionnaire, m. *[deeksyohnehr]* dictionary
différent *[deefayrah(n)]* different
difficile *[deefeeseel]* difficult
difficulté, f. *[deefeekewltay]* trouble
dimanche *[deemah(n)sh]* Sunday
diminuer *[deemeeneway]* to diminish
dinde, f. *[da(n)d]* turkey
dîner *[deenay]* to dine
dîner, m. *[deenay]* dinner
dire *[deer]* to say
directeur, m. *[deerehktewr]* director, manager
direction, f. *[deerehksyoh(n)]* direction
disque, m. *[deesk]* record
distance, f. *[deestah(n)s]* distance

divorcé *[deevohrsay]* divorced

dix *[dees]* ten

dix-huit *[deez-weet]* eighteen

dix-neuf *[deez-nuhf]* nineteen

dix-sept *[deez-seht]* seventeen

doigt, m. *[dwah]* finger

dois/doit *[dwah]* must (see devoir)

donc *[doh(n)k]* then, therefore

donner *[dohnay]* to give

dormir *[dohrmeer]* to sleep

dos, m. *[doh]* back

douane, f. *[dwahn]* customs

doublé *[dooblay]* dubbed (film)

douce f. *[doos]* sweet, soft

douche, f. *[doosh]* shower

douleur, f. *[dooluhr]* pain

doux, m. *[doo]* sweet, soft

douzaine, f. *[doozehn]* dozen

douze *[dooz]* twelve

drame, m. *[drahm]* drama

drap, m. *[drah]* sheet (bed)

droit, m. *[drwah]* right

droite, f. *[drwaht]* right (direction)

du, m. sing. *[dew]* of the, from the

durer *[dewray]* to last

E

eau, f. *[oh]* water

eau de toilette, f. *[oh duh twahleht]* toilet water

eau minérale, f. *[oh meenayrahl]* mineral water

échanger *[ayshah(n)zhay]* to exchange

échelle, f. *[ayshehl]* ladder

éclair, m. *[ayklehr]* éclair (type of pastry)

école, f. *[aykohl]* school

écouter *[aykootay]* to listen

écrire *[aykreer]* to write

écrit *[aykree]* written

église, f. *[aygleez]* church

électricité, f. *[aylehktreeseetay]* electricity

elle, f. *[ehl]* she

elles, f.pl. *[ehl]* they

emballer *[ah(m)bahlay]* to wrap up

embrasser *[ah(m)brahsay]* to kiss

employer *[ah(m)plwahyay]* to use

emprunter *[ah(m)pruh(n)tay]* to borrow

en *[ah(n)]* in, to

en bas *[ah(n) bah]* below, downstairs

en haut *[ah(n) oh]* up, upstairs

en plein air *[ah(n) pleh nehr]* outside, outdoors

enceinte *[ah(n)sa(n)t]* pregnant

enchanté *[ah(n)shah(n)tay]* delighted

encore *[ah(n)kohr]* again, still, yet

endroit, m. *[ah(n)drwah]* place

enfant, m. or f. *[ah(n)fah(n)]* child

enregistrement, m. *[ah(n)rehzheestruhmah(n)]* recording, registration, check-in

enregistrer *[ah(n)rehzheestray]* to register, to check in

enseigne, f. *[ah(n)sehnyuh]* (shop) sign

ensemble *[ah(n)sah(m)bl]* together

ensuite *[ah(n)sweet]* next, afterward

entendre *[ah(n)tah(n)dr]* to hear

entendu *[ah(n)tah(n)dew]* agreed, understood

entier *[ah(n)tyay]* whole

entre *[ah(n)tr]* between

entrée, f. *[ah(n)tray]* entrance

envie, f. *[ah(n)vee]* desire, wish

envoyer *[ah(n)vwahyay]* to send

épaule, f. *[aypohl]* shoulder

épeler *[ayplay]* to spell

épicerie, f. *[aypeesree]* grocery

épinards, m.pl. *[aypeenahr]* spinach

épingle, f. *[aypa(n)gl]* pin

épingle de sûreté, f. **épingle de nourrice** *[aypa(n)gl duh sewrtay]* *[aypa(n)gl duh noorees]* safety pin

épouse, f. *[aypooz]* spouse

époux, m. *[aypoo]* spouse

épreuve, f. *[aypruhv]* print

épuisé *[aypweezay]* exhausted

équipe, f. *[aykeep]* team

équipement de ski, m. *[aykeepmah(n) duh skee]* ski equipment

erreur, f. *[ehruhr]* error

escale, f. *[ehskahl]* layover, stop

escalier, m. *[ehskahlyay]* staircase

escargot, m. *[ehskahrgoh]* snail

Espagne, f. *[Ehspahnyuh]* Spain

espagnol *[ehspahnyohl]* Spanish

espérer *[ehspayray]* to hope

essayer *[ehsayay]* to try

essence, f. *[ehsah(n)s]* gasoline

est, m. *[ehst]* east

est-ce que *[ehskuh]* is, do (introduces a question)

estomac, m. *[ehstohmah]* stomach

et *[eh]* and

étage, m. *[aytahzh]* story (of a building)

étang, m. *[aytah(n)]* pond

état, m. *[aytah]* state

Etats-Unis, m.pl. *[Aytahzewnee]* United States

été, m. *[aytay]* summer

êtes *[eht]* are (see être)

étranger *[aytrah(n)zhay]* foreign

étranger, m. *[aytrah(n)zhay]* foreigner

à l'étranger *[ah laytrah(n)zhay]* overseas, abroad

être *[ehtr]* to be

étroit *[aytrwah]* narrow

étui, m. *[aytwee]* case

étui à cigarettes, m. *[aytwee ah seegahreht]* cigarette case

euro, m. *[uhroh]* euro

excellent *[ehksehlah(n)]* excellent

excursion, f. *[ehkskewrsyoh(n)]* excursion

s'excuser *[sehkskewzay]* to apologize

excuses f.pl. *[ehkskewz]* apology

exemple, m. *[ehksah(m)pl]* example

F

en face de *[ah(n) fahs duh]* opposite (prep.)

facile *[fahseel]* easy

faible *[fehbl]* weak

faim, f. *[fa(m)]* hunger

faire *[fehr]* to do, make

faire cuire *[fehr kweer]* to cook

faire des achats *[fehr day zahshah]* to shop

fait main *[feh ma(n)]* handmade

faites *[feht]* do/make (see faire)

faites le plein *[feht luh pla(n)]* fill it up

falaise, f. *[fahlehz]* cliff

famille, f. *[fahmeey]* family

fard, m. *[fahr]* (makeup) rouge

farine, f. *[fahreen]* flour

fatigué *[fahteegay]* tired

faut *[foh]* is necessary

faute, f. *[foht]* mistake

fauteuil, m. *[fohtuhy]* arm-chair

faux *[foh]* false

félicitations! *[fayleeseetahsyoh(n)!]* congratulations!

femme, f. *[fahm]* woman, wife

femme de chambre, f. *[fahm duh shah(m)br]* maid

fenêtre, f. *[fuhnehtr]* window

fer, m. *[fehr]* iron

ferme, f. *[fehrm]* farm

fermer *[fehrmay]* to close

fermeture éclair, f. *[fehrmuhtewr ayklehr]* zipper

fête, f. *[feht]* holiday, party

février *[fayvreeyay]* February

feu, m. *[fuh]* fire

feu de circulation, m. *[fuh duh seerkewlahsyoh(n)]* traffic light

ficelle, f. *[feesehl]* string

fiche, f. *[feesh]* card

fièvre, f. *[fyehvr]* fever

figue, f. *[feeg]* fig

filet, m. *[feelay]* fillet, net

fille, f. *[feey]* girl, daughter

fils, m. *[fees]* son

fin, f. *[fa(n)]* end

fin d'autoroute *[fa(n) dohtohroot]* highway ends

finir *[feeneer]* to finish

fixe *[feeks]* fixed

flan, m. *[flah(n)]* custard

fleur, f. *[fluhr]* flower

fleuve, m. *[fluhv]* river

flûte, f. *[flewt]* flute

foie, m. *[fwah]* liver

folklorique *[fohlklohreek]* folkloric

foncé *[foh(n)say]* dark

fond d'artichaut, m. *[foh(n) dahrteeshoh]* artichoke heart

fontaine, f. *[foh(n)tehn]* fountain

footing, m. *[footeeng]* running, jogging

forêt, f. *[fohreh]* forest

format, m. *[fohrmah]* format, size

formulaire, m. *[fohrmewlehr]* form

fort *[fohr]* strong

forteresse, f. *[fohrtuhrehs]* fortress

four, m. *[foor]* oven

fourchette, f. *[foorsheht]* fork

frais *[freh]* cool, fresh

fraise, f. *[frehz]* strawberry

framboise, f. *[frah(m)bwahz]* raspberry

franc, m. *[frah(n)]* franc

français *[frah(n)seh]* French

France, f. *[Frah(n)s]* France

frapper *[frahpay]* to knock

freins, m.pl. *[fraa(n)]* brakes

frère, m. *[frehr]* brother

frit *[free]* fried

froid *[frwah]* cold

froid, m. *[frwah]* cold (weather)

fromage, m. *[frohmahzh]* cheese

frontière, f. *[froh(n)tyehr]* border

fruit, m. *[frwee]* fruit

fruits de mer, m.pl. *[frwee duh mehr]* seafood

fruits secs, m.pl. *[frwee sehk]* dried fruit

fumé *[fuwmay]* smoked

fumeurs, m.pl. *[foomuhr]* smokers

G

gagner *[gahnyay]* to earn, win

galerie d'art, f. *[gahlree dahr]* art gallery

gant, m. *[gah(n)]* glove

garage, m. *[gahrahzh]* garage

garçon, m. *[gahrsoh(n)]* boy, waiter

garde d'enfants, f. *[gahrd dah(n)fah(n)]* baby-sitter

garder *[gahrday]* to keep
gare, f. *[gahr]* train station
(se) garer *[(suh) gahray]* to park
garniture, f. *[gahrneetewr]* accompanying vegetables
gas-oil, m. *[gahzwahl]* diesel fuel
gastronomique *[gah-strohnohmeek]* gastronomical
gâteau, m. *[gahtoh]* cake
gauche, f. *[gohsh]* left
gazeux *[gahzuh]* carbonated
gêner *[zhehnay]* to bother
genou, m. *[zhuhnoo]* knee
genre, m. *[zhah(n)r]* type, sort
gens, f.pl. *[zhah(n)]* people
gentil *[zhah(n)teey]* nice
gérant, m. *[zhayrah(n)]* manager
gibier, m. *[zheebyay]* game
gingembre, m. *[zha(n)zhah(m)br]* ginger
glace, f. *[glahs]* ice, ice cream
glacé *[glahsay]* iced, frozen
glaçon, m. *[glahsoh(n)]* ice cube
glissant *[gleesah(n)]* slippery
gorge, f. *[gohrzh]* throat
goûter *[gootay]* to taste
grand *[grah(n)]* big
grande cuisine, f. *[grah(n)d kweezeen]* gourmet cooking
grand magasin, m. *[grah(n) mahgahza(n)]* department store
grand-mère, f. *[grah(n)-mehr]* grandmother
grand-père, f. *[grah(n)-pehr]* grandfather
grenier, m. *[gruhnyay]* attic
grenouille, f. *[gruhnooy]* frog
grillé *[greeyay]* grilled
gris *[gree]* gray
gros *[groh]* fat

grossir *[grohseer]* to gain weight
grotte, f. *[groht]* cave, grotto
guerre, f. *[ghehr]* war
guichet, m. *[gheeshay]* ticket window
guide, m. or f. *[gheed]* guide
guidé *[gheeday]* guided

H

s'habiller *[sahbeeyay]* to dress
habiter *[ahbeetay]* to live
handicapé *[a(n)deekahpay]* handicapped
haricot, m. *[ahreekoh]* bean
haricots, m.pl. *[ahreekoh]* string beans
haricots verts, m.pl. *[ahreekoh vehr]* green beans
haut *[oh]* high
en haut *[ah(n) oh]* up, upstairs
hauteur, f. *[ohtuhr]* height
herbe, f. *[ehrb]* grass, herb
heure, f. *[uhr]* hour, time
à l'heure *[ah luhr]* on time
heureux *[uhruh]* happy
hier *[eeyehr]* yesterday
histoire, f. *[eestwahr]* history, story (tale)
hiver, m. *[eevehr]* winter
homard, m. *[ohmahr]* lobster
homme, m. *[ohm]* man
hôpital, m. *[ohpeetahl]* hospital
horaire, m. *[ohrehr]* schedule
hors d'oeuvre, m. *[ohr duhvr]* appetizers
hôtel, m. *[ohtehl]* hotel
hôtel de ville, m. *[ohtehl duh veel]* town hall, city hall
hôtesse de l'air, f. *[ohtehs duh lehr]* flight attendant
huile, f. *[weel]* oil
huile solaire, f. *[weel sohlehr]* suntan oil

huit *[weet]* eight
huître, f. *[weetr]* oyster

I

ici *[eesee]* here
il, m. *[eel]* he
il y a *[eel yah]* there is, there are, ago
île, f. *[eel]* island
illimité *[eeleemeetay]* unlimited
ils, m.pl. *[eel]* they
impair *[a(m)pehr]* odd
impasse, f. *[a(m)pahs]* dead end
important *[a(m)pohrtah(n)]* important
impossible *[a(m)pohseebl]* impossible
incroyable *[a(n)krwahyahbl]* unbelievable
indicatif, m. *[a(n)deekahteef]* area code
indiquer *[a(n)deekay]* to indicate
infirmière, f. *[a(n)feermyehr]* nurse
infusion, f. *[a(n)fewzyoh(n)]* infusion
intelligent *[a(n)tehleezhah(n)]* intelligent
interdire *[a(n)tehrdeer]* to prohibit
interdit *[a(n)tehrdee]* forbidden
interdit aux piétons *[a(n)tehrdee oh pyaytoh(n)]* no pedestrians
intéressant *[a(n)tayrehsah(n)]* interesting
s'intéresser à *[sa(n)tayrehsay ah]* to be interested in
inutile *[eenewteel]* useless
inviter *[a(n)veetay]* to invite
issue, f. *[eesew]* way out
ivoire, f. *[eevwahr]* ivory
ivre *[eevr]* drunk

J

jamais *[zhahmay]* never
jambe, f. *[zhah(m)b]* leg
jambon, m. *[zhah(m)boh(n)]* ham
janvier *[zhah(n)vyay]* January
jardin, m. *[zhahrda(n)]* garden
jardin zoologique, m. *[zhahrda(n) zohohlohzheek]* zoo
jaune *[zhohn]* yellow
je *[zhuh]* I
je voudrais *[zhuh voodreh]* I'd like
jeton, m. *[zhuhtoh(n)]* token
jeudi *[zhuhdee]* Thursday
jeune *[zhuhn]* young
jogging, m. *[zhohgeeng]* jogging, running
joli *[zhohlee]* pretty
jouer *[zhooay]* to play
joueur, m. *[zhoouhr]* player
jour, m. *[zhoor]* day
jour férié, m. *[zhoor fayreeyay]* holiday
journal, m. *[zhoornal]* newspaper
journaux, m.pl. *[zhoornoh]* newpapers
journée, f. *[zhoornay]* day
juger *[zhewzhay]* to judge
juillet *[zhweeyay]* July
juin *[zhwa(n)]* June
jupe, f. *[zhewp]* skirt
jus, m. *[zhew]* juice
jusqu'à *[zhewskah]* until

K

kasher *[kahshehr]* kosher
kilomètre, m. *[keelohmehtr]* kilometer
kilométrage, m. *[keelohmehtrahzh]* mileage
kiosque, m. *[keeohsk]* kiosk, newsstand

247

L

la, f. *[lah]* the, herself, itself
là *[lah]* there
lac, m. *[lahk]* lake
laid *[leh]* ugly
laine, f. *[lehn]* wool
laisser *[lehsay]* to leave, let
lait, m. *[leh]* milk
laitue, f. *[lehtew]* lettuce
lampe de poche, f. *[lah(m)p duh pohsh]* flashlight
langouste, f. *[lah(n)goost]* lobster
langue, f. *[lah(n)g]* tongue, language
lapin, m. *[lahpa(n)]* rabbit
lard, m. *[lahr]* bacon
large *[lahrzh]* wide
laver *[lahvay]* to wash
laverie automatique, f. *[lahvree ohtohmahteek]* laundromat
le, m. *[luh]* the, himself, itself
lecon, f. *[luhsoh(n)]* lesson
lecteur CD, m. *[lehktewr sehdeh]* CD player
léger *[layzhay]* light
légume, m. *[laygewm]* vegetable
lent *[lah(n)]* slow
lentille, f. *[lah(n)teey]* lens, contact lens
lentement *[lah(n)tuhmah(n)]* slowly
les, pl. *[lay]* the
lettre, f. *[lehtr]* letter
leur/leurs *[luhr]* their, them
se lever *[suh luhvay]* to get up
levier, m. *[luhvyay]* lever
librairie, f. *[leebrehree]* bookstore
libre *[leebr]* free
au lieu de *[oh lyuh duh]* instead of
ligne, f. *[leenyuh]* line
lime à ongles, f. *[leem ah oh(n)gl]* nail file
limonade, f. *[leemohnahd]* lemonade (fizzy)

lin, m. *[la(n)]* linen
liqueur, f. *[leekuhr]* liquor
lire *[leer]* to read
liste, f. *[leest]* list
lit, m. *[lee]* bed
litre, m. *[leetr]* liter
livre, m. *[leevr]* book
local *[lohkahl]* local
loger *[lohzhay]* to stay, lodge
loin *[lwa(n)]* far
long *[loh(n)]* long
longtemps *[loh(n)tah(m)]* for a long time
louer *[looay]* to rent, hire
loup, m. *[loo]* wolf
lourd *[loor]* heavy
loyer, m. *[lwahyay]* rent
lui *[lwee]* her, him
lumière, f. *[lewmyehr]* light
lundi *[luh(n)dee]* Monday
lune, f. *[lewn]* moon
lunettes, f.pl. *[lewneht]* eyeglasses
lunettes de soleil, f.pl. *[lewneht duh sohlehy]* sunglasses
lotion, f. *[lohsyoh(n)]* lotion
lotion après-rasage, f. *[lohsyoh(n) ahpreh-rahzahzh]* aftershave lotion
luxe, m. *[lewks]* luxury
lycée, m. *[leesay]* high school

M

ma, f. *[mah]* my
madame, f. *[mahdahm]* Mrs.
mademoiselle *[mahduhmwahzehl]* Miss
magasin, m. *[mahgahza(n)]* store
magasin duty-free, m. *[mahgahza(n) dewtee free]* duty-free shop
magazine, m. *[mahgahzeen]* magazine
magnétophone, m. *[mahnyaytohfohn ah kahseht]* tape recorder

magnétoscope, m. *[mahnyay-tohskohp]* video recorder

mai *[meh]* May

maigrir *[mehgreer]* to lose weight

maillot de bain, m. *[mayoh duh ba(n)]* bathing suit

main, f. *[ma(n)]* hand

maintenant *[ma(n)tuhnah(n)]* now

mais *[meh]* but

maïs, m. *[mah-ees]* corn

maison, f. *[mehzoh(n)]* house

maître d'hôtel, m. *[mehtr dohtehl]* maître d', host, butler

maître nageur, m. *[mehtr nahzhur]* lifeguard

mal *[mahl]* badly

malade *[mahlahd]* ill, sick

maladie, f. *[mahlahdee]* illness, sickness

malgré *[mahlgray]* in spite of

malheureux *[mahluhruh]* unhappy

malle, f. *[mahl]* trunk

mandarine, f. *[mah(n)dahreen]* tangerine

manger *[mah(n)zhay]* to eat

manque, m. *[mah(n)k]* lack

manquer *[mah(n)kay]* to lack

manteau, m. *[mah(n)toh]* overcoat

manucure, f. or m. *[mah-newkewr]* manicurist

maquillage, m. *[mahkeeyahzh]* makeup

marchand, m. *[mahrshah(n)]* merchant

marché, m. *[mahrshay]* market

marché aux puces, m. *[mahrshay oh pews]* flea market

marcher *[mahrshay]* to walk

mardi *[mahrdee]* Tuesday

marée basse, f. *[mahray bahs]* low tide

marée haute, f. *[mahray oht]* high tide

mari, m. *[mahree]* husband

marié *[mahryay]* married

marjolaine, f. *[mahrzhohlehn]* marjoram

mars *[mahrs]* March

marron *[mahroh(n)]* brown

matin, m. *[mahta(n)]* morning

mauvais *[mohveh]* bad

mayonnaise, f. *[mahyohnehz]* mayonnaise

me *[muh]* me, to me

mécanicien, m. *[maykahneesya(n)]* mechanic

médicin, m. *[maydsa(n)]* doctor

médecine, f. *[maydseen]* medicine

médiéval *[maydyayvahl]* medieval

meilleur *[mehyuhr]* better

melon, m. *[muhloh(n)]* melon

même *[mehm]* same

menthe, f. *[mah(n)t]* mint

menton, m. *[mah(n)toh(n)]* chin

menu, m. *[muhnew]* menu

menu à prix fixe, m. *[muhnew ah pree feeks]* fixed-price menu

menu gastronomique, m. *[muhnew gahstrohnohmeek]* gourmet menu

mer, f. *[mehr]* sea

merci *[mehrsee]* thank you

mercredi *[mehrkruhdee]* Wednesday

mère, f. *[mehr]* mother

merveilleux *[mehrvehyuh]* wonderful, marvelous

mes, pl. *[may]* my

messe, f. *[mehs]* mass

météo, f. *[maytayoh]* weather forecast

métro, m. *[maytroh]* subway

mettre *[mehtr]* to put, put on

meublé *[muhblay]* furnished

meubles, m.pl. *[muhbl]* furniture

midi *[meedee]* noon

mieux *[myuh]* better

milieu, m. *[meelyuh]* middle, environment

249

au milieu de *[oh meelyuh duh]* in the middle of

mille *[meel]* thousand

mille-feuille, m. *[meel-fuhy]* napoleon (type of pastry)

mince *[ma(n)s]* thin

minéral *[meenayrahl]* mineral

minuit *[meenwee]* midnight

minute, f. *[meenewt]* minute

miroir, m. *[meerwahr]* mirror

mise en plis, f. *[meez ah(n) plee]* permanent

mise au point, f. *[meez oh pwa(n)]* tune up

moi *[mwah]* me

moins *[mwa(n)]* less

au moins *[oh mwa(n)]* at least

mois, m. *[mwah]* month

moment, m. *[mohmah(n)]* moment

mon, m. *[moh(n)]* my

monastère, m. *[mohnahstehr]* monastery

monde, m. *[moh(n)d]* world

monnaie, f. *[mohnay]* money, change, currency

monsieur *[muhsyuh]* Mister, sir

montagne, f. *[moh(n)tahnyuh]* mountain

monter *[moh(n)tay]* to go up

montre, f. *[moh(n)tr]* watch

montrer *[moh(n)tray]* to show

morue, f. *[mohrew]* cod

mosquée, f. *[mohskay]* mosque

mot, m. *[moh]* word

mouchoir, m. *[mooshwahr]* handkerchief

mouchoir en papier, m. *[mooshwahr ah(n)pahpyay]* tissue

mouille *[mooyay]* wet

moules, f.pl. *[mool]* mussels

mousse, f. *[moos]* mousse

moustache, f. *[moostahsh]* moustache

moutarde, f. *[mootahrd]* mustard

mouton, m. *[mootoh(n)]* lamb

moyen, m. *[mwahya(n)]* way

moyens, m.pl. *[mwahya(n)]* means

mur, m. *[mewr]* wall

musée, m. *[mewzay]* museum

musique, f. *[mewzeek]* music

N

nager *[nahzhay]* to swim

navet, m. *[nahvay]* turnip

né *[nay]* born

nécessaire *[naysehsehr]* necessary

neige, f. *[nehzh]* snow

neiger *[nehzhay]* to snow

nettoyer *[nehtwahyay]* to clean

nettoyer à sec *[nehtwahyay ah sehk]* to dry clean

neuf *[nuhf]* nine

nez, m. *[nay]* nose

niveau, m. *[neevoh]* level

noir *[nwahr]* black

noix, f. *[nwah]* nut

nom, m. *[noh(m)]* name

nombre, m. *[noh(m)br]* number

non *[noh(n)]* no

nord, m. *[nohr]* north

nos pl. *[noh]* our

note, f. *[noht]* bill

notre *[nohtr]* our

nouilles, f.pl. *[nooy]* noodles

nourriture, f. *[nooreetewr]* food

nous *[noo]* we, us

nouveau *[noovoh]* new

nouvelle cuisine, f. *[noovehl kweezeen]* new cuisine

novembre *[nohvah(m)br]* November

nuit, f. *[nwee]* night

numéro, m. *[newmayroh]* number

numéroté *[newmayrohtay]* numbered

O

objectif, m. *[ohbzhehkteef]* lens

objet, m. *[ohbzhay]* object

obtenir *[ohbtuhneer]* to obtain

obturateur, m. *[ohbtewrahtuhr]* shutter

occasion, f. *[ohkahzyoh(n)]* opportunity

occupé *[ohkewpay]* busy

océan, m. *[ohsayah(n)]* ocean

octobre *[ohktohbr]* October

oeil, m. *[uhy]* eye

oeuf, m. *[uhf]* egg

offrir *[ohfreer]* to offer

oie, f. *[wah]* goose

oignon, m. *[ohnyoh(n)]* onion

omelette, f. *[ohmleht]* omelette

on *[oh(n)]* one, we

oncle, m. *[oh(n)kl]* uncle

ongle, m. *[oh(n)gl]* nail

onze *[oh(n)z]* eleven

opérateur, m. *[ohpayrahtewr]* operator

or, m. *[ohr]* gold

orange, f. *[ohrah(n)zh]* orange

orangeade, f. *[ohrah(n)zhahd]* orangeade

orchestre, m. *[ohrkehstr]* orchestra

ordinaire *[ohrdeenehr]* ordinary

ordonnance, f. *[ohrdohnah(n)s]* prescription

oreille, f. *[ohrehy]* ear

oreiller, m. *[ohrayay]* pillow

origan, m. *[ohreegah(n)]* oregano

os, m. *[ohs]* bone

ou *[oo]* or

où *[oo]* where

oublier *[oobleeyay]* to forget

ouest, m. *[wehst]* west

oui *[wee]* yes

ouvert *[oovehr]* open

ouvreuse, f. *[oovruhz]* usher

ouvrir *[oovreer]* to open

P

pain, m. *[pa(n)]* bread

pain complet, m. *[pa(n) koh(m)play]* whole wheat bread

pain de mie, m. *[pa(n) duh mee]* white bread

pain grillé, m. *[pa(n) greeyay]* toast

paire, f. *[pehr]* pair

palais de justice, m. *[pahleh duh zhewstees]* courthouse

pamplemousse, m. *[pah(m)pluhmoos]* grapefruit

panier, m. *[pahnyay]* basket

panne, f. *[pahn]* car breakdown

panne d'essence, f. *[pahn dehsah(n)s]* out of gas

panorama, m. *[pahnohrahmah]* panorama

pantalon, m. *[pah(n)tahloh(n)]* pants

pantoufles, f.pl. *[pah(n)toofl]* slippers

papeterie, f. *[pahpehtree]* stationery store

papier, m. *[pahpyay]* paper

papier à lettres, m. *[pahpyay ah lehtr]* stationery

papier hygiénique, m. *[pahpyay eezhyayneek]* toilet paper

paquet, m. *[pahkay]* pack, packet

par *[pahr]* by

parapluie, m. *[pahrahplwee]* umbrella

parc, m. *[pahrk]* park

parce que *[pahrs kuh]* because

parcmètre, m. *[pahrkmehtr]* parking meter

pardon! *[pahrdoh(n)]* Excuse me! Sorry!

pardonner *[pahrdohnay]* to forgive

parfait *[pahrfeh]* perfect

parfois *[pahrfwah]* sometimes

parfum, m. *[pahrfuh(m)]* perfume, flavor

parking, m. *[pahrkeeng]* parking lot

parler *[pahrlay]* to speak

parmi *[pahrmee]* among

partager *[pahrtahzhay]* to share

partie, f. *[pahrtee]* part

partir *[pahrteer]* to leave

partout *[pahrtoo]* everywhere

pas *[pah]* not (negates verb)

pas du tout *[pah dew too]* not at all

passage, m. *[pahsahzh]* passage

passage à niveau, m. *[pahsahzh ah neevah]* railroad crossing

passage clouté, m. *[pahsahzh klootay]* **passage piétons,** m. *[pahsahzh peeyaytoh(n)]* pedestrian crosswalk

passeport, m. *[pahspohr]* passport

passer *[pahsay]* to pass, spend (time)

pastèque, f. *[pahstehk]* watermelon

pâtes, f.pl. *[paht]* pasta

patinoire, f. *[pahteenwahr]* skating rink

pâtisserie, f. *[pahteesree]* pastry shop

patron, m. *[patroh(n)]* boss

pauvre *[pohvr]* poor

payer *[payay]* to pay

pays, m. *[payee]* country (nation)

paysage, m. *[payeezahzh]* landscape

en P.C.V. *[ah(n) pay say vay]* collect (phone call)

péage, m. *[payayzh]* toll

peau, f. *[poh]* skin

pêche, f. *[pehsh]* peach

peigne, m. *[pehnyuh]* comb

peintre, m. *[pa(n)tr]* painter

peinture, f. *[pa(n)tewr]* painting

pellicule, f. *[pehleekewl]* film cartridge, roll of film

pendant *[pah(n)dah(n)]* during

pendule, f. *[pah(n)dewl]* clock

penser *[pah(n)say]* to think

pension complète, f. *[pah(n)syoh(n) koh(m)pleht]* room with all meals

perdre *[pehrdr]* to lose

perdu *[pehrdew]* lost

père, m. *[pehr]* father

période, f. *[payryohd]* period

permettre *[pehrmehtr]* to permit

permis, m. *[pehrmee]* license

persil, m. *[pehrsee]* parsley

personne, f. *[pehrsohn]* person

personnel *[pehrsohnehl]* personal

personnes âgées, f.pl. *[pehrsohn zahzhay]* senior citizens

persuader *[pehrswahday]* to persuade

peser *[puhzay]* to weigh

petit *[puhtee]* small

petit déjeuner, m. *[puhtee dayzhuhnay]* breakfast

petit déjeuner complet, m. *[puhtee dayzhuhnay koh(m)play]* continental breakfast

petit fils, m. *[puhtee fees]* grandson

petit pain, m. *[puhtee pa(n)]* roll

petite fille, f. *[puhteet feey]* granddaughter

petits pois, m.pl. *[puhtee pwah]* peas

peu *[puh]* little, few

peu de *[puh duh]* few

peur, f. *[puhr]* fear

avoir peur de *[ahvwahr puhr duh]* to be afraid of

peut-être *[puh-tehtruh]* perhaps

peux *[puh]* am able to (see *pouvoir*)

phares, m.pl. *[fahr]* headlights

pharmacie, f. *[fahrmahsee]* pharmacy

photo, f. *[fohtoh]* picture, photograph

photographier *[fohtohgrahfyay]* to photograph

phrase, f. *[frahz]* sentence

pièce, f. *[pyehs]* play (literature), room (of the house), coin

pied, m. *[pyay]* foot

à pied *[ah pyay]* on foot

pierre, f. *[pyehr]* stone

pierre précieuse, f. *[pyehr praysyuhz]* precious stone

piéton, m. *[pyaytoh(n)]* pedestrian

pile, f. *[peel]* battery

pillule, f. *[peelewl]* pill

piment, m. *[peemah(n)]* spice

piscine, f. *[peeseen]* swimming pool

place, f. *[plahs]* town square, seat

plafond, m. *[plahfoh(n)]* ceiling

plage, f. *[plahzh]* beach

plainte, f. *[pla(n)t]* complaint

plaisanterie, f. *[plehzah(n)tree]* joke

plaisir, m. *[plehzeer]* pleasure

plan, m. *[plah(n)]* map, plan

planche à voile, f. *[plah(n)sh ah vwahl]* windsurfing

planche de surf, f. *[plah(n)sh duh sewrf]* surfboard

plancher, m. *[plah(n)shay]* floor

planétarium, m. *[plahnaytahryuhm]* planetarium

plat *[plah]* flat

plat, m. *[plah]* dish

plein air *[pleh nehr]* outdoors

pleurer *[pluhray]* to cry

(il) pleut *[(eel) pluh]* (it's) raining

plongée sous-marine, f. *[ploh(n)zhay soo-mahreen]* deep-sea diving

pluie, f. *[plwee]* rain

plus *[plew]* more

plusieurs *[plewzyuhr]* several

plutôt *[plewtoh]* rather

pneu, m. *[pnuh]* tire

poche, f. *[pohsh]* pocket

poids, m. *[pwah]* weight

poignet, m. *[pwahnyay]* wrist

pointure, f. *[pwa(n)tewr]* shoe size

poire, f. *[pwahr]* pear

poireau, m. *[pwahroh]* leek

pois, m. *[pwah]* peas

poisson, m. *[pwahsoh(n)]* fish

poitrine, f. *[pwahtreen]* chest

poivre, m. *[pwahvr]* pepper

pomme, f. *[pohm]* apple

pomme de terre, f. *[pohm duh tehr]* potato

pont, m. *[poh(n)]* bridge

porc, m. *[pohr]* pork

port, m. *[pohr]* harbor

porte, f. *[pohrt]* door

porte-feuille, m. *[pohrtuhfuhy]* wallet

porter *[pohrtay]* to carry

portier, m. *[pohrtyay]* hall porter, doorman

porteur, m. *[pohrtuhr]* porter

portion, f. *[pohrsyoh(n)]* portion

posséder *[pohsayday]* to possess

poste de radio, m. *[pohst duh rahdyoh]* radio

poster *[pohstay]* to mail

poterie, f. *[pohtree]* pottery

poule, f. *[pool]* hen

poulet, m. *[poolay]* chicken

pour *[poor]* for

pourboire, m. *[poorbwahr]* tip

pourquoi *[poorkwah]* why

pourrions *[pooryoh(n)]* could (see *pouvoir*)

pousser *[poosay]* to push

pouvez *[poovay]* can (see *pouvoir*)

pouvoir *[poovwahr]* to be able to

pratique *[prahteek]* practical

préférer *[prayfayray]* to prefer

premier *[pruhmyay]* first

prendre [prah(n)dr] to take

préparer [praypahray] to prepare

près (de) [preh (duh)] near

présenter [prayzah(n)tay] to present, introduce

presque [prehsk] almost

pressing, m. [prehseeng] dry cleaner

pression, f. [prehsyoh(n)] pressure

prêt [preh] ready

prêter [prehtay] to lend

prêtre, m. [prehtr] priest

printemps, m. [pra(n)tah(m)] spring (season)

priorité, f. [preeohreetay] priority

privé [preevay] private

prix, m. [pree] price

prochain [prohsha(n)] next

proche [prohsh] near

profession, f. [prohfehsyoh(n)] profession

promenade, f. [prohmuhnahd] walk

faire une promenade [fehr ewn prohmuhnahd] to take a walk

promettre [prohmehtr] to promise

prononcer [prohnoh(n)say] to pronounce

propre [prohpr] clean, own

propriétaire, m. [prohpreeaytehr] owner

propriété privée, f. [prohpreeaytay preevay] private property

protéger [prohtayzhay] to protect

prune, f. [prewn] plum

pruneau, m. [prewnoh] prune

public [pewbleek] public

puis-je . . .? [pweezh] can I . . .?

pyjama, m. [peezhahmah] pajamas

Q

quai, m. [keh] wharf, platform

qualité, f. [kahleetay] quality

quand [kah(n)] when

quarante [kahrah(n)t] forty

quart, m. [kahr] quarter

quartier, m. [kahrtyay] neighborhood

quatorze [kahtohrz] fourteen

quatre [kahtr] four

quatre-vingt-dix [kahtruh-va(n)dees] ninety

quatre-vingts [kahtruh-va(n)] eighty

que [kuh] that

quel m. [kehl] what, which

quelle f. [kehl] what, which

Quelle heure est-il? [Kehl uhr eh teel?] What time is it?

quelque(s) [kehlkuh] some

quelque chose [kehlkuh shohz] something

quelque part [kehlkuh pahr] somewhere

quelqu'un [kehlkuh(n)] someone

qu'est-ce que [kehskuh] what

Qu'est-ce qu'il y a? [Kehs keel yah?] What's the matter?

question, f. [kehstyoh(n)] question

queue, f. [kuh] line (of people)

qui [kee] who

quiche, f. [keesh] quiche

quincaillerie, f. [ka(n)kahyree] hardware store

quinze [ka(n)z] fifteen

quoi [kwah] what

quotidien [kohteedyeh(n)] daily

R

rabbin, m. [rahba(n)] rabbi

raconter [rahkoh(n)tay] to tell

radiateur, m. *[rahdyahtuhr]* radiator

radio, f. *[rahdyoh]* radio, X ray

rafraîchissant *[rahfrehsheesah(n)]* refreshing

raisin, m. *[rehza(n)]* grape

raisins secs, m.pl. *[rehza(n) sehk]* raisins

raison, f. *[rehzoh(n)]* reason

raisonnable *[rehzohnahbl]* reasonable

ralentir *[rahlah(n)teer]* to slow down

rapide *[rahpeed]* rapid, fast

rappeler *[rahplay]* to call back

se rappeler *[suh rahplay]* to remember

raser *[rahzay]* to shave

rasoir, m. *[rahzwahr]* razor

rayon, m. *[rayoh(n)]* shelf, section

rayure, f. *[rayewr]* stripe

récent *[raysah(n)]* recent

recevoir *[ruhsuhvwahr]* to receive

recommander *[ruhkohmah(n)day]* to recommend

reçu, m. *[ruhsoo]* receipt

réduction, f. *[rayduhksyoh(n)]* reduction

refuser *[ruhfewzay]* to refuse

regarder *[ruhgahrday]* to look at

régime, m. *[rayzheem]* diet

règle, f. *[rehgl]* rule

regretter *[ruhgrehtay]* to regret

remarquer *[ruhmahrkay]* to notice

rembourser *[rah(m)boorsay]* to reimburse

remercier *[ruhmehrsyay]* to thank

rencontrer *[rah(n)koh(n)tray]* to meet

rendez-vous, m. *[rah(n)day-voo]* appointment

rendre *[rah(n)dr]* to return

renseignements, m.pl. *[rah(n)sehnyuhmah(n)]* information

renseigner *[rah(n)sehnyay]* to inform

rentrer *[rah(n)tray]* to return

réparer *[raypahray]* to repair

repas, m. *[ruhpah]* meal

repas léger, m. *[ruhpah layzhay]* light meal

repasser *[ruhpahsay]* to iron

répéter *[raypaytay]* to repeat

répondre *[raypoh(n)dr]* to answer

réponse, f. *[raypoh(n)s]* answer

repos, m. *[ruhpoh]* rest

se reposer *[ruhpohzay]* to rest

représentation, f. *[ruhprayzah(n)tahsyoh(n)]* performance

représenter *[ruhprayzah(n)tay]* to represent

réservation, f. *[rayzehrvahsyoh(n)]* reservation

réservé aux autobus *[rayzehrvay oh zohtohbews]* reserved for buses

réserver *[rayzehrvay]* to reserve

responsable *[rehspoh(n)sahbl]* responsible

ressembler *[ruhsah(m)blay]* to resemble

restaurant, m. *[rehstohrah(n)]* restaurant

rester *[rehstay]* to stay, remain

résultat, m. *[rayzewltah]* result

retard, m. *[ruhtahr]* delay

retoucher *[ruhtooshay]* to touch up

(de) retour *[(duh) ruhtoor]* returned

retraite, f. *[ruhtreht]* retirement

rétréci *[raytraysee]* shrunk
réunion, f. *[rayewnyoh(n)]* meeting
réveil, m. *[rayvehy]* alarm clock
revenir *[ruhvuhneer]* to return, come back
rez-de-chaussée, m. *[ray-duh-shohsay]* ground floor
rhume, m. *[rewm]* cold (virus)
rien *[ryeh(n)]* nothing
de rien *[duh ryeh(n)]* you're welcome
rire *[reer]* to laugh
risque, m. *[reesk]* risk
rivière, f. *[reevyehr]* river
riz, m. *[ree]* rice
robe, f. *[rohb]* dress
robe de chambre, f. *[rohb duh shah(m)br]* bathrobe
robinet, m. *[rohbeenay]* faucet, tap
roman, m. *[rohmah(n)]* novel
romarin, m. *[rohmahra(n)]* rosemary
rosbif, m. *[rohsbeef]* roast beef
rose *[rohz]* pink
rôti, m. *[rohtee]* roast
rouge *[roozh]* red
rouge à lèvre, m. *[roozh ah lehvr]* lipstick
rouler *[roolay]* to roll, drive
route, f. *[root]* road
ruines, f.pl. *[rween]* ruins

S

sa, f. *[sah]* his/her
sable, m. *[sahbl]* sand
sac, m. *[sahk]* handbag, bag, pocketbook
saignant *[sehnyah(n)]* rare (meat)
sais *[seh]* know (see *savoir*)
saison, f. *[sehzoh(n)]* season
sale *[sahl]* dirty
salé *[sahlay]* salted

salle, f. *[sahl]* room
salle à manger, f. *[sahl ah mah(n)zhay]* dining room
salle d'attente, f. *[sahl dahtah(n)t]* waiting room
salle de bain, f. *[sahl duh ba(n)]* bathroom
salle non-fumeurs, f. *[sahl noh(n) foomuhr]* non-smoking section
salon, m. *[sahloh(n)]* living room
salon de beauté, m. *[sahloh(n) duh bohtay]* **salon de coiffure**, m. *[sahloh(n) duh kwahfewr]* hairdresser's, beauty shop
salon de thé, m. *[sahloh(n) duh tay]* tearoom
samedi *[sahmdee]* Saturday
sandales, f.pl. *[sah(n)dahl]* sandals
sang, m. *[sah(n)]* blood
sans *[sah(n)]* without
santé, f. *[sah(n)tay]* health
saucisse, f. *[sohsees]* sausage
saucisson, m. *[sohseesoh(n)]* type of sausage
sauvage *[sohvahzh]* wild
savez *[sahvay]* know (see *savoir*)
savoir *[sahvwahr]* to know (facts)
savon, m. *[sahvoh(n)]* soap
sculpture, f. *[skewltewr]* sculpture
se *[suh]* reflexive pronoun for third person
sec *[sehk]* dry
sèche-cheveux, m. *[sehsh-shuhvuh]* hair dryer
secours, m. *[suhkoor]* help
seigle, m. *[sehgl]* rye
seize *[sehz]* sixteen
séjour, m. *[sayzhoor]* stay
sel, m. *[sehl]* salt
selon *[suhloh(n)]* according to
semaine, f. *[suhmehn]* week
sembler *[sah(m)blay]* to seem

sens, m. *[sah(n)s]* direction, meaning

sens unique *[sah(n)s ewneek]* one-way

se sentir *[suh sah(n)teer]* to feel

sept *[seht]* seven

septembre *[sehptah(m)br]* September

sera *[suhrah]* will be

sérieux *[sayryuh]* serious

serrez à droite *[sehray ah drwaht]* keep right

serveur, m. *[sehrvuhr]* waiter

serveuse, f. *[sehrvuhz]* waitress

service d'étage, m. *[sehrvees daytahzh]* room service

serviette, f. *[sehrvyeht]* towel, napkin, briefcase

serviettes hygiéniques, f.pl. *[sehrvyeht eezhyayneek]* feminine napkins

servir *[sehrveer]* to serve

ses (pl.) *[say]* his, her, their

seul *[suhl]* alone

seulement *[suhlmah(n)]* only

shampooing, m. *[shah(m)pwa(n)]* shampoo

si *[see]* if

s'il vous plaît *[seel voo pleh]* please

signer *[seenyay]* to sign

signification, f. *[seenyeefeekah-syoh(n)]* meaning

site, m. *[seet]* site

six *[sees]* six

ski, m. *[skee]* skiing

ski de fond, m. *[skee duh foh(n)]* cross-country skiing

ski nautique, m. *[skee nohteek]* waterskiing

slip, m. *[sleep]* underpants

snack-bar, m. *[snahk-bahr]* snack bar

soeur, f. *[suhr]* sister

soie, f. *[swah]* silk

soif, f. *[swahf]* thirst

avoir soif *[ahvwahr swahf]* to be thirsty

avec soin *[ahvehk swa(n)]* carefully

soir, m. *[swahr]* evening

soirée, f. *[swahray]* evening party

soixante *[swahsah(n)t]* sixty

soixante-dix *[swahsah(n)t-dees]* seventy

sol, m. *[sohl]* ground

soleil, m. *[sohlehy]* sun

somme, f. *[sohm]* sum

sommet, m. *[sohmay]* peak

son (m. or f.) *[soh(n)]* his, her

sortie, f. *[sohrtee]* exit

soucoupe, f. *[sookoop]* saucer

soufflé, m. *[sooflay]* soufflé

souhaiter *[soowehtay]* to wish

sourire, m. *[sooreer]* smile

sous *[soo]* under

sous-sol, m. *[soo-sohl]* basement

sous-vêtements, m.pl. *[soo-vehtmah(n)]* underwear

souvent *[soovah(n)]* often

spaghetti, m.pl. *[spahghehtee]* spaghetti

spécialité, f. *[spaysyahleetay]* specialty

spectacle, m. *[spehktahkl]* show

stade, m. *[stahd]* stadium

station, f. *[stahsyoh(n)]* station

station de métro, f. *[stahsyoh(n) duh maytroh]* subway station

station-service, f. *[stahsyoh(n)-sehrvees]* service station

stationnement, m. *[stahsyohn-mah(n)]* parking

stationnement interdit *[stahsy-ohnmah(n) a(n)tehrdee]* no parking

statue, f. *[stahtew]* statue

steak, m. *[stehk]* steak

stylo, m. *[steeloh]* pen

sucre, m. *[sewkr]* sugar

sucré [sewkray] sweet
sud, m. [sewd] south
suis [swee] am (see être)
Suisse, f. [Swees] Switzerland
suisse [swees] Swiss
suivre [sweevr] to follow
super [sewpehr] great
supérieur [sewpayryuhr] superior, higher
supermarché, m. [sewpehrmahr-shay] supermarket
supplément, m. [sewplaymah(n)] supplement, extra
sur [sewr] on
sûr [sewr] sure
synagogue, f. [seenahgohg] synagogue

T

ta, f. [tah] your
tabac, m. [tahbah] tobacco
table, f. [tahbl] table
tableau, m. [tahbloh] painting
taille, f. [tahy] waist, size
tailleur, m. [tahyuhr] tailor
talon, m. [tahloh(n)] heel
tampon, m. [tah(m)poh(n)] tampon
tant [tah(n)] so many, so much
tant mieux [tah(n)myuh] so much the better
tant pis [tah(n) pee] so much the worse
tante, f. [tah(n)t] aunt
tapis, m. [tahpee] rug
tard [tahr] late
tarif, m. [tahreef] price, rate
tarte, f. [tahrt] pie
tasse, f. [tahs] cup
taxe, f. [tahks] tax
taxi, m. [tahksee] taxi
te [tuh] you (reflexive)
téléphone, m. [taylayfohn] telephone
téléphone portable, m. [taylay-fohn pohrtahbl] cell phone

téléphoner [taylayfohnay] to telephone
télésiege, m. [taylaysyehzh] ski lift
téléviseur, m. [taylayveezuhr] TV set
télévision, f. [taylayveezyoh(n)] television
tempête, f. [tah(m)peht] storm
temps, m. [tah(m)] time, weather
tennis, m. [tehnees] tennis
tente, f. [tah(n)t] tent
tenue, f. [tuhnew] outfit, way of dressing
terminer [tehrmeenay] to end
terrain de golf, m. [tehra(n) duh gohlf] golf course
terrain de jeu, m. [tehra(n) duh zhuh] playground
terrasse, f. [tehrahs] terrace
terre, f. [tehr] land
tes, pl. [tay] your
tête, f. [teht] head
TGV, m. [tay zhay vay] bullet train
thé, m. [tay] tea
théâtre, m. [tayahtr] theater
thym, m. [ta(m)] thyme
timbre, m. [ta(m)br] stamp (postage)
tire-bouchon, m. [teer-booshoh(n)] corkscrew
toi [twah] you, to you
toilettes, f.pl. [twahleht] toilet
toit, m. [twah] roof
tomate, f. [tohmaht] tomato
tombe, f. [toh(m)b] grave
tomber [toh(m)bay] to fall
ton, m. or f. [toh(n)] your
avoir tort [ahvwahr tohr] to be wrong
tôt [toh] early
toucher [tooshay] to touch
tour, f. [toor] tower
tour, m. [toor] turn, tour
tourisme, m. [tooreezm] tourism

258

touriste, m. or f. *[tooreest]* tourist

touristique *[tooreesteek]* touristic

tourner *[toornay]* to turn

tournevis, m. *[toornuhvees]* screwdriver

tousser *[toosay]* to cough

tout *[too]* all, everything

tout de suite *[tood sweet]* right away

tout le monde *[too luh moh(n)d]* everybody

toutes directions *[toot deerehksyoh(n)]* all directions

toux, f. *[too]* cough

traduire *[trahdweer]* to translate

train, m. *[tra(n)]* train

trajet, m. *[trahzhay]* trip

tranche, f. *[trah(n)sh]* slice

tranquille *[trah(n)keel]* calm

travail, m. *[trahvahy]* job, work

travailler *[trahvahyay]* to work

à travers *[ah trahvehr]* through

traverser *[trahvehrsay]* to cross

treize *[trehz]* thirteen

trente *[trah(n)t]* thirty

très *[treh]* very

triste *[treest]* sad

trois *[trwah]* three

troisième *[trwahzyehm]* third

trop *[troh]* too many, too much

trottoir, m. *[trohtwahr]* sidewalk

trou, m. *[troo]* hole

trouver *[troovay]* to find

truite, f. *[trweet]* trout

typique *[teepeek]* typical

U

un, m. *[uh(n)]* one, a

une, f. *[ewn]* one, a

uni *[ewnee]* united, solid

unique *[ewneek]* unique

université, f. *[ewneevehrseetay]* university

urgence, f. *[ewrzhah(n)s]* emergency

urgent *[ewrzhah(n)]* urgent

usine, f. *[ewzeen]* factory, plant

utile *[ewteel]* useful

V

vacances, f.pl. *[vahkah(n)s]* vacation

vais *[veh]* am going (see aller)

valeur, f. *[vahluhr]* value

valise, f. *[vahleez]* suitcase

vallée, f. *[vahlay]* valley

varié *[vahryay]* varied

vaut *[voh]* is worth

veau, m. *[voh]* veal

velours, m. *[vuhloor]* velvet

velours côtelé, m. *[vuhloor kohtuhlay]* corduroy

vendeur, m. *[vah(n)duhr]* salesman

vendeuse, f. *[vah(n)duhz]* saleswoman

vendre *[vah(n)dr]* to sell

vendredi *[vah(n)druhdee]* Friday

venir *[vuhneer]* to come

vent, m. *[vah(n)]* wind

vente, f. *[vah(n)t]* sale

verglas, m. *[vehrglah]* frost

vérifier *[vayreefyay]* to verify

vérité, f. *[vayreetay]* truth

vernis à ongles, m. *[vehrnee ah oh(n)gl]* nail polish

verre, m. *[vehr]* glass

verre de contact, m. *[vehr duh koh(n)tahkt]* contact lens

vers *[vehr]* toward

vert *[vehr]* green

verveine, f. *[vehrvehn]* vervain (infusion)

veste, f. *[vehst]* jacket

vêtements, m.pl. *[vehtmah(n)]* clothes

veuf, m. *[vuhf]* widower

veuve, f. *[vuhv]* widow
veux *[vuh]* want (see *vouloir*)
viande, f. *[vyah(n)d]* meat
vide *[veed]* empty
vie, f. *[vee]* life
vieille, f. *[vyehy]* old
vieux, m. *[vyuh]* old
vignoble, m. *[veenyohbl]* vineyard
villa, f. *[veelah]* villa
village, m. *[veelahzh]* village
ville, f. *[veel]* town, city
vin, m. *[va(n)]* wine
vin blanc, m. *[va(n) blah(n)]* white wine
vin doux, m. *[va(n) doo]* sweet wine
vin du pays, m. *[va(n) dew payee]* local wine
vin léger, m. *[va(n) layzhay]* light wine
vin mousseux, m. *[va(n) moosuh]* sparkling wine
vin rosé, m. *[va(n) rohzay]* rosé wine
vin rouge, m. *[va(n) roozh]* red wine
vingt *[va(n)]* twenty
violet *[vyohlay]* purple
virage, m. *[veerahzh]* turn
visage, m. *[veezahzh]* face
visite, f. *[veezeet]* visit
vite *[veet]* quickly
vitesse, f. *[veetehs]* speed
vitrine, f. *[veetreen]* store window
voici *[vwahsee]* here is
voie sans issue, f. *[vwah sah(n) zeesew]* dead end
voilà *[vwahlah]* there, there is

voir *[vwahr]* to see
voisin, m. *[vwahza(n)]* neighbor
voiture, f. *[vwahtewr]* car
vol, m. *[vohl]* flight
vol direct, m. *[vohl deerehkt]* direct flight
volaille, f. *[vohlahy]* fowl
voler *[vohlay]* to fly, steal
voleur, m. *[vohluhr]* thief
vos, pl. *[voh]* your
votre *[vohtr]* your
voudrais *[voodreh]* would like (see *vouloir*)
vouloir *[voolwahr]* to want
vouloir dire *[voolwahr deer]* to mean
vous *[voo]* you, yourself
voyage, m. *[vwahyahzh]* trip
vrai *[vreh]* true
vraiment *[vrehmah(n)]* really
vue, f. *[vew]* view, sight

W

wagon-lit, m. *[vahgoh(n)-lee]* sleeping car
W.C., m.pl. *[vay say]* toilet

Y

y *[ee]* there
y a-t-il *[yah teel]* are there, is there
yaourt, m. *[yahoort]* yogurt

Z

zéro *[zayroh]* zero